Paths Of Darkness

A True Story

Charles Williams, Ph.D.

PublishAmerica

Baltimore

First printing

ISBN: 1-59286-107-5
PUBLISHED BY PUBLISHAMERICA BOOK PUBLISHERS
www.publishamerica.com
Baltimore

Printed in the United States of America

Dedication:

This book is for my beautiful wife,
Ellen,
who is my inspiration,
my loving partner,
and the one who encouraged me every step of the way
and to my relatives and friends throughout
the state of West Virginia and especially those friends in the small
community of Harlem Heights,
those who are still living and those who have passed,
for giving me courage and a sense of determination.
This is a special dedication to late
Mr. Lewis Hillard and Mr. Harold Robinson who
took special interest in my warfare and vicarious training to help me see
through the paths of darkness.

Acknowledgment

I want to thank my friend and editor,
Faith Berlin,
for helping me through the difficulties
of developing this book and finally bringing it to publication.

Also I want to thank the many friends and
the West Virginia State information Bureau
for helping me with historical information and
dates of significance for this book.

Table of Contents

INTRODUCTION

Growing up as a young Africa-American boy in the Appalachian coal fields and mining camps of West Virginia, there was a bloody battle going on during the late 1930's and into the middle 1940's over the right of the coal miners to unionize. The will to win that battle was fierce and unrelenting on both sides, and somewhere in the middle of that horrific war — for that is what it was — I was caught between the struggle of the miners and my own struggle to survive.

The struggle to survive.

Now that's something I know a lot about. I learned it early; I learned it with my empty belly; I learned it by seeing my sisters and baby brother sick with hunger and neglect; I learned it by the bruises, even darker than my own dark skin, that came from little white boys who didn't want no "nigger" in their school; I learned it from my mama, and from her mama; I learned even more from my step-daddy, and his daddy. Survive? That's what I learned to do better than anything else, except remember.

Remembering is right up there with surviving. "You don't remember your beginnings, then you'll never find your future," my mama used to say. She remembered. She remembered everything when she was sober, and it was the pain of that remembering got her drinking again.

I, too, remember.

I remember the truth of my young growing-up years, the truth of what happened — no matter what some folks would rather believe. I'm going to tell it all here because I did survive, because I do remember, and because it needs telling.

My grandmama's parents were slaves for all their lives. The chains they wore didn't offer them any choice when it came to survival. My granddaddy's father, of African-Puerto Rican ancestry, sailed to the United States from Cuba. He knew something about survival, too, as you will see.

Actually, my story begins with the moment I first realized my being — my sudden and sharp awareness of myself and my surroundings — when I was five years old. To this young black child, that startling self-awareness was like waking from a calm and uneventful dream and finding myself in a frightening world of schizophrenics where alcoholism reigned and wherein I saw my own drunken parents. Add to that picture the unsettling rootlessness caused by constant pilgrimages to various Appalachian mining camps, trailing along with my parents, where I and my younger siblings were consumed by the scramble to survive under the imprudent guidance of alcoholic grownups and the tatter and profanity of coal miners.

In such harsh surroundings even an itinerant five-year-old could see the bitter bleakness, the punishing misery, the poverty, and the deadly entrapment of those hell holes blasted into the belly of the earth.

I'll never forget the first time I saw the "tipple;" a tall, horribly noisy, giant-spider-looking monster made of metal that functioned primarily as a "sift," and was used for sorting coal. This metal monster savagely gobbled up great quantities of the "black gold" — as miners sometimes called the coal — like a hungry predator devouring its prey. It was like watching a live animal crouching overhead, defecating its mangled meal in black lumps destined for Northern furnaces.

To me that process — that unending cycle of swallowing, digesting, and spewing forth the globs of black coal on the looping conveyers — was an allegorical pathway that seemed to personify my own never-ending anguish. Years later, with the memories still burning in my mind, I transformed those haunting images of the West Virginia coal fields and the mining camps into a poetic impression called, *"Life Is A Journey,"* which I sometimes recited as a prayer:

Life Is A Journey

Life is a journey for this young boy.
The path of a pilgrim, not a playtime of joy.
Across every hurdle I reckon my way
As through valleys of deep indecision I stray.
Life is a journey, pond'ring which path to take.
My path is a road someone else would forsake.

Premonitions, intuition and inspiration all glisten
And the message they offer impels me to listen.
Oh, Father above, God Divine, take my hand,
Help me keep my eyes open . . . do the best that I can.
There's no compass, no signposts, no maps point the way,
Just the same endless struggle through every long day.
Oh, save me from darkness, from wickedness, from the hater,
For I'm a proud warrior on a path to something greater.
Life is a journey. Dreams and fantasy some say.
*But despite what it seems, it is **my** path. I'm on my way.*

To me, the dark passages I experienced above ground in my youth, equal the cavernous passageways traveled by the men working underground in the mines. Those dark encounters suggested the descriptive title of this true-life memoir: *"Paths of Darkness."*

CHAPTER 1
Going Back To Minden

"Your mama's dying, son." Dad squatted down, level with my eight-year-old height. "You've got to go back to Minden tomorrow. She wants to see you one last time."

"Dying?" I repeated, stunned. Mama had been fine when I'd left only three months ago to come to Buckingham and live with my dad's family on their farm. Well, not fine, but she'd been her same old self, drinking to where she didn't even know she had four children to care for, beating on me with anything she had in her hand, taking off and forgetting about feeding us kids and letting TC's dirty diapers pile up till our shanty stunk like an outhouse.

News about her raising hell like that, stumbling around the house and yelling out bad language had somehow reached my dad and he'd come and taken me out of that living hell. What had made her so sick all of a sudden? How could she be dying?

I couldn't believe it. Maybe she was drunk and just actin' sick...tellin' Dad stuff to get me back. She'd do *anything* when she was drinking; lie, call me ugly names, take off and be gone all night, leave me to beg the neighbors for food for us kids.

Dad saw the disappointment on my face. "I'm sorry," he said. "I don't want you to go back there, but how can I let you stay on here when she's, you know, begging to see you one last time?"

"But she's..." I stopped before the word "lying" slipped out. Mama wouldn't lie about dying...would she? That was a terrible thing to think, much less say out loud, but still it was exactly what I was thinking. She *would* lie. She'd say anything when she was drunk. She'd promised I could stay with my dad and now she was dragging me back into that broken-down shanty in Minden and the life I hated. How could she do that?

"She's sick, son. Real sick."

Turning away, I ran off to the back bedroom to be by myself, overcome with a confusion of feelings. What if it was true? What if Mama really was going to die? I pressed my hot face against the cool pillow of my bed. I was burning with guilt and shame for in my deepest heart — whether Mama was dying or not — the truth was I didn't want to leave Daddy's parent's farm.

Grandma Ayers helped me pack. I could tell she was upset about my leaving by the way she threw the cardboard box on the bed and started slamming my clothes in it, her lips pressed together and her eyes snapping fire... but there was no help for it.

I stood at the window staring out at Grandpa's corn fields, at the dirt road he tractored down when he hauled us kids to school, at the oak that shaded the kitchen roof and Grandma's fresh-churned butter all summer. At that moment I knew I would never see them again.

Grandma calmed down and was folding my shirts, pressing them into the box with little love pats like they were precious garments. "Maybe your mama will get well," she said, her voice strong with hope. "Maybe she'll let you come on back to us here." She tried to smile, but I saw the tears gathering in her eyes.

"No she won't, Grandma." I turned away, not wanting her to see the truth in my eyes. I didn't believe Mama was dying. I couldn't believe it. She was just feeling sorry about letting me go live with my dad, wanting me home 'cause I was her "little man," and maybe missing me some when she was sober. "Naw, Grandma," I said, "she won't let me come back. I know she won't." Tears blurred my eyes.

"Well, don't fret about it any more, honey." Grandma hugged me tight. "You just be a good boy. Your mama's dyin' and she needs you."

"But Grandma..."

"Now you be strong."

"I will."

The next morning I climbed into the family car beside my dad. All his kin were out on the porch to wave me off. I fought back the tears for I'd promised Grandma I'd be strong. Turning around with my knees on the seat I waved one last farewell as Dad pulled away. Grandpa and Grandma waved too, and I could see my grandma was crying. Looking back at them through the rear window I thought my heart would break.

All the way home to Minden I sat quietly beside my dad in the front seat, thinking about what I was going home to, and wondering how Mama had come so far down this dark pathway. How had she let things get so bad for her and for my two younger sisters, Marguerite and Inez and for my baby brother, TC? I knew it was her drinking that had made her so sick, but before the drinking took her down... that was the part bothering me. How had she managed to drag us kids with her so far down the path of darkness?

Maybe it had something to do with her growing up on that plantation in Alabama where her mother worked in the kitchen and her daddy hoed corn for slave wages. Had being from a slave family put a mark on my mama that made her feel so low about herself? Made her feel different? Or was it just being in the Appalachia mountains, in the dirt and the coal dust and the poverty that sunk everybody into the depths of sadness and into a whiskey bottle. When she was drinking, she talked about being at the bottom of the pit, whatever that meant. "Always on the bottom," she'd say. "Ain't worth nothin'!" and she'd go on like that. And she'd cry.

I knew that both my mama's grand-parents were born into slavery, raised in servitude, having to bow and scrape for white folks who could have had either one of them whipped to death if they'd wanted to. Back before she started drinking so hard, Mama had told me those slave stories so many times I knew each one of them by heart. Did all that have something to do with my mama being like she was?

I began thinking about those stories... and how Mama had repeatedly told me, "Knowin' your slave history is important, son." The more I thought about it, the more I began to believe that those stories and her low state of mind were all connected somehow. "You don't ever want to forget your family's beginnings," she'd said.

Our family's beginnings —

I didn't know how to put all the pieces together, but I had a strong feeling that the answer to Mama's moody unhappiness, and maybe even the reason for her drinking like she did — well, part of it, anyway — had something to do with those beginnings.

I closed my eyes and let my head fall back on the plush upholstery of Dad's Packard, and as we drove on to whatever was going to be my future, I let my mind wander back... way back... as far back as I could remember.

CHAPTER 2
Beginnings

Mama's mother was the child of a slave named Elizabeth. No last name. Just "Elizabeth." Slaveowners in the Deep South rarely bothered about slaves having a last name. "Liz'beth" was good enough for a "house nigger" like she was, born and raised on her owner's plantation. She was slim and fair, a light-skinned mulatto woman of mixed blood, mostly African and American Indian. However, the pale, creamed-coffee shade of her smooth skin, her small nose and her beautiful almond-shaped eyes proved that a white man had been involved in her creation somewhere along the line.

Good-looking, light skinned black women were usually favored to serve in the master's house over the coal-black darkies who toiled like machines in the fields.

A born storyteller with a good memory, Elizabeth was known as being a kind of "seer." Not a fortune teller, she was just one of those deeply insightful women who didn't need to look at a person's palm or read tea leaves to feel the good or the evil lurking in a person's soul.

It was said that she could sense a storm coming, or a drought, illnesses and impending disasters by the smell of the air, the dry feel of her own skin, the way the overseer might slump his shoulders walking across the fields, or by the look of the dusky skies and a smoky moon at twilight.

The riveting slave stories Elizabeth told were carried on in the minds of her eleven children — the youngest of which was Malissie, who grew up to marry Charlie Martin and become my grandparents on my mama's side — and were repeated through the years, mother to daughter. Those haunting stories were the reason our family's slave history was so well-fixed in Mama's memory. As I was growing up, she passed the stories on to me.

My grandma's parents, Elizabeth and Jessie, belonged to a plantation owner in Tennessee. Jessie was a tall, strong, light-skinned man with blue eyes and blond kinky hair. It was his pleasant, ever-smiling personality that kept him in favor with the whites. His light skin and blue eyes — which had to come from white ancestors — didn't elevate him in any way to his owners. A person born with the merest fraction of African blood was automatically a black person, or a Negro, and labeled "nigger" by white folks.

As a house slave, Elizabeth cooked and cleaned and cared for the white owner's children. Jessie was a "body slave" who served his master as valet and personal messenger. On most plantations, the majority of "field slaves" regarded the "house slaves" as those "without a race," and they lived in a kind of an ostracized limbo, for they were neither true blacks, nor pure whites. They were considered very close to white, because of their privileges and their station, but they certainly were *not* white. At the same time they were very close to black, but not *really* black; not "field slave" black. Because of their mixed-blood heritage — Elizabeth with her light skin and Jessie with his blond hair and blue eyes — the couple quickly learned to endure the painful sting of racial hatred, for even between slaves, it was vividly alive on those plantations. The African slaves regarded my great-grandparents' "mixture" as no better than a mongrel dog, and the whites regarded them as the lowest life form on earth, so they existed in a hellish limbo between those two alien worlds.

Still, to other slaves, house slaves like Elizabeth and Jessie functioned as a source of news and personal information; an inside spy who could pass on happenings, events, news of the day, tales of punishments or escapes and household gossip to those who had no knowledge of such things. Field slaves, who craved this information for it sometimes gave them a warning about certain events, had no way to get such knowledge for they spent their lives laboring in the heat of the sun. Only house slaves like Elizabeth and Jessie could pass on tidbits of news and gossip, and this serendipitous arrangement, encouraged by both sides, was sometimes the only link the "field niggers" had to the outside world.

Like countless numbers of slaves on southern plantations, Elizabeth, and Jessie, too, had been produced by "matching;" specifically bred by the slaveholders to work in the master's home. "Matching" was what they called it, but in reality it was a forced rape by a black male upon a black female at the will of her owner, commonly done at the time. It was the same practice used to breed race horses, cows and hunting dogs, observed and commented upon by the spectators as bluntly as a dog owner would stand over a bitch looking for a successful coupling. After all, owners considered their slaves as no more than animals and treated them accordingly.

In 1864 it cost $7.50 to $15.00 a year to feed a slave. The monthly ration was a peck of corn meal and three or four pounds of salt pork, not enough to stave off the hunger generated by twelve-hour work shifts or more. As a result, field slaves found ways to use anything the owner's family threw away, like pig intestines (chitterlings), pig tails, ears, feet, nose, head and so on.

Habitually, after a slaughter, the owner buried the swine entrails because they were considered unfit for human consumption, but those leavings were often dug up later by the hungry slaves, cleaned and used for food any way they could devise. Called "shiterlings" at the time, the slaves took the still-warm, steaming guts and cleaned away all the waste until they had a bucket full of glistening, pink entrails which, after being boiled in two waters, were dropped into smoking-hot fat to curl and crisp up much like thin-sliced bacon. Eventually, the name was changed to "chitterlings," and they became part of the slave's daily provisions.

One terrible practice Elizabeth told about was the sadistic "breaking" of a slave, a strategy used to break his will, eliminate all feelings of self-respect; lower him in his own eyes beyond redemption and trample on his soul. To make things easier for the slaveowner, induction into the slave work force was always done at an early age. As a child, my grandma remembers being brought outside and made to stand in the yard by the post and watch slaves being whipped. Bull whips with braided leather thongs, some as thick as twined rope, could open up a "nigger's" back till his bone was gleaming through the river of blood. It was mandatory for the little slave children to stand and listen to his screams; to see his body writhe in agony. It was part of their introduction to the discipline. Sometimes a whipped slave would have to be dragged from the yard for he was too injured to stand. Sometimes they'd leave him tied and walk away. Let his kin undo the rope and get him back to his shack. Let them wipe off the streaming blood and deal with his agony.

Sometimes, in order to enforce the rule of discipline, certain resistive blacks were castrated — tied and forced to spread their legs where their manhood was then slashed from their bodies — and then hung from trees as examples, to remind other blacks not to question the white man's superiority in all things. Also, reports raged during those times that disobedient blacks were punished other ways, too. Some were tarred and feathered — an agonizingly painful, skin-searing procedure involving boiling hot pitch — and then burned to death.

Elizabeth, and even five-year-old Malissie, witnessed those scenes and passed them on to her children. When Mama told those recollections to me, her words seemed to seep into my young mind and induce the ghosts of those poor human beings whipped sometimes to their death, and those phantoms lingered long in my memory and still visit my own sorry dreams to this day.

Slavedrivers were free to rape slave women at their leisure, sometimes not even for satisfaction, but simply to foul and demoralize the black female who might have cast her eyes, or positioned her self away from him, in some manner that fostered his anger. And no matter what is said about it now, it is a known fact that many white owners, whose families strongly deny the practice today, often pleasured themselves with the most beautiful of the African slave females, even abusing little black girls of no more than ten or twelve. After her first "monthly," which often came early in young black females, her body was at her white owner's disposal.

To hear my grandma tell it, one of the worst things ever shackled to the black race — even more damaging than the whipping — was the deliberate repression of learning. Elizabeth told how the slavemasters would rather kill a slave, no matter how valuable, just to set an example, and to impress the others about the wages of learning to read or write or speak in their own language. White owners didn't want any kind of "book learnin'," any kind of intellectual advancement that might open a door to the black man's fertile mind.

"Them niggers don't even *want* to learn all that stuff," Elizabeth heard her master telling one white gentleman who was questioning the practice.

"But wouldn't it be a good thing if they could read the Bible? If they could understand the word of God?" the visitor asked.

"Naw, it'd just make trouble. Whatda they need it for anyway? They ain't goin' nowhere. We see they got food and shelter. Go on with yer books and learnin'. Leave my niggers alone. Strong bodies and empty minds... that's just the way I like em."

Of course, if a slave was bold enough to try to escape these inhuman conditions it usually meant death, and not always a sudden one. When the dogs were finished with the escapee, the bull whip began and if the body was still breathing they strung up the remains on the nearest tree limb using a noose that slow-choked the victim until life finally bubbled from his mouth and stopped his pounding heart. Of course, all the slaves on the plantation from the tiniest tot to the oldest gray-haired granny, were made to watch this ordeal. Another lesson in obedience… in "breaking" the black's will… in ruling by fear of death

On some of the plantations, staged fights were not uncommon when a group of owners wanted a little entertainment. Young, strong, black men were forced into the arena where they'd be set upon, one to another, goaded and pushed by pitchforks, into savage fighting, so the slave owners could enjoy a little side bet on which of the two niggers would live the longest.

If the deadly, bare-fist fights didn't kill a black man, the field work he was made to do often did. "Keep 'em out in the fields. Work the black bastards to death," was the attitude of some slaveowners. "Makes the most profit that way." Many owners went along with that philosophy. Besides, slaves could be made to produce offspring that required little food and clothing, offspring who would replace the older, worked-out slaves much like a young mule replaces the sway-back mare or the hobbled puller of the plow.

But the black man survived.

Tough sinews, strong backs, long-muscled legs and arms, sharp-eyes from needing to see what was coming at them at all times. And the women: supple, strong, tall and proud-postured, dark beauty hidden under the heavy dust of the field, capable and fearless in childbirth, cunning, skilled and enduring. They survived. Malissie said it was the constant oppression, the labor, and the unrelieved trials they met, and conquered every living day of their lives made black Americans the most durable human beings on the face of the Earth.

Shortly after Elizabeth and Jessie passed on, their youngest child, Malissie, found her life's mate in Charles Alfred Martin. A fiery, dark-skinned man, he had a lighting flash of Spanish temper, swifter than a machete slicing through cane. Born in Puerto Rico in the early 1860's, Charlie came to this country as Carlos Alberto Martinez, lured from the cane fields of Cuba with false promises of good wages in the United States. But once on board the ship, young Carlos became suspicious, and when the ship arrived in Savannah, he slipped away.

Making his way west to the Georgia-Alabama border, Carlos met a white farmer named Helmut Martin who coaxed him to work on his plantation. Helmut Martin called himself a Christian, but paid Carlos the lowest wage possible, and would have been pleased to work him for no wages at all, keeping him as a slave. Although slavery was outlawed in 1864, antebellum ideas lingered on in the minds of many southerners who cherished the old habits and satisfactions and couldn't bring themselves to quit the practice as long as they could get away with it.

Actually, at that time in the deep south, if a black man wanted to move about freely in any of the local communities, it was best if he took his white employer's name. I'm using the word "employer" because mostly, after abolition, blacks were given something in the way of wages — food or small amounts of cash — but the whites still thought of them as property. They had been property, owned flesh and blood, body, mind and soul, and now it took more than a recently-passed law by legislators way off back East to change southern thinking. Besides, it made the white folks nervous when a black man tried to keep his name and his own personal identity. My Grandpa Martin overheard many of the white folks' expressing their outraged indignation.

"Damn uppity niggers," one would say. "Ain't got any real names anyway; just that African mumbo-jumbo stuff don't make any sense. Hell, let 'em use the good Christian names -a their owners...uh, 'employers,' I mean. Least we'd know who's responsible for 'em when they get into trouble." The fact that they had no legal right to impose a social restriction like that made no difference. Everybody knew that blacks didn't have any "rights" anyway.

In my Grandpa Charlie's case, the farmer Helmut Martin demanded and succeeded in changing Carlos Alberto Martinez's name to Charles Albert Martin, and in doing so, forced my Grandpa to assume what whites called "negritude;" a humble attitude of respectful subservience in facial expression and in physical posture expected by most whites dealing with blacks at that time. God help the black man who dared hold up his head and stand proud. That single act brought such terrible wrath upon his bony black skull he did not often survive the blows and live to tell the proud story to his progeny.

On farms and plantations all over the Deep South hundreds of black men toiled like my Grandpa Charlie. In return, the plantation owner paid little cash money, but gave all they wanted of turnip greens, yellow corn, sweet potatoes, white potatoes and fruits. It was supposed to be a barter system, but since the blacks, in fear of punishment, had to accept whatever the white man offered, it was not always a fair exchange. Of course, it was easy to exploit uneducated black people in the early years after slavery. How could it *not* be easy to cheat someone who was not allowed, under threat of death, to study reading or writing or figuring?

It was the slaves, using knowledge brought over from Africa, who cultivated the tropical vine we know today as the sweet potato. Subsequently, plantation owners found that their livestock also craved this tropical vine. Vines like the sweet potato, and other edible roots, were very cheap to grow. It's easy to believe that slave owners saw the Africans eating these roots and quickly figured out that if the fast-growing sweet root was good enough to nourish their slaves, then it was probably good enough to feed their prized heifers out in the pasture.

Mama always spoke of her daddy as a mean man, and sometimes maybe he was, but Charlie was a hard worker and was the unquestioned patriarch of the family... till he took off one day and never came back.

Malissie nearly went crazy waiting and listening for Charlie's footsteps on the porch that evening, but he never arrived. "He musta let his temper fly," she sighed. "Lord, how many time I told Charlie he can't sass a white man an' live." As the hours went by she stared out into the darkness, knowing in her deepest heart her Charlie had to be dead. "If he could walk or crawl, he'd a come on home."

And that's what she told her six children.

"I don' want you thinkin' your daddy run off," she said, her dark eyes flashing with the force of her true belief. "He never leave you like that. He mus' be dead, babies. I think he mus' be dead." And she hugged her children tight. "That overseer been runnin' him real hard lately, and you know he boil over sometimes an' can't hold back." She touched the sweet faces of each of her children in turn. "Sally, Samantha, Nora... you, too, Ruth. Virgil, honey, look at Mama, baby. Albert. I want you all to remember your daddy love his children. You hear now?"

"Yes, Mama," was the plaintive chorus echoing in that squalid shack on that sad day. Mama often mentioned the fearful feeling came over her when she realized her daddy had most likely been hung for sassin' his white boss. Hung. For back talk. For bein' what white folks called "uppity." Killed for saying angry words. That was a terrifying idea to a child of no more than seven or eight who was already getting swatted now and again for letting her own temper get away from her.

As sure as Charlie was the undisputed patriarch of our family, Malissie, was the beloved matriarch. Malissie was a small, shy woman of African, White and American Indian blood. Her straight black hair, very light skin, small eyes, straight nose and small, well-shaped mouth were all attractive features. She was the lightest and best-looking of all her four sisters and six brothers, and proud to be a woman of such a richly-mixed heritage.

Malissie, who worked many years as a paid cook for white families, regarded her cooking as an art, and she had a special knack for pleasing the palates of her white bosses. With a two-wheel buck-board wagon and one old horse she traveled to adjoining farms to select fresh meat and vegetables in season. Those white farmers, knowing her sharp eyes and prideful attitude about her cooking, didn't try more than once to pass off any inferior cuts or old produce on that "good-lookin' light-skinned nigra woman" who was running the neighbors kitchen. Soft-spoken Malissie Martin got her respect. All her white employers loved her. She was considered a most valuable person to every white family she ever worked for. She never recovered from Charlie's disappearance that sad evening. "My Charlie never woulda left his family like that," she'd say. And then her voice would get all whispery and melancholy and her eyes looked off, distant like. "He love his kids," she'd whisper. "He love me. I know he did." After that, it wasn't long before she grew despondent and sickly and then, weary of the struggle, lay down and died. At the time of her mother's passing, my mama was only nine years old.

CHAPTER 3
My Mama, Elnora

Elnora is my mama's name.

Her birth name was Nora Martin, but to her "Nora" was too plain. By the time she was a teenager she knew she was a good-looking, light-skinned woman with a fine eye for stylish clothing, even though she didn't own any, and as such, she preferred a name that had more of a special ring to it. "Elnora" lifted the old-fashioned sounding "Nora" to something more exotic, something different, and it suited her. Mama's heritage is Puerto Rican from Charlie, American Indian, White, and African-American from Malissie. She was always proud of the mixed blood in her veins which created her fine bones and her attractive facial features.

All four of Mama's older sisters had moved away from the Alabama farm by the time Malissie died, leaving Mama and her brother Albert in a kind of limbo until Aunt Rose came and reluctantly took them in. I say reluctantly because my grandma's sister Rose was not a family-type woman herself. Treasuring her independence and her private way of life, Aunt Rose accepted her duty to her sister, but she was by nature a wild, impulsive, brilliant woman of instant and varying moods and violent emotions. Also, with her own health deteriorating at the time, she viewed caring for Mama and Albert as a tremendous burden, but nonetheless a duty she would not turn away from. As a result, life with Aunt Rose was not a happy one, and she was not always kind to the two children.

Aunt Rosie loved both her sister's children, but she was a perfectionist who was quick to kiss, and quick to slap. Mama found her extremely hard to please and reluctant to praise for a job well done. At nine, grateful for the roof over her head and the food she was given, Mama would have jumped

24

through fire to please her Aunt Rose, and lived every day feeling like she was walking on a tightrope where one wrong step would send her falling into rejection and despair.

After Mama and Albert had been settled in with Aunt Rose for several months — trying to accustom themselves to her fussy ways, her constant Bible reading, her flashes of temper and her low moods — Albert Junior went off by himself one day, hopped a passing freight and Mama never heard from him again. From then on, Mama endured the awesome responsibility thrust upon her, and at the age of ten she rose to that burden from sheer necessity.

Aunt Rose's health steadily deteriorated. Every weekday morning Mama walked to the local church-school— "for Nigras only" — to learn a little reading, writing and spelling, and then came home to cook and clean house while tending to the demands of her dying aunt. It was only after Aunt Rosie's death that Mama, a very grown-up thirteen-year-old by then, was able to set down the burden thrust upon her and move on with her own life.

The day after Aunt Rosie's funeral, Mama moved in with a nearby farm neighbor whose family name was Johnson. The Johnson's young daughter, Marcie, had become a close friend of Mama's, and the only friend she could turn to during the last stages of her aunt's sickness, when the burden was almost too much for such a young girl to bear.

Marcia Johnson, whom Mama called "Mert," was two years older than Mama. The two young ladies were schoolmates together and a close friendship had blossomed between them. Fifteen-year-old Mert, a smart-looking young girl with a mature figure, some dark freckles across her nose, a wide smile and short-cropped straight hair taught Mama many things and was always exceedingly kind to her. However, in spite of how happy my mama was to be living with Mert's family, after she turned sixteen she began to realize that she could not stay with the Johnsons forever, so she began trying to find her four sisters, Ruth, Sally, Virgil and Samantha.

With Mert's help, Mama wrote letters, fixed on the required two-cent stamp, and mailed one to each of her sisters' last known address. She didn't know what to expect in reply, since it had been five years or more since she'd had contact with any of them. Several weeks later a letter arrived from Summerslee, West Virginia, where Mama's older sister Samantha lived in a coal mining camp with a man named Rudy.

Elated to find one of her living relatives, Mama replied at once, and then letters were exchanged for several weeks, each one offering a little more information about the town and the living conditions of Summerslee. Coal mining camps were not part of Mama's experience and she plied her sister with questions about the place and the people.

Eventually, Mama and Mert decided to leave Alabama and migrate to Summerslee. After all, they told each other, how bad could it be? Worse than working for the rest of their lives on a tenant farm in Alabama? Worse than having to marry one of the poor, uneducated black boys who had been coming around every now and then?

Samantha had described the coal mining town of Summerslee saying there was a lot of hard working black men living there because of the paid wages for mining work. Maybe they could meet someone and get married and have a little house of their own someday and maybe even a family. Mama and Mert burst out laughing just talking about that possibility, but my mama was a dreamer, eager and high-spirited, and she was convinced life held more for her than a tenant farm in Alabama. Once the decision to leave was made — and with the Johnsons' blessings, for it would be two less mouths to feed — the girls saved every penny, nickel and dime they could get their hands on to pay their way.

It took several weeks of extra jobs, asking around to the neighbors for house cleaning work or hand laundry, and baby sitting some evenings for the more prosperous white families in the area, but finally they had enough money for the two of them to cover train fare to West Virginia.

There were no lingering farewells. The girls shared one old, beat-up cardboard suitcase — they had very little in the way of clothing to carry anyway — and that was packed in fifteen minutes. A box lunch was made up for their travel and Mert's tearful goodbyes were said at the house, for her parents and her older brothers could not spare the time away from the fields to see them off at the train. Mert and Elnora walked, carrying the suitcase and the box lunch between them, laughing and chattering like magpies all the way to the train station. Mert, as the oldest, stepped up to the clerk's window and paid out their cash money, all in nickels and dimes and quarters, to the station master for two one-way tickets to Summerslee.

In spite of her nervousness about what might be waiting on down the line, and some fear she was hiding from Mert, Mama was happy to be on the way to whatever it was life was holding for her. Of course, she and Mert were forced to sit in the Jim Crow passenger car which had broken seats, windows that didn't open, smelled of urine and had no accommodations of any kind. And, since Negroes were not served in any of the white cafes at the train stops along the way, once their box lunch snack was consumed, Mama and Mert had to make do with the half-eaten sandwiches and scraps of food thrown away by white passengers. Toilet facilities for blacks were not available at all. As Mama told it, that was one unforgettable ride.

It was only when the locomotive stopped to replenished water, fuel and supplies that the conductor grudgingly allowed the two young women to disembark in order to relieve themselves behind some bushes. Mama and Mert always remembered how humiliating that posture was; how dehumanizing, and for the rest of their lives that incident — having to slide their panties down under their skirts and squat in the dirt like a bitch dog behind some shrubs — reinforced their deep disdain for white people and their cruel racist attitudes.

For a long part of the run, Mama and Mert sat on the hard wooden seat, listening to the frightening sound of the train as it picked up speed heading away from the towns where it had stopped. It was a scary noise to country girls never on a train before, all that huffing and hissing while the loud clickity-clack of the wheels, racing on those gleaming rails, caused the car to jolt from one side to the other. Scared half to death, they clung to each other and began to pray, thinking that maybe the train had gone out of control and was never going to stop.

On the third day the young women arrived at the station in Thurmond, West Virginia, a small community eighteen miles southeast of Fayetteville. The date was May 9, 1929. Mama never forgot the date that marked such a significant change in her life. She and Mert gathered their belongings and stepped off the train onto the boarding walk, a pathway formed by oak planks set side-by-side on the soft earth. The two girls walked along those fresh-sawed planks on their way to the station house.

Thurmond was an embarkation and debarkation point for Fayette County and southern West Virginia. It was sunny morning and many people were bustling about. Mama had never seen so many folks in one place before, hurrying back and forth, and she was about to ask Mert what she thought, but she was distracted by seeing a shoeshine boy — really a shoeshine man — for the first time. She just stood stock still in her tracks letting people push around her as she stared at the jolly old black man who was polishing leather with his rag, snapping it rhythmically as he worked, almost dancing at the job, his eyes sparkling with joy and looking like he was still fifteen years old. His red cap bobbed up and down as he popped the rag, seeming almost to play a song with it as he struck it across his white patron's shoes with studied expertise.

In those days, the shoeshine man was the eyes and ears of the mining community, using his entertaining manner as a show while he soaked up everything that went on and every word that was said around him. With his almost supernatural intuition and sharp eyes, in only two steps off the train and he could spot the aimless drifters, the puffed up business man with a hot deal, the weary traveler just passing through, the sharpie looking to find his next sucker, and the hired thugs — hard knuckles brought in by the union to keep some strays in line in this rough-hewn mining town. The shoeshine man smiled and laughed and kept his rag popping. Street smart as well as wise, that nappy-haired old black gentleman knew how to work all the angles to earn a dime or two.

"Come on, Elnora," Mert urged, taking her by the elbow and pulling her toward the far side of the station house. "We can wait over there outta this mess of people. What in the world are you starin' at?" She followed Elnora's fascinated eyes. "Aw, honey, he just a shoeshine man."

"Yeah, hey, I know what he is, but watch him, Mert. Look how he poppin' that rag. Ain't that smart lookin' how he does that? An' he's an old man, too. See them gray streaks in his hair?"

Mama moved on with Mert, but her mind was still busy with what she'd seen. "Looks like the years crept up on him and he just don't know it yet...the way he jumps around with his eyes sparkin' like that. Makes me smile just lookin' at him."

"He's just tryin' to earn a living," Mert said in her practical way. "You always see more in somethin' than there is, Elnora." Mert sat her skinny body down on the flimsy suitcase while Mama kept stepping around, keeping her bright eyes busy, too high-spirited to relax and just sit and wait for her sister. "Come on, I'll skooch over and you sit here with me."

"Naw, two of us goin' to bust that old case."

"Well, stand still then, will you?"

"Yeah, Mert." Elnora sighed. Her sixteen-year-old body seemed about to burst out of her clothes. She could feel the blood pulsing in her throat and racing through her arms and legs; she felt alive, ready to jump into life with both feet. This was a new town, a mining town. Lots of activity and excitement. She forced herself to stand still, wanting to dance or whirl around just to burn off energy. What was takin' Samantha and Rudy so long to get here to pick them up?

CHAPTER 4
To Summerslee, West Virginia

Samantha and Rudy finally wandered into the train station. Mert recognized them first because she remembered what Mama had told her previously. Samantha would be a dark, brown-skinned woman escorted by a tall, slender, light-skinned man with slicked-back straight dark hair. Samantha said she'd be wearing a short fur coat and a white hat cocked to one side.

"There they are," Mert yelled, waving her arm to catch their attention.

"Where?"

"Over there near the door. YooHOO..." Mert yelled.

"YooHOO, Samantha! Samantha!" Mama called from across the room. "Here we are."

Samantha waved back, motioning them toward her.

Mert and Mama grabbed up their belongings and rushed to meet Samantha and Rudy. For a few moments it was pandemonium. Squealing with happiness, Mama hugged her sister and got hugged back as tears rolled from her eyes. This was a happy moment for Mama, knowing she had finally left her old life behind and was standing there in Summerslee ready to make a new beginning. After the hugging, Mama introduced Mert, and Samantha introduced Rudy, who had been standing back, smiling and waiting on the women to finish greeting each other. Mama liked Rudy at once. He was a handsome man with a wide smile and just oozing with contagious charm. Only his light-skin and his large, dark eyes betrayed him as an African-American.

"Right this way, ladies," Rudy said with an exaggerated sweep of his arm as he took the lead marching them out of the station.

Samantha turned back to grin at her sister and Mert following close behind.

"My Rudy, he always take over like that," she whispered. "He's a born leader, I tell him. Ought to make his mark, you know, Nora? But he's too happy-go-lucky to listen about stuff like that." She laughed and followed along behind Rudy, adjusting her pretty white hat to an even jauntier angle over her lovely dark eyes.

The happy foursome soon found Rudy's brand new 1929 Packard Sedan out in the lot, settled in with Mama and Mert in the plush rear seat, and with a good-natured toot of the horn motored off toward Summerslee. Neither Mama nor Mert had ever ridden in a motor car before. Although they had seen pictures and heard talk about them, their real life experiences up to now had been confined to a horse and buggy. They were farm girls, used to walking barefoot most of their lives, and wearing home-made clothes. With the activity of the train station and all the people coming and going and seeing Samantha's lovely fur coat and her darling white hat, and now riding like royalty in Rudy's brand new automobile, they felt like country hicks coming to the big city, yet Thurmond was truly a very rural community.

"Oh, you gonna love it here in Summerslee, Nora," Samantha chattered as they rode along. "Well, mostly, anyway. 'Course, they some things we just have to tolerate."

"Like what?" Mama wanted to know.

"Well, just a few days ago there was a tornado touch down in one of the minin' camps. Lord, what a sight that musta been! You ever see a tornado, Nora? You, Mert? Me neither. But Rudy here told me all about it. He said the wind comes roaring down out of the Rockies like a livin' thing, twistin' its way through the trees, all them big ol' oaks an' pine and chestnuts snap off like matchsticks. Forty years of growin'... gone like that!" and she snapped her fingers. "And once it got down in the valley, it took up a whole lot of dust, you know, and it just rushed on like a fast-movin' freight, only it twirls in a circle. Tornados they swirl round and around, knockin' people down, blowin' over their little shanties an' turnin' 'em into splinters. 'Course them little shanties no more 'n shacks in the first place. Wonder a little breeze don't knock 'em over."

"That sounds terrible," Mama said. "But if there's tornadoes comin' down here, then why do people keep on livin' in them little shanties, like you call 'em. Aren't they scairt they get blown away?"

Rudy laughed. "They don't have much choice, Nora. It seems like the coal companies — they're the ones who built most of the housing here — didn't know the tornadoes came here to West Virginia. If they had, you'd think they woulda done better, instead of puttin' up a shanty town, like we call it. No basements, no strong walls or decent roofs. But come to find out they just didn't think it mattered that much. All they aimed to do was provide cheap housing for the miners, see? Spend the least amount they could. You think they cared if it wasn't very sturdy?"

"Yeah, I see," Mert said, and Mama nodded.

"Mostly the folks here just live with it," Samantha went on, turning half around as she spoke to her sister. "They just ignore it much as they can, hide from it when it gets too bad. And some don't even think about it." She crinkled up her pretty nose. "Poor things. I guess it compares kinda favorable to the shacks they live in before and the hard time they left behind."

There was a short silence then in the car as they bounced along in the sunshine on the rutted country road.

"Hey, Rudy," Mama piped up from the back seat, "while we was waitin' for you folks, me and Mert heard people talkin' about some union leader name of Ella Mae Wiggins. She was murdered, they said. You know about that?"

Rudy did not answer right away. He just kept staring at the road and steering the car, sorting through the thoughts in his mind. Lately there had been a lot of talk and newspaper articles telling about the violence between coal mining companies and the union organizers. Hearing about people randomly gunned down almost every day was common. It was true that coal company had been accused of hiring thugs who had murdered Ella Mae a few days earlier. She was the mother of nine children. The murder occurred as she and companion strikers were riding along a public highway.

"I don't want you talkin' about that, Nora," he said quietly. "It happened, yes, and it was a terrible thing."

"Oh, I feel so bad for her little children," Samantha said, her voice teary.

"How many she have?" Mert asked.

"Nine."

"Oh, God, nine little orphan kids." Mama's eyes got teary too.

"Just don't talk about it, Nora, honey," Rudy said again. "I don't want you sayin' the wrong thing to the wrong person, you understand? Somethin' might happen."

"Don't scare the girl, Rudy," Samantha admonished, frowning.

"Well I'm just tellin' her the truth... "

"I know, Uncle Rudy," Mama said. "Don't worry. I know how to keep my mouth shut."

"Yeah," Mert added. "But it's sad to know that stuff like that is goin' on in Summerslee... people gettin' killed for standin' up for what they believe in... It ain't right."

"No," Rudy said, staring at the road again. "It sure ain't right."

As the sedan rumbled along the tar-laden one-lane highway, Mama and Mert enjoyed seeing the heavily forested mountains blanketed with such a wealth of oak, walnut, hemlock, spruce, yellow popular, ash and birch trees. Mama and Mert had never seen so many varieties of trees, and so many tall mountains. The Appalachian mountains were so tall their peaks reached up beyond the clouds and the lush greenery hugged both sides of the highway as the car motored on. Drizzling rain began to fall and a gusty wind smashed rain drops against the car windows as it imparted sweet fragrances of the surrounding woodland.

In West Virginia the month of May is magnificently alive with wild flowers which thrive along the road sides. Spring beauties were everywhere, blackberries blooming, oak trees spreading lacy green and June bugs beginning their early plumage. Along the roadside paraded exquisite groups of slippery elm, appearing suddenly as the road twisted through the mountain slopes which lay carpeted by yellow dandelion buds. There was a hint of morning frost left in the high mountains and overhead wild Canada geese formed their familiar V-shape as they migrated north. Mama shifted her body in the plush back seat of the car trying to look out of every window at once as the landscape rushed by.

Even with the troubles they'd already spoken of and such, Mama thought West Virginia was going to be a much better place to live than anywhere in the Deep South for black folks like her and her family. *Freedom at last,* she thought, knowing she already liked the beautiful state of West Virginia. She was going to have a good time, for like Samantha had written, there were a great many more men than women, and that was a fact any young girl could appreciate.

CHAPTER 5
Money Of Her Own

It was high noon when the group arrived in Summerslee. As they drove through the town itself, Mama couldn't get over seeing so many houses all painted the same color and all built in the same style.

"Don't pay to get too drunk in this town," Rudy said, laughing. "You never be able to find your way home."

Mama and Mert giggled, liking Rudy's joking around.

"These houses belong to the mining company," Rudy explained. 'They rent 'em out to the miners, and they ain't cheap neither."

To the young girls staring out the windows in the back seat of that shiny Packard, this was a city compared to the rural Alabama backwater they'd come from. The plank sidewalks and the street corners were crowded with young men — more single men than Mama or Mert had ever seen in their young lives. Mert, feeling her eighteen-year-old juices rising, nudged my sixteen-year-old mama. and said jokingly, "Hey, look at that handsome fool standin' over there by the barbershop... the one with the spiffy hat and the white shirt. Eooee! Ain't he som'thin'!"

"Yeah, he is. But so's that one. An' that one, too." She pointed.

Rudy and Samantha started laughing in the front seat. "Settle down, now," Rudy admonished gently. "You don't want to forget that you are refined young ladies."

"Yes, Uncle Rudy," Mama said, but she was still giggling when she added, "I'm not forgettin' my raisin' but, Lord, Mert and me is gonna have some fun in this town."

"Bet on that," Mert added, feeling like a Queen Bee in a hive.

In those early years, countless men — from all over the country — had ventured to West Virginia, looking for work in the coal mines, looking for decent pay, looking for opportunity. Lots of them had left their wives and children behind in their driving need to better the squalid lives they had, and hoped to earn enough to send for their families later. And there were hundreds of young, unattached adventurers just looking… looking for what, they sometimes couldn't say. Honest work and good pay was what most of them were seeking, and it was there for them when the mine was working. If you had a strong back, tough hands and the ability to swing a pick for hours at a time while you might be lying on your belly or squatting on your knees and breathing in the pulverized granules that blacked your lungs along with every crevice in your skin, well, come on; they had a job for you. Summerslee was no better and no worse than any of the mining "camps" strung out along those West Virginia mountains.

"I'm hungry," Samantha said, turning to Rudy, "and I sure don't feel like cookin' this afternoon. You s'pose we could stop for something?"

"Sure thing, honeybunch," Rudy said, swinging his Packard sedan carefully to the side of the road. "Buster's Beer Garden serves the best bar-b-que ribs and blackberry pie in the whole state. You girls like blackberry pie?"

"Oooh, that sounds good," Mama said, scrambling out of the car with Mert just behind her. "Is this where all them men eat, too?" They entered Buster's and found an empty table.

"Well, see, these miners," Rudy said, after he'd ordered sweetened iced-tea all around and pointed out the menu chalked on the wall, "most a them live in boarding houses around here."

"All these good-lookin' single men you girls are so high on meetin'," Samantha said with a smile, "got to have big, healthy meals. With the kind a work they do, they can't get by with just a plateful like they'd get in a reg'lar restaurant, you know?"

Rudy laughed. "Bunchie's right. They like eatin' good. So the mining companies set up these free rent boarding houses and got really good cooks givin' 'em three man-size meals a day. Like Annie Trotter's place over there just down the street."

"An the men get all this for free?" Mama asked, incredulous.

"Naw, baby," Samantha answered. "They pay a good price every week for their board. Ain't nothin' free in this world as I know of," she laughed. "Come on, now, girls. What you havin' for lunch? I'm starvin'."

Annie Trotter had established one of the better boarding houses in

Summerslee where she was known as the "housemother." In order to provide the excellent service and food she was famous for, Mrs. Trotter required a lot of kitchen help. Only a few days after Mert and Mama had settled in with Rudy and Samantha and were making themselves at home, they got word that Mrs. Trotter, who had to deal with transient employees a large part of the time, was looking for good cooks, housekeepers and dishwashers for her place.

This was good news to Mama and Mert, for despite their young ages, coming up as they had in big families and enduring the daily grind of country life, they were both excellent and experienced southern cooks. With her sister Samantha's strong recommendation, both young ladies were hired immediately.

For the first time in her young life Mama was earning money. The work was hard, but Mama didn't mind. She was strong and full of the vitality common to healthy young girls. Eager to make good and prove herself a valued worker, Elnora was up and cooking at Annie Trotter's place as early as four a.m., making rolls and biscuits for the men's breakfast and packing up lunches for them to take to the mine. Many times she couldn't quit the kitchen, even with extra dishwashing and cleanup help, until ten at night.

During the year Mama worked in Annie Trotter's, she found many opportunities to perfect her recipes, and it wasn't long before Elnora Martin was known as the finest cook in Fayette Country. Coming home late in the evening to Samantha and Rudy's place, sometimes too bone tired to sleep, Mama would make herself a cup of tea and sit out on the front porch in the dark, just enjoying the night air, her sweet drink, and sometimes she'd be recalling the days before her mama died and the meals they used to enjoy. All her life, my mama believed — in spite of her own growing fame as a cook at Annie Trotters — that her mother Malissie was the best cook in the world, and nobody could tell her different.

"You name it," she had often heard her daddy Charlie say, "an' my Malissie here can make it." That included pound cake, egg custard, blackberry cobbler, ambrosia, rice pudding, corn pudding, rhubarb and sweet potato pies. Those white families Grandma Martin served "ate like Kings," Grampa Charlie used to say. Mama often told me that she counted the happiest memories of her childhood by Sunday meals and what was cooking on the stove. Grandma Martin had all kinds of secret recipes which she passed on to her daughters, but one in particular was her way of cooking greens, which, if boiled by themselves, are quite strong-tasting. She rarely used vinegar or lemon squeezings as most cooks did to cut the bitter taste. She cooked her turnip tops or collards or field-pulled mustard greens slow and easy on the back of the stove, and to get the special flavor she tossed in scraps of fatty meat, generally pork, that her white employer gave her. Served up on Sundays with some tender pork neck-bones, corn bread and one her special deserts, it was no wonder everybody praised Grandma's cooking.

From the start of her employment, Mama was highly praised for her ability to prepare and bake biscuits and dinner rolls. Her dinner rolls were so light and fluffy, all the miners bragged that they "damn near floated out of my hand at the table," and no matter how many batches of those light rolls she baked, they never got enough.

Mert, on the other hand, proved an expert in preparing the meats and vegetables. The miners said she was the only cook they knew could make a scrap of pork taste like prime steak and tough beef to taste as tender as pork. And Mert's Bar-B-Que ribs and chitterlings were unbeatable. As might be expected, these two pretty young ladies did not go unnoticed in that mining camp. The young men were always flirting with them, but Mert and Mama were having too good a time to consider narrowing the field quite yet. They were just taking their time.

CHAPTER 6
"Who Is That Man Gonna Wrestle The Bear?"

One weekend, after the girls had been at Annie Trotters for only a few months, Mrs. Trotter chaperoned Mama and Mert on an outing. The girls dressed in their best clothes and they all made their way via the back seat of a city bus to the nearby town of Oak Hill, ten miles west of Summerslee. They were going to see a minstrel show where some of the performers were black folks. You didn't see many blacks on the stage in those years — at least not when the show was mainly for white folks' entertainment.

When they got to Oak Hill, Annie Trotter left the two girls in front of the bandstand while she went to find them some refreshments. "Keep your eye on Elnora, Mert," Mrs. Trotter cautioned. "She's so excited she's liable to walk straight into a wall. I'll go get us some R.C. Colas."

Mama couldn't take her eyes off the performers. Her country upbringing had not included seeing such famous stars as cowboy Hoot Gibson or showmen Cab Calloway and Peg-leg Bates. Mama was thrilled, and as she watched the show she remembered how Grandma Martin had always bragged about her favorite cowboy, a black man who had wrestled his fame from the white man's arena the hard way. His name was Bill Pickett, and to Grandma he was one of the greatest cowboys who ever lived. Grandma always said it was a shame the first professional rodeos weren't open to blacks. "Those white boys wouldn't allow any blacks to compete for money," she said, and then she'd laugh. "Prob'ly scairt they'd show 'em up." Then she'd shake her head. "Sure did thrill the crowd though with their ridin' and ropin' demonstrations."

Elnora smiled to herself. Hoot Gibson was good... real good... but Grandma — and lots of other knowledgeable blacks — had always said the most spectacular show they'd ever seen was the "101 Ranch Wild West Show," with Bill Pickett. Billed as the "Dusky Demon" Pickett would jump on the steer's back, twist the animal's head around and sink his teeth into the animal's upper lip. Stunned, this would completely immobilize the animal. Then Pickett would throw his arms up in the air and the crowd would go wild. Originated by Bill, this kind of steer wrestling, called "bull doggin'" was a real crowd pleaser. Pickett was the first black cowboy to be elected to the Cowboy's Hall of Fame.

As fascinated as the girls were by the performances of the stars, it wasn't until after lunch when they got around to looking at the fabulous side shows that Mama saw something that made her heart leap up in her throat with fear and yet pound in her pulse with sheer excitement. They had stopped to see a show where they were exhibiting a black bear — a wrestling black bear — who would take on all comers.

For one dollar, any strong man clever enough to slam the savage bear to the canvas would win a prize of $25.00. Of course the bear had a muzzle over his mouth and it had been declawed, but any full-grown bear is a powerful beast. His enraged roars during the contests sent shivers tingling up Mama's spine. She was shocked to see that several men took up the challenge. Mama was gripping Mert's hand so hard it almost went numb, and she was half-hiding behind Mrs. Trotter, as one at a time three different men went into the ring to engage the bear. Within less than one minute the huge animal had defeated them.

There seemed to be no more challengers and the audience was about to leave when a young black fella who'd been sitting in the back row of the arena approached the ring and blurted, "I'll wrestle this bear! And I will defeat him."

Mama gasped. "Oh, Mert, who *is* that man gonna wrestle the bear? He's the best lookin' thing I've ever seen!" A powerfully-built young man, even his posture as he stood in the ring exhibited tremendous confidence.

The ringmaster called out the young man's name. "Edward Sherrod," he shouted. "All right, Ladies and Gentlemen, we have a contestant. Mr. Edward Sherrod's going to take up the challenge." Mama caught her breath. He couldn't be more than nineteen, she decided, staring at him with wide eyes. Tall for his age, he was muscular, full-chested and brawny; his eyes were a deep, soft brown and his hair was wooly and jet black. Somewhere in his family background, she thought, there was probably a trace of Arab blood, but she could see he was mostly African. His skin was not coal or blue-black;

it was a warm brown shade, much like bronze.

"Edward Sherrod." Mama whispered his name to herself as she braced to watch him wrestle the bear.

An astute challenger, Edward obviously realized he would need to employ some tricks or special techniques in order to wrestle the bear to the canvas. No one else had been able to accomplish that feat so far. The mixed crowd shouted cat-calls and hoots and some yelled out words like "Get 'em, Sherrod," as the black man took his time about climbing into the arena. While he'd watched the previous matches, he'd noticed that every time the animal charged he would stand on his hind legs and batter the opponent into the ropes, consequently the bear himself was often tangled. Edward believed that he had figured out a way to defeat the brute. It would be a back-breaking attempt, but he was the man to do it.

He jumped up to the ring and climbed though the ropes. Immediately the bear's handlers turned him loose. The animal raced toward Edward. Quickly Edward side-stepped the bear's charge, letting the beast crash head-on into the ropes. Fortunately, the bear's head and front paws became entangled between the ropes as had happened before. That was exactly what Edward had counted on. Wrapping his long, muscular, bronze arms around the beasts' rear legs, Edward yanked the creature backward with all his strength. Down went the bear, slamming into the canvas. Instantly, Edward pounced on the bear, ending the match, as it was only necessary to put the animal on the canvas. It was a thrilling show. The crowd applauded Edward Sherrod and cheered when he collected his money. Mama stepped away from Mert and applauded with the others, thrilled that this handsome bronze giant she so admired had floored the bear.

Edward left the ring and without hesitation climbed up to where Mama, Mert and Mrs. Trotter were standing. Mama never did tell just exactly what Mr. Sherrod said to Mrs. Trotter, something flattering no doubt, but it made her laugh and earned him an introduction to the girl he'd been showing off for with that bear. He never would have wrestled the beast, he admitted later, but once he'd spotted Mama in her smart-looking pink dress and her flashy smile, he could think of no better way to impress her than by throwing that bear on the canvas.

The four of them toured the rest of the fairgrounds together that afternoon, Edward happily spending his $25 prize money, and somehow he ended up holding Elnora's arm, looking cocky as a red-tailed rooster in the hen house. The romantic feeling between the two of them was so strong, Mert said, it fairly snapped sparks whenever they touched. Nobody knows for sure, since Mama would only blush like a young girl when his name was mentioned years later, but from that day on Edward Sherrod was her hero, and for a while rumors were rampant that Mama and Mr. Sherrod had an affair.

CHAPTER 7
"A Little Moonshine Never Hurt Nobody"

As the time went by and Mama continued working at Trotter's boarding house, she was surprised to find that every now and then she felt a little homesick for Alabama. Sometimes she'd sit by herself under one of the old maples at Samantha's place, wondering about her future and thinking about her childhood. All through her younger years, it seemed, what she'd felt most was fear and loneliness. Lord, how scared she'd been of displeasing her Aunt Rose. That old woman was so stern, and so quick to jump all over you. Made her shiver just thinking about it. But the loneliness was worse; far worse than the fear.

Mama's sense of loneliness was difficult to explain. Growing up she'd always felt inadequate and not quite as good as other girls. She never liked the person she saw herself to be, and yet she couldn't help bending over backwards to please people. It was just in her nature. Like most young women on their own for the first time, Mama was searching for her place in society, and searching for truth.

During those first months at Summerslee, whenever Mama felt blue and depressed, she would pray, asking God to help her take the right path. She prayed frequently and hard, but when nothing happened, and she was still feeling lonely and unhappy, she began doubting the power of prayer. The more she thought about it, the more she realized that none of her prayers had ever been answered. Not one. As a child she'd prayed for her daddy to come home... but he never did. She prayed, Lord how she'd prayed! for her mama not to die... but she'd died anyway. Then she listened to Aunt Rose and all her Bible reading and she'd prayed that she could please her, that she could just one time do something right... but it never came out that way.

As she analyzed her feelings, she realized that throughout her life all her teachers of religion — all of them, white and black alike — had assumed God was white. She'd seen the pictures of Him with that shining halo lighting his sad white face, surrounded by his chubby white angels. She'd seen statues of His son Jesus on the cross, and remembered his pale skin. And hanging over the choir section in the black folk's church in Alabama was a picture of "The Last Supper" where He was sitting with all His white disciples. Nothing but white men. How could it be, Mama wondered, that blacks came to worship a God who did not reflect their own heritage? It seemed clear then that as long as she knelt to pray to a white male figure she'd never overcome her feelings that white folks were superior.

Worried, she spoke to her sister about it, but Samantha was mired in the mud of the old slave mentality, and could not lift herself away from being an acquiescent Uncle Tom; doing things the white folk's way. Samantha wasn't able to give Mama any explanation as to the whiteness of God's image, and she insisted that Mama continue to pray and worship the Lord Jesus. But Mama closed her heart to the white man's symbol of God and refused to bow her head to an image that did not acknowledge her blackness or her being. She remembered her mother Malissie saying that because of the harsh repression during slave times, blacks in American are the only people in the world who worship a God whose image they did not choose.

Mama stopped praying, but with no relief from her sad moods, she got more profoundly depressed. In an attempt cheer her, Mrs. Trotter stirred up a remedy made of sugar and clover powder mixed with a little moonshine whiskey. "Here, honey, try this," she said. "A little moonshine never hurt nobody. Make you feel better."

From that point on Mama was a changed person.

Whenever she felt the old sadness, she prepared a glass of Mrs. Trotter's moonshine remedy, and her troubles faded away. Mama did not know it then, but that "remedy" — so good-heartedly offered by Mrs. Trotter — eventually changed her world and took her into the bottomless pit of alcoholism.

CHAPTER 8
Mine Shafts, Murder, And Mert Gets Married

Samantha's man, Rudy, never was an alcoholic, but he surely did love to party. In Summerslee, all the black folks knew him as a lucky and successful gambler and a bootlegger of moonshine whiskey. Good-looking with a ready smile, Rudy was a man who knew how to keep money in his pockets. He loved his good times, but one afternoon, Mama and Mert discovered Rudy had a more serious side.

Mama and Mert were sitting out in the back yard in the shade of the old maple tree, sipping some ice tea that Mama brought out on a tray, and Rudy started telling the girls about how young Bennie Thompson — a hard-working miner with a wife and four kids — had just got himself killed because he'd been drinking the night before and griping about how he couldn't earn enough to live on and saying they should all support the union so the company'd be forced to pay better wages. His friends tried to hush him up, for there were some company men sitting at the back of the bar, but he was feeling his liquor and was not going to be silenced. When the shift was over today, Rudy said, the goons were waiting for him.

"Won't his killers be caught?" Mama asked. "Won't they do somethin'?"

"Who?" Rudy asked, his brow furrowed. "Who's gonna bother? Just one more dead nigger. God, I don't see how them miners do it," he went on. "Facing that grind five days a week."

"You sayin' it's a dangerous way to make a livin'? " Mert's sweet face looked worried.

"Dangerous?" Rudy repeated, incredulous at her innocence. "Men die down there of suffocation, and bein' trapped by a cave in, or a shaft collapses on 'em, or they drown if they tap into some underground spring and can't get out in time. All kinds of terrible accidents happen in them mines."

"Can't they do somethin' else for a living?" Mama clinked the ice in her glass.

"Like what, Nora? How many other jobs you hear of for a workin' man in Summerslee but the mines? Men come here — some leave they families behind thinkin' they bring 'em on later, if they don't die first — they come dreamin' of prosperity, thinkin' they earn a fortune and all like that, but that dream turn into a nightmare of hard work and low wages under company bosses.

"Doesn't anybody care about the miners?"

"Sure, Nora. That's what the union's all about. That's why they need to organize one."

"Well, shoot, how hard could it be for the miners to get together and… "

Rudy started laughing. He rolled on his side, laughing till tears came to his eyes. "Nora, you're worse than a ten-year-old. What's the owner gonna do, honey? Sit back an' just let these miners take over? Let 'em get together so's they can demand more pay and then be forced to fix things better for 'em? They ain't lookin' to spend money to make things better. What do they care? You want to dig coal and get paid for it then you gonna do it *my* way, is what they say. You don't like it? Well, then don't *do* it, boy. Just go sit out in the woods and starve to damn death, an' take your family with you. You ain't gonna get no mine owner to treat a coal miner right just out of the kindness of his heart. Hell, Nora, they ain't even *got* a heart in the first place. Why do you think they's all this shootin' and killin'? If you start talkin' about organizing, trying to force the owners to treat you right… well, they'll kill a man. Hell, didn't they just knock off Bennie Thompson?"

Rudy was through talking for the time being. He went into the house for his jar of white lightning before returning to the maple shade. "Your sister really likes this view."

Nora didn't answer. She was looking at her friend. "Mert, what's botherin' you, honey? You been real quiet now."

Mert lowered her head and her voice was very small. "I… I'm in love, Elnora. Really in love. His name's Kemp. Now Rudy's sayin' how bad it is working in them mines, makes me scared. But Kemp don't have any other way of makin' a livin'."

"Hey, Mert, don't cry, honey," Rudy said. "I know Kemp. He's fine. He be good to you, honey, I know that for sure."

"Oh, I know he will, Rudy… but…" and she turned to Nora, "he left…"

she began and then hesitated… "he left…" she tried again and had to stop to wipe her eyes.

"What you sayin' Mert? Kemp ain't left. I just seen him yesterday."

"No, I mean, he had to leave his…" she stopped again, sniffing her nose.

"You tryin' to say Kemp's got a family someplace off from here? That's what he left?"

Mert nodded, her dark eyes brimming with tears.

"Well, he can't change that, honey. And he's sending money home to 'em, right?"

"Yeah."

"Well, when two people fall in love, that's just a happenin' you can't help. Kemp is a good man, Mert. He don't want to hurt nobody."

"I'm not goin' to give him up. I love him. But I'm worried about him workin' down in them shafts. Don't want nothin' to happen to him."

"Well, how else can the man make a livin' Mert? What else is here for him?"

"Nothin'. I know that."

"Listen, don't worry so much." Rudy took a swig from his jar and leaned back, feeling the breeze in the sweet Maple shade. "Some men can take it, and others fold. Kemp ain't the foldin' kind, way I see it. He's left his family behind to start a new life, then you might as well stay with him an' help him start it. He lucky to have a sweet thing like you, Mert." Rudy laughed to see Mert blush.

"Thanks, Rudy. We'll work it out. I ain't plannin' on lettin' this one get away."

They lingered there in the back yard under the maple, Mama with her dreams, Mert with her hopeful plans, and Rudy with his jug of white lightnin'. It was a nice yard, even had some flowers Samantha had planted by the back porch. Compared with other black folks at the time Samantha and Rudy lived well.

CHAPTER 9
Mama's In Love

Up until my mama's arrival, Samantha was considered the best looking and most popular black lady in the county. Mama was a younger, more vivacious woman, with a gleaming smile, the prettiest brown eyes and a petite body that attracted men like ants to a picnic. Samantha felt that Mama was an interloper, invading and taking over her own personal territory.

Mama never gave all competition business a thought. She had gotten used to the longing looks she been receiving from the young men — that had been going on ever since she arrived in Summerslee almost a year ago — and she was thrilled that they found her exciting, but she wasn't getting bent out of shape by anybody... at least not yet.

That Friday night, however, Samantha threw one of her famous weekend parties.

In those days, it wasn't a party unless you had music; real, live music made by the party-goers themselves. One of the most uplifting sources of joy and self expression available to the miners and their families, white or black, was music. As poor as the miners were, each family had some sort of musical instrument — home made or borrowed or saved up for — that the children learned to play. Washboards were used to rub out a rhythm with bare knuckles, or a thimble if you owned one; a home made bass was created out of taut string, wire or stretched gut fastened onto a wood slat from an apple crate, or across a wash tub... anything that produced some kind of a note or sound was used. If you owned a store-bought instrument and could play it, other musicians — or anyone musically inclined — would join in with whatever they had in hand, harmonicas, jewsharps, or horns, while somebody thumped out the beat on an empty wooden keg for a drum or slapped a couple of brushes on a slick magazine cover to get the sound of the rhythm. On weekends when people gathered, they played music, sang well-known or newly invented songs, and danced. The music created by the mountain people — with its rambunctious joy and its scraping sorrow — appealed to the blacks in the region mainly because it sounded like a combination of the familiar blues and gospel music they'd known from the farms and cotton fields of the Deep South. Of course, "hillbilly music" always had undertones of sadness, and sometimes a harsh melody, too, for it sprang out of the brutal history of the mountain people themselves and their struggles. So people brought their instruments, a pot of baked beans or a platter of fried chicken, and came on.

Samantha's parties always drew large crowds, but that Friday it seemed there were a number of young black men who'd come just wanting to get a look at — and an introduction to — the beautiful young woman from Alabama. And on that dewy April evening, while stars glittered in the velvet sky, Mama had no idea she was about to fall in love for the first time in her young life... with the man who would be my father.

She did know, however, that the well-built older man with the deep dimples, a couple of cowlicks and a gracious smile, was somebody she wanted to meet. He looked to be around 30 or so, Mama thought, watching him closely from across the room as he spoke eloquently to several of the women guests. It was his sophisticated manner and calm demeanor that caught Mama's eye. When they met and started talking, she was impressed when he kept using words she'd never heard before, and appeared so confident and self-assured. His name was Charles Ayers, a semi-educated man, who spoke openly and frankly about his work, his philosophy, even his religious beliefs, and his knowledge on all those subjects seemed to mesmerize Mama. She never felt so enthralled by a man before, not even the bear wrestler had impressed her in this way. Oh, Edward had been real sweet... but Charles Ayers was a grown man, not a nineteen-year-old kid.

Maybe, she told herself, this was what falling in love felt like.

The musicians began thumping out something by Scott Joplin. Charles's eyes lit up for he loved ragtime music and told Mama playing piano was his favorite pastime. As they danced, Mama didn't hear half of what all Charles was saying, but she felt the excitement of the ragtime music and her face flushed with the heat of her happiness. While she was moving around the floor, melting into his strong arms and listening to his smooth voice, Mama knew she was in love.

The party ended, just as the sun was coming up on Sunday morning, and

Mama was certain she'd found the man she wanted to marry. They were together the entire evening and ended up sitting on the porch in the dawning light where he told her about his work and she told him about hers. He hadn't wasted any time letting her know how he felt, and earlier, after they'd shared their first kiss, they both knew their attraction to each other had ceased being a flirtatious little game they were playing. It had quickly turned into a deeply-felt relationship.

CHARLES AYERS taken in 1932.

Charles Ayers was a part-time coal miner, part time farmer, and a peddler of produce and coal. He had a truck which he used in strip-mining coal and hauling it for barter or cash payment. He would haul coal to farms over in Virginia, return to West Virginia with a load of farm produce and sell that off the tailgate to families living in rural coal mining camps. He made Mama laugh when he told her that he was kind of "Safeway on wheels."

From that night on Charles and Mama stayed together, talking, laughing, loving and learning more about each other. Right away Charles told Mama about his family in Buckingham County, Virginia. Listening to Charles talk about his family was exciting to Mama. He was an experienced older man with a solid family upbringing who knew a lot about life. She felt secure with Charles and with every passing day her feelings for him became even more profound.

Samantha, however, was not happy with her sister's affair and wasted no time making her feelings known. "You are gonna grow restless, Nora. You wait and see. He'll get impatient with you. You're too young to be tied down like he's talkin' about, goin' back to his family on the farm. They educated people, you young fool! He talks about stuff you don't even know about."

"I like that he's smart. I don't want to marry no uneducated man who don't even…"

"You don't know *what* you want. You still a kid. I'm warnin' you, you gonna regret tyin' up with a man his age."

"I love him. He thinks I'm very special. You just jealous, maybe, 'cause…"

"Jealous! Me? Jealous a you? You dreamin' or drinkin', I don't know which, but you got it wrong. I'm just worried, I'm tellin' you. You only a seventeen-year-old child! I want you to be happy, Nora. You know that."

Mama hung her head. "I know. I know you do. Lettin' me and Mert come out here and stay with you all this time… I know you been good to me, Samantha. I 'preciate it, too. Honest. But I'm gonna marry Charles Ayers. He's the smartest, the finest man I'm ever gonna meet and I ain't plannin' to let him get away. We'll get on fine. I'll work at it. You'll see."

CHAPTER 10
Living In A Different World

Despite the dismay of her sister Samantha, later that same April in 1930, Mama and Charles Ayers were married. Mama quit her job at the boarding house — much to Annie Trotter's regret — and moved to the farm owned by the Ayers in Buckingham County, Virginia.

As Charles Ayer's young bride, Mama was once again back on a farm. She was used to farm life, having spent most of her childhood on one, but this farm was run in a more disciplined way, with all the family members carrying out certain tasks. Orderly and well planned, it seemed different than anything she had ever experienced. Charles had many sisters and brothers. His father Daniel and his mother, Bethy (Elizabeth), were very kind to Mama, and Mama tried hard to fit in with her new family and to please her husband.

The only thing Mama was really apprehensive about was trying to deal with — and understand — the Ayers' religion, for Grandpa Ayers had adopted the Jewish faith from one of his white neighbors. The Jewish religion was alien to Mama, as it would be to any young woman whose background was of the Baptist tradition and who had been raised to enjoy pork products from ribs to chitterlings and the yearly ritual of celebrating Christmas.

While Charles accepted and respected his folks' religious faith, he had cultivated his own beliefs, and he took every opportunity to expound his theories of religion, death and dying. He enjoyed talking, especially a chance to argue the difference between his views and the views of his father. The best moments for this ongoing conversations were at supper, after a long day of farm work. Charles lingered over his coffee taking aim at his father's views, pummeling away at his father's views of life after death and the question about the coming of the messiah. These discussions were always conducted in reasonable calm, with very little raising of voices, and Mama, who had left the table with the others long before, would sometimes listen from the kitchen where she was helping to clean up the dishes.

Charles believed that people proclaim religion because they were told — even as children — that if you were good and followed God's will, your body would die here on earth, but your spirit would live on forever in Heaven. Charles said, quite forcefully, that because of this promise, people wanted to learn how they must behave on earth in order to earn the blessing of life ever after. Consequently, it was not piety that drove people into the churches, he argued. "When the clergy promises to inform people how they can wind up in Heaven, then folks are going to sit down and listen." Grandpa Ayers expressed his opinions with no less ardor and the conversation would often continue for over an hour.

As time went on at the Ayers' farm, although she had more material things than she'd ever had in her life, Mama — as Samantha had predicted — did become unhappy. Charles at home on his family's farm was a much different Charles than the one she'd seen at the party where she'd fallen in love. That Charles — the fun-loving Charles — had been happy-go-lucky, smiling, fun-loving and generous, dancing with her till all hours, telling her all kinds of sweet nonsense that she'd loved. Here, he seemed almost stern with her sometimes, all the laughter and tickling fun had seemed to be wrung out of him in front of his parents, and he was constantly bombarding her with his religious philosophy — which she found utterly boring — and he treated her as a child.

It was a most unhappy discovery to find that she had married too quickly, and had been fooled by charms that seemed to have vanished along with what she'd thought was his fun-loving nature. She was always required to do what he wanted to do, when he wanted to do it, and listen to all his sophisticated talk, most of which she didn't understand and didn't even *want* to understand since it was all so complicated about life and death and Jews and the messiah supposed to arrive or that he'd already arrived. She just wasn't interested anymore.

She stuck it out for a little over a year, staying with Charles on the farm, motoring periodically to Summerslee to visit Samantha and her friend Mert. She worked as hard as she could with the family, trying to be a good daughter-in-law and a good wife. During that time Mama believed that Charles was trying to be a good husband. He was a kind and compassionate man who tried to teach her many different perspectives of life from his point of view, but he was terribly staid in his ways, too mature in his thinking, always knew best, and by the time she was eighteen, Mama was thinking seriously of leaving Charles. However, discovering she was pregnant prevented her taking any steps in that direction.

It was during the second year of their marriage, in the late summer of 1932, Mama gave birth to a baby boy who was stillborn. Charles was devastated at the loss, and somehow seemed to blame Mama, though she, too, was grieved by the death of her first child and could not understand his unforgiving attitude. After the baby's death, Mama felt a disturbing change in her husband. He became cold toward her, treating her unkindly and sometimes even cruelly. To her young eyes, Charles had become selfish and unreasonable.

Yet, she was his wife. She had married him, and she felt obligated to stay with him on the farm, although everything inside her wanted to run away... run away and find a kinder man, some one gentler and wiser, someone who would see all that she was and treasure her own specialness, not constantly try to educate her and change her into somebody she'd never be.

As the irrevocable agony of her situation hit her for the first time, she went off by herself and wept sorry tears. She could never be anything to Charles Ayers, or him to her anymore. It was over. Their happy time of playing, of trusting and seeking each other innocently and openly, with love and abandon, was over.

They still tried to make the marriage work, but there was too much anger between them now. The loss of the baby had provoked deep animosity between them and could never be put right. In spite of her strong feelings, Mama stayed with Charles at the farm a few months longer, but after her 20th birthday she left him in the summer of 1933 and they divorced. Unknown to either of them at the time, Mama was carrying me — Charles's second child — in her womb.

Lost and unhappy, feeling terribly let down and despondent over the failure of her marriage and the loss of her first baby, Mama returned to Summerslee and once again moved in with her sister Samantha. With tears the sisters greeted each other in a close embrace. At first there were a few heated words about "I told you so," from Samantha, who could not restrain herself, but her remarks were quickly forgotten for there were too many other things to tell and talk about. For Mama there was the unpacking and the settling into the same back bedroom she'd shared with Mert, and all the while pouring out how things had gone wrong with her and Charles. She wept again as they talked about the stillbirth of the child she and Charles had so desired, and how her husband had changed toward her afterward.

Samantha was truly glad to have Mama back again. She could hardly wait for Mama to get done with her story because she had one of her own she wanted to talk about. Finally it was Samantha's turn and as the two women went into the kitchen to start supper, she began telling Mama about her troubles. She'd been having a hard time with Rudy. Lately he'd been making her life miserable, she said, "an' he's goin' around actin' like a fool."

The two sisters sat down and poured themselves a drink and soon it was just like it had always been between them... loose, comfortable, funny and emotional. Samantha wiped away her tears as she told Mama that for the past several months Rudy'd been runnin' around like a wild man. "He's out chasing every woman he can find!" she said, her eyes flashing anger. "The man's gone skirt crazy. I swear I don't know what's come over him. And after all this time we been together. How can I keep on with a man actin' like that?"

Mama sympathized and poured herself another "tonic."

"You know that fool is runnin' so wild," Samantha said, laughing now, "I heard he's chasing cows across the pasture." She wasn't quite ready to admit she didn't care all that much anymore about Rudy and his philandering ways. After all this wasn't the first time Rudy had stepped out on her or revealed his not-too-hidden interest in some other woman. Rudy couldn't help being a good-timing man. It was his nature. Well, Samantha admitted to herself, when it came to that, she had seen a few young men looked pretty good to her, too, now and again. Before long, the two young ladies had cheered themselves up, decided to accept what life had handed them, dusted off their hands like they'd just cleaned out the wood stove and dismissed both of the current men in their lives. They were young, and good looking, and life must have something more to offer. They'd just have to go looking for it, Samantha said, with one of her sly smiles. "And that's what I'm plannin' on doin'." Mama nodded and the two of them agreed that Rudy would quickly become a shadow in the past, and as for Charles Ayers he could keep all his smart talk and his bossy ways.

Mama and Samantha giggled and drank a little bit more of that white lightnin' and fixed themselves a fine dinner... feeling free and independent and ... well, there was still this little bit of sadness in Mama made her stare out the window at the maple tree in the back yard and wonder how Mert had found somebody who'd worked out so fine. She'd been lucky.

One Sunday, about three weeks after Mama came back, a late July sun shone warmly down on the old church in Summerslee and a soft wind blew through the trees, moving the heavy green branches high overhead. It was still warm that evening when the setting sun began to send streamers of gleaming light through the lower branches of the trees, and the bees raced by on some last hurried errand. Mama didn't care to go, she said — she'd heard all she wanted to hear about religion for a while — so Samantha dressed for church and went out, never guessing she was about to lose her heart.

The moment Samantha set foot inside the black folks' church that evening, it was the glory of a young teacher and musician visiting the congregation who caught, and held, her eye as he skillfully directed the performance of a highly talented quartet. Upon first meeting this man, Samantha knew he was exactly what she wanted. Flamboyant, debonair, intelligent and well-educated, his name was Henry Sherrod, and Samantha called him "Sherry." As it turned out, Henry Sherrod was the father of Edward Sherrod — Mama's young hero who'd wrestled the bear — and Henry laughed when Samantha told him of his son's courageous showmanship.

Like a lightning bolt, love struck the two of them on first sight, and before anyone or anything could interfere, they married and moved away to the town of Leslie, a mining camp in the southern part of West Virginia in Greenbrier county. It happened so fast, in a flurry of joy and excitement, Mama was swept away during those busy days by her sister's happiness, and it wasn't until she'd stood on the porch waving goodbye to the newlyweds that she realized she was going to be alone. Alone in that little old house. Fixing meals by herself, sleeping by herself. Lord, but Mama hated being alone.

Then, as if her own personal sadness, and going through a divorce with Charles, wasn't enough for a young woman to cope with, one week later, a week full of worry and anxiety, her monthly period didn't come around... for the second time. When she missed in July she'd just thought it was nerves, being upset over leaving Charles and all, but now it was early August and Mama sighed, accepting the fact that she was pregnant.

CHAPTER 11
A Birth... A Brawl... and Bullets Are Flying!

Thank God for Mert.

"There's no two ways about it," Mert said on learning of Mama's condition. "You can't live there by yourself, Nora, cryin' and feelin' lonely all the time. I won't have it. Kemp won't mind you comin' in with us. I'll come get you this afternoon."

Mama packed up her things, all the while her mind buzzing with worry about what she was going to do about the baby. She was *not* going to go back to Charles, that was for sure. Yes, it was his child, but the thought of returning to the farm and his domineering ways chilled her to the bone. On the other hand, she was not going to be one of those poor black women everybody stares at because their baby didn't have no daddy. Her child was not going to be born illegitimate with the sad record on his birth certificate to carry with him all his life.

Mert and Kemp treated Mama with great tenderness and affection, but Mama knew it was a strain for her to be there, sleeping on the couch in the front room of the tiny one-bedroom house, and everybody missing their own privacy. Within a day or two she'd done all her crying about it, and she knew there was only one thing for her to do. Now that she'd made a plan, she didn't waste any time putting it into action.

In a very short time she re-kindled an old relationship with a coal miner and part-time preacher she'd known since first coming to Summerslee. He'd always had an eye out for her — women always can tell about things like that — and he'd been very kind to her since she'd arrived from Alabama. His name was Virgil Williams. Virgil, thrilled that this beautiful 20-year-old woman was interested in his company, didn't ask too many questions and grabbed at the chance for happiness, no matter if it might prove to be fleeting. Within three days they were married.

Mama always felt badly about marrying Virgil, knowing she wasn't telling him the whole truth about her condition. Oh, she told him she was pregnant shortly after the wedding, but she just let him assume it was his child. Holding back on the truth though was like a dark cloud over Mama's heart. She felt bad seeing his joy at them being together and knowing she was holding a secret. Virgil was good to Mama all during the hardest months of her pregnancy, but every time he brought her a cup of tea or helped with some of the house chores to save her spending too much energy — small and petite like she was — she felt guilty. In fact, the nicer he was to her the worse it made her feel. But still, she defended, what else could she have done but find a good man to give her child a name? Seven months after their August wedding — prematurely, Mama insisted to Virgil — on the 9th day of March, 1934, I was born.

Mama chose to name me Charles after my biological father Charles Ayers and my last name became Williams after her new husband. Mama felt forced to keep up the ruse that I was born a little early, and that I was Virgil's son, because of Virgil's strong-minded moralistic feelings about the marriage relationship and the fact that he'd often mentioned how he'd hate it if Mama ever lied to him. So, in spite of all her misgivings, Mama knuckled down and stayed on with Virgil, trying to make a go of it. After all, his willingness to marry her so quickly had saved her a lot of humiliation, and for that she was grateful to the man. Grateful, yes, but Mama didn't truly love Virgil. There wasn't anything she could do about that.

Sensing Mama's half-hidden withdrawal from him, it wasn't long before Virgil became disenchanted with his new bride, and began to listen to the rumors that she's been pregnant by her first husband, Charles Ayers, before she married him. Try as he did to overlook the gossip and go on as if it weren't true, that thought kept eating at Virgil. Every time he looked at me, Mama saw him wondering, staring at my features as if trying to find some resemblance that could convince him and squelch all the gossip, but the resemblance just wasn't there. This dark shadow between them caused a great strain and a festering resentment began to rise in Virgil.

By June, it became evident that I resembled him in no way at all. At that point, he began grousing about it aloud to his friends, and they were quick to agree I was not his son. It was more than a man like Virgil could take.

It was at dusk on a warm June night when Mama and Virgil engaged in a bitter argument. After a few drinks, and a lot of angry shouting, with accusations flying through the air like darts in a pool hall, Mama gave it up. She turned around, put her hands on her hips and said the words he'd been trying to push out of her. "All right, Virgil. You want to know? Well, the rumors are true." She spoke in a quiet voice. "I'm sorry, but that's the way it is. This boy is Charles's son. I been holding all this for too long, Virgil, but there's no gettin' away from the truth. I didn't mean to hurt you, but I had to protect my baby." And then Mama smiled. Her smile wasn't meant to mock him, she wasn't laughing at him, it was just that despite the pain and frustration that still gnawed at the edges of her mind she was suddenly immensely happy. She'd finally told him the truth. That confession filled her with such relief and sudden joy it made her smile, but Virgil didn't know that. He stared at her for no more than two seconds, feeling his rage mounting like a geyser inside him. She had lied to him. She had betrayed him. In a blind fury Virgil raced to his closet and reached for his .22-caliber rifle.

Believing Virgil would kill her, Mama snatched me from the crib and dashed to the door. Cuddling me her arms she ran, terrified, toward Mert's, knowing her friend would help her. By the time Virgil roared out of the house with his loaded rifle, Mama was a distance away. But Virgil laid himself on the ground in a prone position and fired at Mama as she sheltered me in her arms and ran for her life. If Virgil hadn't been shaking with rage, he probably would have shot her dead right there, but his hand was not steady and two of the bullets hit Mama in the right thigh. She cried out from the burning pain and felt the warm blood run down her leg, still she ran, knowing if she fell or slowed, Virgil would kill her and most likely, he'd kill me also. Carrying me, Mama staggered against the pain, but somehow she kept running.

Rifle shots brought neighbors to their doors. The sight of a young woman holding an infant to her chest and running for dear life stirred an angry outburst. Yelling at Virgil, they came out to see what was going on. One woman summoned the camp superintendent.

When Mama reached Mert's, she was crying and hobbling along with blood streaming down her leg. Mert lifted me out of my mama's arms, cuddled me for a moment to stop my frightened screaming, and then put me down in a deep upholstered chair by the fireplace. She guided Mama to a bed, and quickly wrapped a thick towel about the wound to hold off the bleeding. Hurrying to the porch where people were gathered, Mert sent a man running off to bring the camp physician, Dr. Benjamin.

Twenty minutes later the doctor arrived in a T-model Ford and bounding up the steps with his black leather bag. "What happened?" he asked, going immediately to Mama's bedside and removing the towel to examine her wounds. Mert told him what Virgil had done. The doctor examined Mama, then shaking his head, he removed bandages and the instruments he'd need for minor surgery from his bag. Knowing it was going to hurt her badly, he asked Mert to come hold her hands and try to keep her still. He had to tie her legs to the bed for he knew any human being would naturally jerk away from such agony. Mert was weeping, but she stepped forward firmly and held Mama down with all her strength. Mama tried not to scream, but she nearly broke her teeth clamping her jaws against the searing pain. The first one, not too deep, came out quickly and Mert wiped Mama's sweating brow. "Just a little more, honey," she said, her eyes tearing over with her sympathy. "Hold on. Hold on."

Carefully, and as quickly as he could, the doctor used a scalpel skillfully to dig out the second bullet imbedded in Mama's upper thigh. Mercifully, Mama passed out.

"Praise God! She won't feel it no more," Mert sobbed.

After a minute Mert got Mama to open her eyes. "It's all over, Nora," Mert soothed. "The bullets are out. You gonna be fine now." She plumped the pillows. "Just lie still, honey, and let the doctor finish up." She untied Mama's legs and brushed back her hair.

The doctor told Mama how lucky she was to have been out of range of the full force of Virgil's bullets. Otherwise, he said, they could have hit her squarely in the back, shattering her spine and penetrated her stomach or lungs causing sudden death. Just as Dr. Benjamin was leaving, the Superintendent and his entourage arrived at Mert's house. The doctor spoke with them on the front porch — the Superintendent stuck his head in the door to see Mama on the bed with her bandaged leg — and after assessing the situation they promptly arrested Virgil.

Virgil hadn't run off. He was so angry about Mama lying to him he'd just sat there on his own front porch, muttering to himself, shaking his rifle at the neighbors who were watching him through the windows, and trying to drink himself into the forgetfulness of an alcoholic stupor.

Within only a few days, my biological father — Mama's first husband, Charles Ayers — got word of the situation. Bad news always travels fast, and the shooting — along with the gossip about me not being Virgil's baby — was passed on quickly. Worried for Mama's welfare — putting two and two together and guessing the truth of the circumstances of my birth — Charles didn't hesitate a moment. Grabbing up his hat and coat he jumped into his car and motored from Buckingham, Virginia, all the way up to Summerslee. As could be imagined, his arrival prompted apprehension on Mama's part... and yet compassion, too. She immediately understood that Charles now knew he had a son. A boy. An heir. The child he'd always wanted.

The thought that kept racing across Mama's mind was, "Will he take my baby away from me?" Charles was a well-off, settled, responsible, mature man; a property owner along with his highly respected family; he was a hard worker and a part-time preacher of the word of God. He was powerful, and had well-placed friends. Was he going to try to say that she wasn't able to raise the child as well as he could? Was he going to hurt her like that?

Sunlight glimmered through the shutters of Mert's house as Mama lifted her chin and pulled up the covers on her bed. She was trembling, but she wasn't going to let him know how scared she really was. Worry wrinkles pleated her forehead but shook her head and forced a pleasant expression as his car stopped in front of the house.

"Charles Ayers is here." Elnora heard the whispers of the neighbors who had gathered on Mert's porch, fascinated by the drama unfolding before their eyes. As Mama watched through the window, his long, loose-limbed figure emerged from the gleaming automobile, ambled confidently up the walk and onto the porch. He didn't knock, sensing that she already knew who was coming to see her; he just swung the door open and came to her side.

Taking her hand, Charles gazed into her dark eyes and spoke in his low, well-modulated voice... a voice that any actor would cherish... a voice she'd heard raised to her in chastisement so many times, but he wasn't chastising her now. Surprisingly, he seemed tender and caring.

"Nora, why did you not tell me you were pregnant with my son?"

It was a simple question, yet Mama felt her heart leap up to her throat. She flashed many excuses — lies, really — in her mind, but she held his gaze and told him the truth. "I was afraid," she responded. "I... I was afraid you'd try to force me to come back to the farm." She saw a shadow of pain pass fleetingly in his eyes.

"I wouldn't force you to do anything, Nora," he said, but then he glanced away, realizing that perhaps he might well have tried... if he'd known. "How's your wound? Does it hurt badly?" He had not released his hold on her cold fingers.

"No, it's not too bad. Doctor said I was lucky I wasn't killed."

Charles shuddered. "I'm sorry that happened." They sat together in silence then for a moment. "Can I see him?"

"Sure. He's a beautiful baby."

Charles arose and moved lightly over to my crib. Mama told me he stared down at me for the longest time, finally reaching down and adjusting the blanket away from my round face, and touching my fingers.

"I guess... I guess I understand why you didn't want me to know," Charles said, coming back to Mama's side. "He really is a handsome lookin' baby."

Mama saw the hint of a smile touching his firm lips and she smiled warmly up at the man she had lived with for those long, difficult years. They stared a long moment at each other, their eyes saying things that words never could. Mama finally spoke. "Your son's eyes are the exact pattern of yours. Did you see that?"

His eyes remained fixed on Mama as he nodded, as if to say, "I know." And suddenly he smiled, really smiled at her as gladness about his son welled up in his heart. He had a son. "What is the boy's name?"

"I named him Charles after you," Mama said, feeling his emotions. "Of course, 'cause of Virgil, his last name is Williams."

"Charles," he repeated, and his voice sounded pleased. Then, in a practical manner, he asked Mama if she would consider surrendering me to his care until she was well, until her leg had healed.

Mama turned her eyes away from him and hardened her heart to his easy charm. She knew how persuasive he could be when he wanted to. Firmly Mama shook her head. "No, I couldn't do that, Charles."

My father left some money with Mama — just to help her get through this hard time, he said, since Virgil had been put in jail — and then he left. His eyes were gleaming with pride, Mama said, and she always remembered how jauntily he walked, almost floating on air, to his shiny car. He had a son. Damn! He had a *son!*

As for my Mama's wounds, she was a strong woman and after only a few days she was up and about and as good as new... except for the scars marking the smooth skin of her right thigh.

CHAPTER 12
A Dashing Young Man From The Carolinas

When I was one year old, one hot summer day in June of 1935, a twenty-nine-year-old mining-partner of Kemp's came by Mert's place to drink "white-lighting" and discuss the effect of the impending walk-out by the coal miners. The young partner's name was James Leadbetter, a dashing young man from the Carolinas. Kemp knew that most folks spelled James' last name as "Leadbetter" or "Ledbetter" and sometimes "Lead Belly," but James always preferred to be called "Leadbelly," which seemed to personify his hardness toward society. Indeed, Led was a powerful man with his slim build, his smooth black skin, a straight nose and pearly-white teeth.

Mama knew the instant he walked into Mert's house that this man would steal her heart. Her marriage to Virgil had been annulled a year ago, right after the shooting, so she was free to indulge the instant attraction she felt for this handsome stranger.

James told Mama — whom he was taken with the moment they were introduced — that he was the son of a street musician named Huddie Leadbetter, a man known throughout the Deep South as Huddie Leadbelly. After a few drinks, more of James's story, and the story of his father, came out.

It seems Huddie was only fifteen years old when he fathered James by a seventeen-year-old chocolate skinned, almond-eyed young lady named Irene. Irene's heritage was African-American, Chinese, French Creole and West Indian.

Huddie had met Irene in 1905 during his rambling sojourns throughout rural northwest Louisiana and Texas. As Huddie strayed across the Deep South, his keening, high-pitched vocals and powerful, percussive guitar playing commanded attention. Beautiful women were no exception and they flocked around Huddie, competing with each other to be in his company. According to James, his mother Irene was mesmerized by fifteen-year-old Huddie Leadbelly's enormous strength, talent, good looks and sexual prowess. Unable to resist such a powerful combination, she gave in to his needs and became pregnant. Irene had then followed Huddie when he took off for the Carolinas, but she eventually lost track of him. A kind black family took Irene in and helped her deliver her baby boy. James had no birth certificate, but he told Mama he was born in 1906 in a one-room log cabin.

It's been said that Huddie intended to leave his common law wife, and that was what inspired him to write "Goodnight, Irene," a song made famous by white musicians many years later. James survived a life that included brutal poverty and hardship. Like his father, he was talented musically, and in many other ways; good-looking, and had a remarkable way with women. When he grew to manhood, he was, as they say, the "spitin' image" of his father, Huddie Leadbelly.

Following his father's footsteps, James became a common-law husband at age seventeen to a stunning older lady named Essie Mae, six years his senior. According to James, Essie Mae was a tall, slim beauty, who added immensely to her attractiveness by the way she carried herself.

Long, dark hair framed her well-featured face which was never adorned with anything more than the rosy glow produced by plain soap and water and the warm southern winds. The two lovers had a daughter named Castmay. Sometime later, James left North Carolina and made his way to West Virginia to work in the coal mines.

James never did explain why he left his common law wife and daughter behind. His friend Kemp believed that James — or "Led" as Mama called him — had intentions to move his family to West Virginia once he found a job. But Mama's friend Mert contended that once Led laid eyes on Elnora, he totally forgot his family back in North Carolina.

Led's quixotic nature made him a strange type of man, a sojourner, a migrant who never stayed in one place very long and seemed to be always on the run. Short-tempered and moody, Led seldom laughed. His favorite weapon was a straight razor or a switch blade knife, and ugly rumors persisted around the camp towns that he had already killed several men by slitting their throats. Led casually denied this, and whenever the question was put to him, he'd smile sarcastically and say "Nope, not that many." But there was no way to deny that he took pride in his father's reputation of being a killer.

HUDDIE LEADBETTER
Huddie was the father of James Leadbetter. Huddie rose from itinerant street musician to world recognition, and as his son James did in later years,   Huddie often bragged about his sexual prowess and his ability to entertain people... women in particular. This photo was taken around 1928 or '29.

With no formal education, Led was illiterate, but he needed no instruction on being an entertainer like his daddy. At times he told funny jokes or he'd stand up and perform a wild and rhythmic tap dance. He loved to play the guitar or strum a banjo, and just ask him and he'd sing blues or any of the hillbilly songs.

One late evening, a group of men had gathered at Kemp's house, and they were sitting out on his front porch drinking moonshine and listening to Led's jokes. According to people who knew Led best, he could tell a funny story… but only when he was in the mood or sitting around drinking booze.

That night he told them a joke about the tough life of a preacher who was trying to raise money for his church. According to Led, the preacher had tried just about everything legal to raise money, but he wasn't having much luck.

Finally one of the church members told him about horse racing, claiming that a fortune could be made on the horses. Having heard rumors about this before, the preacher decided to buy himself a horse and enter it in a race. However, at the local auction place, the going price for horses was so steep that he ended up buying a donkey instead.

Contemplating that since he had it, he might as well go ahead, he entered it in the races. To his surprise, in the first race his donkey came in second. The next day the racing sheets carried this headline: "*Preacher's Ass Shows!*"

Well, that preacher was so pleased he entered his donkey in another race. For the second time the donkey won, and the racing sheet read: "*Preacher's Ass Out In Front!*"

The local bishop was so upset with this kind of publicity that he ordered the preacher not to enter the donkey in another race and to scratch the donkey from the racing sheet. The next day, the new headlines read: "*Bishop Scratches Preacher's Ass!*" Now, this was too much for the bishop, and he ordered the preacher to get rid of the animal. The preacher gave it to a nun in a nearby convent. The next day, headlines said: "*Nun Has Best Ass In Town!*"

The bishop fainted.

When they revived him, he told the nun that she would have to dispose of the donkey. The nun finally found a farmer who said he would take it off her hands for ten dollars. The paper said: "*Nun Peddles Ass For Ten Bucks!*"

They buried the bishop the next day.

With this, the men fell down laughing. One of the group was a man called "Rat" who was rolling on the ground laughing to bust out his sides. He couldn't stop though tears were streaming down his face. So another man called "Big

Hands" picked Mr. Rat up and shook him like his namesake until he stopped laughing.

Despite his shortcomings, it was not long before Mama fell in love with Led. Not letting anything stand in their way, she and Led took off together, leaving me with Mert and Kemp for a while, and were "married," though no one ever learned any details of the ceremony. They returned as man and wife and after picking me up, they lived in several different coal mining camps as Led kept moving about under the pretense that he was looking for work.

After almost a year of his restlessness, in April of 1936, Led brought Mama, pregnant and in her last month, back to Summerslee where she gave birth to my sister whom Led named Marguerite.

Marguerite was the very image of Led. She was born with a head full of black curly hair and smooth dark skin. Led was proud of his daughter. Like most fathers he was concerned about her future and worried about how he could ensure the survival of his child and the family. This was a primary concern for all the coal miners during the crisis between them and the owners.

At the time, in 1936, mining was slowed in Summerslee, so Led took off by himself, saying he was going to find work in another coal mining field, leaving Mama, Marguerite, who was just an infant, and myself, only a two-year-old, with Mert and Kemp. He sent word to Mama as he crisscrossed central and northern West Virginia. About that time Uncle Henry and Aunt Samantha got word to Mama that some coal loading jobs were available where they lived in Leslie. Uncle Henry had become an activist in Leslie's African-American community and in the coal miner's union. Mama was sure that his influences would help get a job for Led. So Led, Mama and us children packed our belongings, said many thanks and farewell to Mert and Kemp, and moved to Leslie.

CHAPTER 13
Leslie Hollow... Friday Night In "Nigger Bottom"

It was in Leslie, West Virginia, a coal mining community in the Appalachian mountains, where I first realized my being — a sudden and sharp awareness of myself and my surroundings — when I was five years old. It was like awakening from a calm dream and, all at once, every little thing aroused me with wonderment and awe.

All around our run-down little shanty on the mountainside of Leslie Hollow, I saw the picturesque evidence of the wonderment of nature. Steep slopes dominated the topography and their slanted sides gave way to the narrow bottom land where black folks like us lived in almost every conceivable mode of the rural condition. To my eyes it was a mountain paradise, but in my innocence I couldn't see the reality of the squalor that surrounded me.

All Appalachia hollows might appear to be the same, but in reality they are all different. Each has its own uniqueness, its own mysteries and many untold stories. The hollows themselves are the result of the tumultuous upheavals that occurred millions of years ago, of shuddering earthquakes and thrusting ice floes which created towering mountain knobs jutting upward from the melting earth. Maps do not list most hollows in West Virginia. Only the tall mountains that shelter the hollows are named. But in July of 1939, within the Appalachia Hollow of Leslie, my own life story begins, when I suddenly came awake — aware of being myself — at the age of five.

In Leslie Hollow, Mama and Led and me and my three-year-old little sister Marguerite settled in a murky mining camp called Foggy Bottom. The local bigots liked to call it "Nigger Bottom," a slur based on the fact that it was where the largest group of blacks lived. Foggy Bottom's sloping mountain

66

knobs were sprinkled with sagging makeshift shacks built out of tin and cardboard. Slowly I came to see Foggy Bottom as the image of poverty, for it contained all the characteristics of the great depression going on at the time; a spot where pig sties, rotting wood, unwashed clothing and dirty human bodies prevailed.

On the west side of the Hollow, stood Buck Knob, Walnut Knob and Beer Garden Knob. To the east stood Peasor Knob, Sumac Knob, Rich Knob, Laurel Creek Mountain and Mill Creek Mountain. Each knob and mountain had its own kind of hobos and hillbillies. A railroad cut through the Hollow, and it was a childhood ritual of mine to watch the giant steam locomotives pulling empty railroad cars to the Leslie mine, and then pulling the same railroad cars away, loaded with coal. From far off, as I stood observing, I could see the transient hobos, the fugitives and criminals who were illegally aboard, and watched them hitching rides in the empty boxcars.

Misfits looking for refuge often took up residence in Leslie Holler... or hid out on one of the Knobs. Hobos frequently joined up with derelicts and outlaws, or even some of the rebellious coal miners who were hiding out to escape the armed guards hired by coal-mining companies to capture and arrest them. There were others, snuggled into a shack or a shanty in the deep woods, who were moonshine makers. They all lived among themselves in the shanty town shacks that peppered the hillsides. Consequently, bounty hunters did not bother to differentiate one category from the other, and perceived them all as wanted criminals.

Everybody knew that the creek flowing through the Leslie Holler had been poisoned by water drained from coal mines and coal-washing facilities. During rain storms the creek would metamorphose into a river and spill over, flooding Nigger Bottom. Twice a year flooding water turned into colossal funnels, hurtling along unchecked, inundating hollow after hollow. Spewing raw sewage from outhouses, loaded with ghastly coliform bacteria, flooded the ground, killing vegetation and filling the air with a nose-burning sulfurous stench.

In Leslie Hollow, Led quickly discovered that the coal miners only were able to work one or two days a week in the dark, damp, ghostly shafts. During the summer months, the men had to go weeks, and sometime months, without working at all, since at that time there was little demand for coal in the northern communities.

Coal miners who were out of work, drew monthly food rations for their families, but that was never enough. Their children were sick from near starvation, and had stomachs swollen painfully from eating green apples, and anything else they could get their hands on. Unemployed miners would, by necessity, turn to thievery and rustling, tracking down runaway domesticated animals such as cows, goats and pigs — anything they could kill and eat. Life was so hard then, with so many folks suffering rock-bottom poverty, it all seemed like a bad dream to Mama.

Our little shanty, like all the other shacks, was tucked into a small clearing in the trees with only a dirt path leading off into the hills beyond. One evening, Mama sent me to Aunt Samantha's house to deliver a note regarding the up-coming weekend party that was going to be held at our house.

I started off down the path through the clearing. When I got to Aunt Samantha's, I remember she was holding a mean-looking butcher knife and hacking chicken parts. She was putting together a meal of fried chicken with barbecue sauce, corn bread, greens and lemonade which she'd take to Mama's houseparty. I gave her the note from Mama and then stood around watching as she pulled a few pieces of brown chicken from the frying pan. It smelled so good, my mouth was watery as the aroma engulfed the whole house. That delicious aroma even reached the front porch where Uncle Henry was sitting in a porch swing with a glass of bourbon. He called out, "That chicken sure smells good, Bunchy. It's makin' me hungry!"

"It'll be done soon, Sherry. Then we'll be on our way to Elnora's."

"All right," he acknowledged.

After hearing Uncle Henry speak up, I figured I would try my luck. "Hey, Bunchy," I said, smiling up at her, "can I have a piece of chicken?"

My Aunt Samantha looked astonished! Then she began to chastise me in a way that made such a lasting impression, I never forgot. She was already half intoxicated, and with that sharp butcher knife in her hand, waving near my face, I was more than astonished, I was petrified with fear. Bending close to my small frame, she scolded me loudly and severely for calling her "Bunchie," — a diminutive of "Honey Bunch" my Uncle Henry often used for her. Then Aunt Samantha gave me a quick lesson in etiquette, insisting I call her "Aunt-T." At least that was the way I heard it. She said it slowly… "Aunt-T"… slowly and distinctly, stretching her mouth on the "tee" part, so I'd be sure to hear her correctly. In less than five seconds flat she'd made it clear that I must always call grownups "Mr" or "Mrs." or "Miss," using their first or last names, and that as a child, I was being disrespectful by daring to use a nick-name only privileged by her husband. While she was making her point, waving that knife close to my small nose for emphasis, I began to cry, for not only was I terrified, but I had pissed my trousers.

Eyeing that butcher knife, my infantile mind suddenly began to record and comprehend everything she was saying very profoundly. Now I know she was using a scare-tactic to insure I would never forget her instructions, and it worked, for I was rudely awakened right there in her kitchen; awakened to events in my life from that day on, and in that first moment of memory I understood that I was a living being and I was horrified. I can still see her weaving a little as she shook that knife at me. So strong was that image set in my mind, to this very day I remember everything in that kitchen: The tall kitchen cabinet with fancy dishes, the long table with a white table cloth exhibiting some delicately crocheted lace, the light-brown-colored linoleum on the floor. My awakening might be compared to a person's first experience with a violent thunderstorm where lightning flashes across the sky and the roar of thunder jars the human spirit. Somewhere deep in my young soul I "came to" and began to see myself as a human creature who was part of some incredible force and a part of the terrible world around me.

It was not long before the meal was ready to go. Aunt-T said she was exhausted and needed to rest before being able to walk to the party. She pleaded with Uncle Henry to go ahead and take the food, she would come later after taking a nap.

Uncle Henry realized that Aunt-T was tipsy, and if she took a nap, waking her up would have been next to impossible. He insisted they go to the party together. Finally, Aunt-T agreed to leave with us. She went to her closet, primped a bit, donned her dancing shoes, a feathered hat that was high fashion for the time, a little rouge on each cheek and we were ready to go. About half way down the little knoll situated at the back from their house, Aunt-T staggered and finally fell on her rump.

Uncle Henry knew better than to laugh... at least not where she could see. He said, "Hold on, Bunchy. I'll get the wheelbarrow."

"What do you need the wheelbarrow for?" Aunt-T spouted, still sprawled on her bottom.

"You can sit in it, Bunchy. Then I'll push you over to Nora's place!" Uncle Henry raced over to get the wheelbarrow from under the back porch. Then he raced up the steps, found his door key and opened the back door. Meanwhile, I was busy trying to help Aunt-T to her feet, but she was too heavy for me. It was not long before Uncle Henry returned with a thick blanket. He tossed it over the wheelbarrow's bucket so that the dirty residue there would not soil Aunt-T's dress. Then we both helped Aunt-T into the

69

wheelbarrow and away we went.

Being the child I was, I perceived my environment as a giant world where everything was much bigger than I. With a sense of dwarfishness, I trotted behind my Uncle Henry as he pushed the teetering wheelbarrow. He was taking long steps. I could hear his heavy breathing, a steady, laborious sighing as he staggered along, pushing the metal monster. His long steps made it hard for my short legs to keep up. Uncle Henry stalwartly pushed on. The large metal monstrous-looking wheelbarrow was overflowing with the flabby body of my Aunt Samantha. as she sprawled there, intoxicated.

Uncle Henry was panting loudly as he approached the place where Mama, me, Led and Marguerite lived. After helping Aunt-T heave herself from the 'barrow, we entered the kitchen where Mama toiled between the hot fireplace and a big, black, square, coal-burning stove, cooking away.

The houseparty was about to begin. Plenty of fish, battered in corn meal and dipped in hot, boiling grease was in the making. A huge pot of pinto beans, with a large piece of salted pork, was steaming on top of a stove. The stove sat on four iron legs which had a long, black pipe that reached the top of the shanty. One large black skillet was packed with pork barbecue ribs. The menu included Brunswick stew, hush puppies, coleslaw, collard greens, fried chicken and corn bread. I could feel my stomach gnawing with hunger.

I watched Mama prepare ashcakes. Ashcakes were made from a mixture of water, corn meal and butter beaten into a thick batter. When the batter was the right consistency, Mama poured it to the floor of the extremely hot fire-grate, shaping each puddle into a pancake portion before covering it with red-hot cinders. In a little while the red-hot cinders cooled to ash gray, which was a sure sign that the ashcakes had browned. The gray ashes were carefully scraped away and the ashcakes were removed and piled onto a large plate common to the party-folks. I knew what would happen to those ashcakes, and I could hardly wait: A bowl of peach preserves with hunks of peaches would be placed near the ashcakes on the table. The party people would slap a spoon full peach preserve onto an ashcake, curl it up like a slim bread-roll and then consume the mix as a delicious hors d'oeuvre while waiting for the main dishes to arrive from the kitchen.

As Mama continued to prepare for the party, I found my way to the front door and out onto the porch, sitting there on the porch floorboards with my feet dangling over the edge. A brisk summer breeze whisked hot and sticky. Smells of burning slag filled the air with a sulfurous stench. As I surveyed the huge world around me, I was awed by the silhouettes of tall oak trees that stood, black, against a summer moon. In this area, the steep slopes were sprinkled with all types of sagging shacks and the narrow canyon floor smelled of burning kerosene lamps. Almost everyone in the hollow lived in a gray-planked, tar-paper-roofed, one- or two-room dwelling, sometime called "shanties." Attached to each dwelling was a wooden porch. Some porches were broken down and rotting away; others were covered and brought into use as an extra room.

As the light breeze shifted, the stench from outhouses was overwhelming, but that stench blended in with the loud music, the laughter and chatter going on among the good-timin' community dwellers. The sound of blues music echoed through the night with a strangely sad musical mystique. I sat on our front porch, my belly growling with hunger, taking in the sight of everything around me while waiting on Mama to call me to eat. Finally she did and at last I had my fill.

All around me people were jazzin' around, talking and laughing and eating. It was Friday night and all the community citizenry were jolly and spirited as they sat on their porches drinking white lighting made of pig mash. Let me tell you about pig mash. First off, there is no part of a pig in pig mash. It's only *called* pig mash because it used to be fed to the pigs, as well as to the slaves, on the old southern plantations, but it is made from dry corn pounded into very fine, almost powdery cornmeal. People used it to make corn cakes by adding water, maybe a little sugar if you have it. And, if you know how, you can turn that corn mash into corn whisky, a cheap, gut-burning, mind-warping liquor called white lightnin'.

At the time, white lightning was the booze of the day. Mama and Led passed the strong whiskey freely among the party goers jammed into their little shanty, and I watched them dance and stagger around, laughing and talking incoherently.

Periodically folk from nearby communities of Crichton and Little Fork would join the good times. Every once in a while, a few white people attended. Generally they came from Laurel Creek Mountain or Buck Knob. Usually they would hitchhike to Nigger Bottom just to buy a plate of soul food. Those who dared to, mingled with the black folks and stayed on to enjoy themselves while eating aesthetic food, drinking moonshine, and listening to the blues.

Mama's Friday-night party was in full swing. It roared on through the night. At half-past eleven the dancing had become fast and furious. I remembering noticing a fine mist ascending from the wood floor, mingling with cigarette smoke. The mix hung like a gray haze in the room. Through the haze the music whined and moaned and soared. The shuffling of feet, and loud voices and the occasional bursts of laughter merged into a sort of steady, dull hubbub as predominant as a sustained organ note.

The air was suffocating. Collars wilted, men's faces shone, the women's dresses looked bedraggled, and their hair curls were pushed carelessly from flushed damp faces. Soon more neighbors came to join in and they passed more white lightning and home brew around. At the time, an African-American ritual, derived from the old slave mentality, I suppose, was raging in Nigger Bottom and everybody sang, "Let The Good Times Roll." But let me tell you, that party rocked all night.

The next day the whole community slept late into the morning. Mama coerced

Marguerite and me to remain on our sleeping pallet longer than usual. She was tired, and I felt pity for her, but I didn't know how to tell her that.

The sun was climbing higher in the sky and I was tired of playing baby games with Marguerite. My stomach was beginning to feel empty but Marguerite appeared content. Unlike most children, she never cried when she was hungry. It seemed that the habit of sucking her thumb satisfied the emptiness of her stomach. She was a cute-looking three-year-old with a round, black, doll face and long thick black hair. Her hair stood out much like Buckwheat's, the child actor in the *"Little Rascals"* movies.

The house was peaceful compared to the noisy party the night before. Our little room seemed adrift in a sea of quiet as sunlight began to peep through holes in the dark-colored shades. Sometime during the early morning Led had built a coal-fire in the old-fashioned fireplace as summer nights in the hollows were chilly. The fireplace kept the rooms moderately warm, and with that rosy glow, morning in our little shanty seemed as pleasant as if it were a palace.

The fire dwindled down and for a long while I sat with my eyes fixed on the last glowing coals, yawing, tired and restless. Soon the glowing coals died and there was no more popping or cracking. The only noise in the room was the ticking of the clock.

It was late morning when Mama and Led lifted themselves from bed. The house was a total wreck. Discarded paper, glasses and cups, whiskey bottles and cigarette butts were everywhere. All the food was gone; only dirty, empty plates were left. Mama washed both our faces with a damp cloth and then plopped Marguerite into her highchair. She handed me the half-gallon pail and sent me to fetch water from the community pump.

Not far from the pump a big, red, pugnacious rooster pranced cockily around his owner's shanty. He kept his beady eyes on me as if he expected me to invade his territory. But I feared to do that, knowing that as small and skinny as I was, I wouldn't have much chance if attacked by his powerful beak and sharp spurs.

Led drank half of the first pail-full I brought, and poured the rest of it over his head... obviously suffering a great thirst from a pounding hangover. He and Mama began to clean up the shanty, Led sweeping trash and Mama preparing to wash the dishes. Feeling like I was lending a big hand, I rushed out to get another bucket of water.

After the dishes were put away, Mama set up to do some serious cleaning by putting a washtub on the stove and filling it half full of water. When the water was heated, she poured in a cup of Oxydol, her favorite detergent, and with a rag-mop she scrubbed down all the wood floors in our shanty. I kept busy shuttling water from the pump and soon our shanty was clean again.

For our lunch, using whatever scraps we had, Mama gave us some fried-apples and crisp fried saltpork. Led and I peeled the wild apples while Mama made buttermilk biscuits. Then, after we'd eaten, Led packed-up his crude fishing gear and hiked up the mountain to the railroad tracks. I knew he was going to hitch a ride on the coal car like a hobo so he could get to Summersville Lake to snare a catfish.

CHAPTER 14
Attempted Murder

It was April, one month after my sixth birthday in 1940, and mama began her washing one Monday morning. Doing the laundry was a hard job for Mama as she had to scrub everything by hand. After soaking all the white things in her wash tub, she'd lug the heavy tub over to the stove and leave it on the fire until the water boiled up around the clothes. Then she'd haul it over to the wash bench, let the steaming water cool a little, and then she'd rub each piece of clothing on her washboard. In those days' people in the hollow did not know anything about Laundromats or washing machines.

Later in the week, Althea, Uncle Henry's youngest daughter from his first wife, stopped by our house. She and Mama were fairly good friends. I remember Althea as being a shapely, short little lady with buck teeth. Althea carried an intense hatred for Aunt-T, presumably because she had caused the break-up between her papa, Uncle Henry, and his first wife. Consequently Althea did all she could to undermine any relationship between Aunt-T and any potential friend. On this particular day, she was gossiping to Mama about one problem and another. Very protective and jealous she always referred to my Uncle Henry as "papa." During her conversation with Mama I heard her express her strong dislike for Aunt-T.

"Elnora, I know she is your sister," Althea said, "but I will never forgive that bitch for taking papa away from my mother." Then she took a sip of the iced tea Mama had brought her and leaning forward, her eyes became narrowed a mean-looking. "You ought to hear what she said about you." She hesitated, glancing at me.

"Charles," Mama said, "go outside and play."

"Yes, Mama." I got up from where I was playing on the floor. I knew they

74

were about to discuss something they did not want me to hear, and I knew it was something about Aunt-T. But I was obedient and went outside to play. Of course I sat on the back porch with my ear to the door, hoping to hear what they were saying, but they were speaking in low voices and I couldn't make out their words. Even then, I remember thinking that Althea was deliberately trying to set Mama against her own sister by repeating something mean she must have said, but I was too young to understand the significance... or guess the terrible event all this was leading up to.

I sat on the back porch and looked to the mountainside, marveling at the heavily-forested hills surrounding the hollow. Hickory, walnut and acorn-bearing oak trees were scattered about the forest. Meadowlarks were chirping melodies, robins were making rain calls, buzzards circled smoothly looking for dead prey, plus there were chickadees, goldfinches and bluebirds nesting in the wild apple trees or nestled in one of the tall oaks. I watched the little colored birds in the apple trees or the swallows darting under any shelter they could find. There were maple trees too, and in them sometimes would be a hidden robin's nest with a precious cargo of blue eggs. If I were quiet — and very lucky — I'd see the straining necks and gaping beaks of hungry babies searching the air for worms the mother brought back to the nest.

Althea left our house, and the sun had already drifted to the west when Mama summoned me to take a note to her sister. Immediately I began to visualize my journey, and realized I'd have to pass the shanty where a big red rooster lived. In the past I'd had no problem with that rooster, but recently he'd begun loitering about his owner's front porch and I knew he did not like me for some reason. In my mind, he was just waiting for me to pass, and I was scared of that aggressive old bird. I did not tell Mama because I wanted her to think that I was her brave little man.

I took the note and was on by way. When I passed the rooster's place, he was nowhere to be seen, so I skipped along happily thinking, "Maybe that old rooster's not as bad as I thought."

Lucky for me I reached Aunt-T's while she was just finishing putting chocolate icing on a three-layer cake. Giving her Mama's note, I begged her to let me scrape the remaining icing from the bowl and she obliged. That bowl was almost as big as I was, but I held it in my arms and went to the front porch where the double chair-swing was. I was only two-and-a-half-feet tall and the seat of the swing was at least two-feet from the floor. I stood there with this big bowl in my arms trying to figured out how I could get both me and the bowl up into the swing. Finally I sat the huge bowl in the swing first, heaved myself up, grabbed the bowl, parked it in my lap and, using a spoon, tried to scrape out the bits of chocolate. But I was so anxious to get to the chocolate that I dropped the spoon and it fell to the porch floor. Frustrated now, I stared down at the spoon and then at the streaks of chocolate in the bowl. "The heck with it," I said bending my head into the bowl, licking away contentedly. Aunt-T came out with a note for Mama in her hand and she burst out laughing. I guess I must have been a funny sight with my little head completely buried in that big bowl.

"Take this back to your Mama," she said. Once more picturing the feisty red rooster, I wondered if he'd be there to challenge me this time, but he wasn't. I reached home safely, gave Mama the note and trotted out to the porch again. This time I ventured into the tall swamp grass which had been parted by a path leading up the hill and across the railroad tracks. Mama never allowed me to play there so I stopped at the edge of the swamp weeds and stared at the smoky mountains along the tracks where I could see hobos and tramps hiding among the trees.

This rough, woodland territory was my hangout when I had no one to play with.

Mama calling my name ended my daydreaming. I ran to the house. She had written another note for Aunt-T. Mama's face looked angry this time as she folded the paper and handed it to me. I put it in my pocket and started on my way. It was a hot day so I stopped to drink from the public water pump, and I remember that water was icy-cold and very refreshing.

As I was skipping along, having a good time and just plain day dreaming like little boys do, I saw the rooster. Instantly I stopped skipping and began to walk slow. He spotted me at the same time. He reacted by lowering his head, spreading his enormous-looking wings, ruffling up the feather around his neck and stomping his clawed feet.

"Someday I'm gonna catch that rooster head on," I muttered to myself, trying to feel brave, "and I'm gonna kick his sorry ass. I'll grab his ol' neck and pull out every one of his feathers, slowly, one by one. Get even with him for pickin' on me like he does."

In spite of my bold words, I saw that the bird was readying to jump on me and I was very afraid of him. I turned around, like I was going back home, intending to fool the rooster into thinking I was not passing his territory, in the hope he would wander off with his hens. Luckily, he did just as I figured and wandered away out of my sight.

Now I felt good again. I had succeeded in fooling that nasty old rooster.

However, not taking any chances, I sneaked past the shanty. Just when I thought I was out of reach, that mean-minded bird spotted me and the race was on. He cropped his wings and lowered his head and I heard his low, fighting-squawk of a chuckle as he came at me with his feet chopping down faster than a runaway horse. I screamed for mercy and began to cry, but that rooster caught up with me. He half-flew and half-jumped onto my head and began to peck away at my skull and any other part of my head he could reach. I was screaming and trying to shake him off but it wasn't until my bare feet carried me out of his territory that he let go and jumped off and began to crow. He was triumphant and he wanted me and the whole world to know it.

Arriving at Aunt-T's I tearfully told her about my encounter and pleaded with her to walk me home. She agreed, but in a very distracted manner, for she was far more interested in the contents of Mama's note which she read immediately. Entering her bedroom she slipped on a sweater and then went to the kitchen. Finally, in a strange, tight voice of anger, and with a distant look in her eyes, she assured me she'd walk me past the rooster.

As we walked along the dirt path, the pugnacious rooster was parading around his owner's front porch, prancing like a prize fighter who had just won a bout and ready to take on another. "You're nothin' but a big, ol' bully," I thought, walking close to my Aunt-T. "I'll be glad when I grow up 'cause then I'll get even with you."

Aunt-T was holding my hand as we walked on, and I noticed she held her free arm very close to her body as if she was concealing something under her armpit. I remember wondering why she had chosen to wear a sweater in this warm weather, but I was distracted by the rooster who kept dancing in half-circles as we went by, but he did not attack while Aunt-T was with me.

Soon we reached my shanty. Aunt-T stormed up the three steps, across the porch and into the kitchen as it was the first room you entered from our front door. I stayed on the porch, looking in through the screen. Something about Aunt-T, something terrible in her face, now scared me more than the rooster.

Mama turned around to face her sister and abruptly Aunt-T spouted off in an angry voice, "What do you mean, writin' a note like that to me?" She reached into dress and pulled out a butcher knife she'd been hiding between her arm and her body. Without another word she savagely attacked Mama.

Thrusting her arms up to protect herself from the wheeling knife, Mama screamed for help. Blood spurted from Mama's arm. I stood on the porch, frozen with fear, in disbelief and confusion. How could this be happening

77

between sisters who loved each other?

Hearing Mama's screams neighbors came running to our shanty. A curly-haired light-skinned man banged through the door, grabbed Samantha and forcibly took the knife away from her. Mama was covered with blood, dripping it onto the floor. Samantha had collapsed onto her knees and was sobbing into her hands. "What the hell's wrong with you, woman?" the man yelled at Aunt-T as he eased Mama over to a chair. "God damn, this lady's near bleedin' to death. Somebody get a car," he yelled. "Get this woman to a doctor!"

Several other people came into the kitchen attending to Mama. They stopped the blood with towels as best they could, but Mama's wounds were deep and soon the floor was littered with blood-soaked towels. One of the neighbors who owned a Ford coupe came running. He helped Mama into the front seat and they drove off to the doctor's office. In all the excitement, I was ignored, and I stood silently, my eyes pouring tears, watching what I thought was my Mama bleeding to death in our own kitchen and staring at my Aunt-T who was still kneeling on the floor keening a high-pitched wailing sound. All the neighbors came out to watch the Ford drive off with Mama. As soon as the neighbor's left the kitchen, Aunt-T lifted herself up and kind of staggered over to our wash basin. She dampened her face with water and stared around her like she was just coming out of a trance or waking up from a bad dream. She saw me, standing out on the porch, shaking with fear and confusion, and from the look of horror on my face, she must have realized what she'd done. She ran out the door, dashing past me and the other folks just standing around and she ran on down the road like demons were after her.

Later I learned that the good Samaritan had taken Mama to a doctor in a small village south of Leslie called Orient Hill. The physician stopped the blood by covering her multiple stab wounds and lacerations with bandages, but insisted she be rushed over to the nearby hospital.

The neighbors summoned Led and he arrived at our shanty about an hour or so later. After learning the details of the attack from the neighbors, he started pacing the floor. Yelling out his anger, I could hear him snarling like an enraged bulldog. "That bitch took a knife to Nora and she in her sixth month? I didn't know then what someone "in her sixth month" meant, but Led was like a tiger in his unbridled wrath. Some of the neighbor men had to hold him back from running out to avenge Samantha's attack on Mama.

I never did learn whether Aunt Samantha was in jail or had gone into hiding, but she was gone from the community for several days. Led got a neighbor woman who lived next door to us to babysit me and Marguerite while Mama was in the hospital. They said she lost a lot of blood.

Worried as I was about my mama — nobody ever told me anything about how she was — I needed a distraction to help me get through the long wait while she was gone. That distraction came in the form of Mrs. Hattie, our sitter. Hattie was a small young woman with a short stature, a shapely form and a complexion the color of old ivory. Her black, straight hair was long, and hung loosely down her back. She cultivated the appearance of an extreme Christian-type person, but as a child, I still found her to be unkind. Although she had agreed to watch over us, I sensed that Marguerite and I were a great burden to her. She was always using the phrase, "Lord have mercy," and her conversations were sprinkled with talk about the "Holy Ghost" and the saints she had seen in her dreams. After listening to her going on about the evil way of life that surrounded her, and how she strove to rise above it all, she succeeded in making me feel I was covered in sin. I sensed she was referring to the sinful environment I lived in, meaning the sinful drinking parties in our shanty.

I'd been in Mrs. Hattie's shanty several times for one reason or another. She had effigies of Christ hanging everywhere. In fact, it was in her house where I realized for the first time who Christ was and what the Last Supper was all about. She doted on those images as if they were physical beings, and she'd fondle them gently, saying, "I live in the spirit of Christ and the Holy Ghost." When she mentioned "ghost," I was somewhat apprehensive, for Mama always told me if I were a bad boy some ghosts would come and take me away. Now this lady kept saying that people should live in the spirit of the Holy Ghost. I didn't know what in the world she was talking about, but I never told her of my fears. In my mind she was a person to be wary of, for somehow I felt she was a phony, even with all her "God" talk, and I was more than a little bit afraid of her, too. I knew even then that I would never be mesmerized as she was, totally engulfed, with this Holy Ghost of hers. Whatever it was, I was not going to let that happen to me when I grew up I was never going to dress like the men depicted in the Last Supper; in those silly-looking robes and open sandals.

Hattie stayed busy with us children while Mama was in the hospital. I saw Led only once or twice, but it was common for him to go away and stay gone for several days at a time. At Hattie's, she put us children to bed very early. My guess was she did that so she could relax and be her real self out of sight of our eyes.

One night I was almost sleep when I heard a man's voice. Apparently it was a man Hattie was having an affair with, but I was too young to understand that implication. She called him Harold. Curious, I got up from by sleeping pallet, crept to the door and peeped through the key hole. They were smooching and hugging in the fire light. I could see that Harold was a tall, dark- skinned man, and he was sitting there naked to the waist as if he was ready for bed. His pants were skintight, and they bulged with his manhood so pronounced that even if he wore looser trousers his privates would not have been hidden successfully. Harold was peering down at Hattie's form, fascinated by the smooth, shiny black hair which hung in a thick braids down her back. He could not resist touching it; letting his fingers move lightly along its silky fineness. Then he asked her, "You're not a pure nigger woman are you?"

"Why?" she replied, letting her head fall back as she stared up into his eyes.

"Because your hair is not nappy like mine."

She laughed a soft little chuckle. "Well, honey, that's because my daddy was white." She used the tips of her fingers to make light, slow, circular motions on his knee and then on up his inner thigh to his crotch where she encircled and hefted the weight of his testicles.

"That's a mighty big thing you got showin' there," she said, letting her fingers begin their slow, sexy dance on his leg once more. "I juice up just feelin' it, baby. You want me to spread my legs for you now?"

Harold sat back, tightening his buttocks and lifting his manhood upward under her touch. "You crazy about makin' love with this thing, aren't you."

"Oh, yes. I want it now, Harold." Mrs. Hattie suddenly arched her body and began a slow rocking motion while pursing her lips and making small, soft sucking sounds. Harold grabbed her breasts and squeezed them so tightly that the veins in his hands and arms popped up clear enough to be seen. I thought for sure she would scream, but instead a low moan of delight escaped her throat and her hips began moving more rapidly. Harold grabbed her by the shoulders, then his hands moved down and, sliding underneath her, began massaging her buttocks. He spoke in a gentle voice, but there was a warning in it.

"I am gonna make you holler for your mama."

Mrs. Hattie smiled and said, "Try me!"

Harold's hands pulled at the pink silk slip she was wearing, drawing it over her head. I could see she was completely naked. He kissed her, and while holding her in his embrace, the two of them rose from the couch and she walked backward as he pushed her as toward the bed where he gently nudged her down. A only a few moments, his body covered hers. Her legs parted willingly to let his fingers probe between them. Then he sank into her as if he'd found his intended target. He arched his buttocks and shoved forward, piercing Mrs. Hattie at the greatest depth. She screamed a tight, almost happy little noise, then started whimpering over and over, "Please don't hurt me, baby... please don't hurt me, baby..." but only seconds later she was crying out, "Oh, baby, it's good... it's good... it's good."

As I watched all this going on, it was mystifying and perplexing to my six-year-old mind. The activity appeared to me as if they were having a physical fight, wrestling about with each other, which was all I could possibly imagine. He was on top of Mrs. Hattie, humping as if he were a human jack-hammer. She responded by moaning, groaning, gyrating and shaking her body in long shudders and caressing his back and his buttocks. In my mind, Harold was beating her up pretty bad, but still, she did not seem to be struggling to get away from him.

In a little while, the activity got even more rambunctious. Mrs. Hattie's moans and groans got louder and more frequent. I started to shiver, for I truly thought he was killing her, yet I was immobilized by my own fear and caught as if in a nightmare. His thrusting humping action appeared brutally punishing and I couldn't see what he was doing with his hands, but my fear finally released my legs and I ran silently back to my pallet on the floor and pulled the covers over my head. All the while I was almost crying, thinking, "Poor Mrs. Hattie is gettin' beat-up." But the moaning from the other room ceased suddenly with what sounded like one last yelp of joy, certainly no more screaming. I couldn't understand what was happening, it was a strange kind of fighting to me, so I closed my eyes and drifted off to sleep.

The next morning when Mrs Hattie woke us, she was smiling more than usual. There were no scars or bruises on her arms or face. As she made our breakfast she was singing, "What A Friend We Have In Jesus." I stared at her in amazement. It seemed a very strange way to behave for someone who'd been beaten up so violently.

Fortunately Mama was in the hospital only seven days. She returned home with orders to rest in bed for at least three days. To my horror she told me that one hundred and eighty-six stitches had been necessary to close the knife wounds. Mama had a long scar from her shoulder to her wrist on the left arm, a long, ugly scar across her back, and many stab wounds. Like always Mama had a mind of her own and paid no attention to the physician's orders. After only a few hours at home, talking to Mrs. Hattie and thanking her for her trouble, Mama was up and about cooking and attending house as usual. Of course, she had to keep her left arm in a sling, but she was in good spirits as she smiled at me. Mama's smile was beautiful; her stunning white teeth were exceptional, straight and well set, and she took pride in her profile. I waited as long as I could — at least till Mrs. Hattie left — before asking Mama about the event.

"Mama, why did Aunt-T cut you?" I asked.

"I don't want to talk about it," she snapped. Obviously she was aggravated at my question and fearing her anger I resolved not to ask her about it again. I never did learn why Aunt-T stabbed and cut her like that. Not from her, anyway. Much later I surmised that Althea had passed on some cruel remark Samantha must have made about Mama — hoping to pit the sisters against one another — and Mama had sent a nasty note in retaliation to Samantha, who then rose to the bait. I don't know. Underneath their appearance of getting along, there was always a thread of jealousy hanging between Mama and Samantha, and a feeling of female competition. Mama was younger, had more flash and vitality about her, was more delicate of form, and much to Samantha's annoyance, young men buzzed around her like bees in a honey comb. But Mama never told me any reason for Aunt-T's knife attack that nearly killed her and left her scared for life.

A few weeks later there was Aunt-T, coming on toward our shanty. At first, I was frightened to see her, thinking she was coming to attack Mama again, but then I could see she wasn't angry. She was weeping and sniffing her nose. I stayed out on the porch as she went into the house crying and begging Mama to forgive her. I wasn't sure what Mama would do — after all she'd been hurt real bad — but the two sisters embraced each other and they both began to cry. Next thing I knew they were drinking together and hugging each other every other minute, telling each other how sorry they were for what all had happened.

Mama stood up and showed Samantha her scars… and Aunt-T covered her face with her hands, rocking in her chair with the agony of her guilt. "Oh, God, Oh, God," she kept moaning through her fingers as Mama pulled her dress back over her shoulder. "Oh, God, I'm sorry, Nora. I'm sorry…" Then they hugged again and Mama refilled both their glasses.

I stayed on the porch lost in my own confusion at their behavior. I never did find out what had made Aunt-T mad enough to try to murder my Mama.

CHAPTER 15
A Friendly Fish Fry Turns Into A Bloody Nightmare

In our shanty I awoke to see rays of the early morning sun stretched across the room through the slits of the window curtains. It was one of those mornings when sunlight burnishes a keen wind and long feathery clouds moved about in lofty skies. That silver morning light turned every blade of grass and every particle of sand into luminous metallic splendor. I lay for a moment in my makeshift bed, nothing more than two heavy quilts sprawled on the hard floor. More quilts were added on as a cover to keep me and my sister Marguerite warm. A mocking bird sang in the distance and all else was quiet except for an occasional snore made by Led who was sleeping with Mama in an adjoining room.

Afraid to awake my parents, I eased up from the bed and out the kitchen door. Party remnants from last night's gathering were still strewn about. Outside the fog began to lift high enough for the white folk's shanties to appear on the rim of the hollow. Down the street, the big red rooster crowed, marking the early morning.

People were sleeping in late now as a result of the coal miner's strike which had been in progress for several weeks. Part of the problem was that in Leslie's camp, the highest position a black man could expect to be hired for was break man, since white men always got jobs as Boss. Most blacks, however, were hired on as coal loaders. The miners constantly complained that coal loading was back-breaking labor and very dangerous work. The owners refused to make any changes so the miners were striking until they agreed to improve the working conditions.

The long strikes were causing a great hardship on all the miners. Without their pay, in order to make ends meet, some miners were now bootlegging white-lightning, or hoping to get lucky with gambling, or even renting out rooms to white hillbillies who brought their prostitutes down to Nigger Bottom. Homemade whiskey was the only commodity that sold well, and most everybody drowned their own depression in a little white lightning now and then.

The fog had burned off and the sky was blue. People begin to emerge from their shanties and stir around the neighborhood. A few folks owned chickens and maybe even some pigs, and most shanties had a planted garden that usually contained peas, corn, potatoes, tomatoes and cabbage. Mostly, it was the women who tended the gardens for the unions needed the men to walk the picket lines around the coal mines. When they were not walking the picket lines, they were off stealing food or gambling.

In our community I was aware that Led was known to be a good maker of white lightning and home brew. Bootlegging moonshine was another one of his many schemes to earn money, along with his ability to make and reconditioned garden and coal digging equipment. Led's skills were exceptional when he felt like applying himself. He regularly made axe and pick handles of hard wood for the miners. But when he was not busy doing this, he was gone up the mountainside gambling with the bums and the hobos.

This morning Mama had wash to do. As I remember we owned only two sheets and Mama would wash them and hang them on a long line strung across the yard to dry in the sun. High upon the hillside I noticed a commotion had begun. You could hear, faintly, loud voices echoing down the slope. Several men sitting on railroad ties and a few standing about had begun arguing about a gambling hand. A fight broke out and soon men began to run. I went back into the house when Mama called out to me, for she'd seen the fight, too, and didn't want me playing outside. A little bit later a tall, bloodied, skinny, white man staggered through our yard and right through Mama's fresh wash. He left blood all over the sheets. He staggered awhile, looking like a drunk, and then he collapsed in a heap on the creek bank. Nobody went to help him for they'd only get blamed for his injuries. Black folks panicked when they saw his bloody body fall and they ran into their shanties. A dead white man in the community could bring nothing but trouble.

At dusk, I could see his body still laying limp in the creek bank. Mama saw me peeking out a window and cautioned me to remain in the house and not to look at the bloodied mess.

The night was tense and quiet. The winds begin to stir, and I knew a storm was in the making. You could hear distant thunder cracking like an awesome bullwhip. Then the rain began to splatter, hard and wet, against the window pane.

The heavy rain didn't end until the next morning. I quietly crept to the window, pulled the tattered curtain aside and looked out to where the body had been left. It was gone! It had just disappeared. Creeping back to my pallet on the floor I pulled the quilts over my face and fell back to sleep, dreaming disturbing dreams about what might have happened to that white man's body.

It was broad day light now and grass glistened in the morning mist. Led tossed his legs over the iron-frame bed and got up slowly. Raising his arms over his head, he stretched his six-foot frame, then ran his hands through his thick black hair. He stumbled over toward the wash basin and poured it half full of cool water. He made a face before shoving both hands under the water and tossed the chilly liquid back onto himself. The shock of the water completely awakened him. He stood looking in a makeshift mirror as he sharpened his shaving razor on a large black leather strap. Mama got up and gazed at our partially empty cupboard, searching for food to prepare breakfast.

I dared not ask about the dead man for I knew they would have severely scolded me. Still, the memory of him staggering through those bloody sheets stayed long in my mind. Later, I heard whispers that somebody had thrown the murdered man's body down an old mine shaft.

Times grew even harder during this striking period. There was very little food. Led's way of looking for work was by traveling to distant counties, hitching rides on coal cars. He wouldn't come back sometimes for days at a time. Mama seemed upset and agitated whenever Led was away like that. She drank too much of her "remedy," trying to forget her sorrows, I suppose, and sometimes she would leave the house and not come home for long hours. Being alone with just us kids seemed to drive Mama into pacing the floor and looking out the windows... restless and nervous. When she couldn't take it any more she'd just grab her sweater and say, "I'll be back in a while, honey. Take care of Marguerite" and off she'd go.

A lot of the time, while Led was on the road looking for work, we had nothing in the house to eat. Mama would have to go to the neighbors and borrow pig mash and use it to make us bread or ash cakes. On some days, if we were lucky, we'd have a fried onion with our pig mash bread. On a really good day we'd have fried apples, or fried green tomatoes which had been dipped in pig mash batter. Pinto beans soaked and boiled with a piece of white meat, cornbread and buttermilk was our primary Sunday dinner.

Occasionally, folks in the hollow would join together and prepare a community potluck dinner. The hollow would become a mecca for a feast of barbecued ribs. I remember these potluck dinners as a good time for me. I saw it as an opportunity to fill my stomach. Once I ate so much I could hardly walk and had to be carried home in my mother's arms.

One hot summer evening, a man named Tom Hall drove his Model-T Ford truck down the steep knoll of Nigger Hollow and motored on down the dirt road. Tom was six-foot-six-inches tall with a large pot belly. He had a big head for his body and very small eyes, and huge feet. His feet were so big that when he walked it was all he could do to keep his feet from stepping on each other. Consequently people called him "BigFeet." When BigFeet laughed, his wide-gaped pearly teeth showed, his belly shook and his pleasant black face glistened.

People in the community regarded BigFeet as a rogue, a petty crook, a bootlegger and a gambler and someone whom they could not trust. BigFeet was known to be a man that would do anything for money. When he appeared in the Hollow, folks knew he had something to trade or sell. This time, in the back of BigFeet's old Model-T truck was a mixture of vegetables stolen from some white person's farm, several bushels of corn, apples, and barrels of pig mash. Pints of white lightning and home made mash were hidden under the barrels of pig mash. And in the cab of the truck was Led who had hitched a ride with Tom.

Mama was happy to have Led home again, but dismayed to learn that he did not have any money for food or other vital necessities. Nevertheless, he tried to calm her fears by claiming to have found a job in a little town near Montgomery, West Virginia, called Sink Clear. The job was working at coke ovens... which are giant, red-hot ovens where they extract various products from bituminous coal.

The glad tidings about Led being home again spread throughout the neighborhood. In spite of his sultry ways when he was drinking, he was a very popular man with his ability to entertain and tell his funny jokes and stories when he was in the mood. His old friends began to plan a Saturday night fish fry to celebrate his return. Usually a fish fry began at dusk. That night as evening began slipping away, the sun hung low in the sky and a full moon made it's welcome appearance. Dusk fell in purple sweeping shadows and neighbors began to appear and the fish (brought by the neighbors and friends) began to fry.

It was the usual crowd for a Saturday night, and they were tossing off their usual quota of mash whiskey and white lightning. A neighbor called Hambone had brought his guitar and was spewing out the blues. Women and men began to congregate in the shanty, on the porch and in the front and back yards. Everyone was having good time, eating, dancing, and drinking white lightning and whiskey mash.

Saturday night in Nigger Hollow is the biggest night of the week. Black folks, bootleggers, hustlers and prostitutes all liked to come to a good party. Some people were friends who worked together as coal-loaders. Others were hobos just looking for some good old white lightning, a free meal, and conversation. Usually, when word scattered that a party was in the making, strangers appeared in the community.

Our fish fry had been under way for an hour or so. Most of the party goers were drinking heavily, some were downright intoxicated. Samantha and Henry entered the smoke-filled room. Uncle Henry was accompanied by an ominous-looking light-skinned man who must have weighed 200 pounds and was at least six-feet tall. Led looked up, and with his usual straight face asked Uncle Henry "Hey, man. Who is your buddy?"

The stranger did not realize that Led was the host, so he took a stand and mouthed-off. "What is it to you?"

"I was asking Henry," Led said, ignoring the tall, heavy-set man.

But the man didn't take kindly to being ignored. He got himself in Led's face and said "I'm here to see Elnora. She's carryin' my baby."

Suddenly Led's casual expression faded and was replaced by a look of genuine shock. Then anger flushed his face and his voice got snarly. "I asked you who is your damn buddy?" Led said again to Uncle Henry.

"Look here, you ugly nigger," the stranger replied, stepping closer to Led than he should have, "don't go talkin' to me in that tone. Don't you know who I am?"

"I don't give a damn who you are," replied Led.

"I work for the mining company and I'll have your dumb black ass thrown out of here if you mess with me." The stranger's mouth had narrowed to a thin angry line in his dark face and his eyes glittered as mean as a junkyard dog.

"Listen, man," Led said, "I'm not lookin' for any trouble with you. Just figured you might be the revenue man, you know."

But that half-jokey answer didn't put off the tall man. He poked a finger at Led's chest and said, "Look, you son-of-a-bitch. I tol' you I want to see Elnora. She's carrying my baby!"

"Nora! Come out here, godammit!"

Mama rushed from the kitchen. "Yes, honey," she said, and then her dark eyes got big and round and she said, "Oh, hello, Crooks."

"This nigger says you carrying his baby!" Led's mouth was twitching, just a tiny little nerve on the left side, but when that happened he was near his breaking point.

"Oh, I…uh," Mama stuttered, looking scared and kind of fluttering her hands.

Before Mama could answer Led flashed his razor before her face. "You lyin' bitch!" he screamed. "I'm gonna cut that baby outta your belly right now!" His eyes were fiery red. Mama screamed at the sight of his wild eyes.

Crooks stepped between Led and Mama and during the tussle Led dropped the razor. He threw a left jab and a quick right at Crooks' head. Both punches hit their mark. One punch landed in Crooks' right eye, the other smashed his mouth sideways and sent him spinning across the room to the floor. Led rushed in and pounded the man with his fists. Chaos erupted in the shanty. Women were screaming and crying; other party-goers were trying to get out of the house and knocking each other down in their hurry. Meanwhile, Led scrambled for his razor. He got it in his hand and was about to cut Crooks' throat when Uncle Henry realized that Crooks was in trouble. Uncle Henry rushed in and wrapped his right arm around Led's neck, applying a choke-hold, trying to pull Led off the man. Believing that he was being attack from behind, Led seemed momentarily to panic. As quick as lightening, he wheeled out of the choke-hold, popped out his straight razor, and with savage speed he slashed at Uncle Henry's throat. Uncle Henry ducked slightly, but the razor still caught him, slashing down the left side of his face and throat. Blood spurted everywhere. Silence dominoed across the room as heads turned toward the gushing blood.

Suddenly, from a dark corner of the room, another figure emerged. It was BigFeet, the burly rogue. He approached Led as Uncle Henry lay bleeding. Everyone knew BigFeet to be one who enjoyed violence. He grabbed Led's hand that held the razor, and with the other hand he clutched Led by the throat. Led was blinded by his rage by now and the men cursed each other.

"Why did you cut him, you black son-of-a-bitch?" BigFeet screamed.

"Take your goddam hands off me, asshole," Led shouted, half choking the words out. Then he suddenly jabbed his free hand, catching BigFeet smack across his nose. BigFeet went down like a tree in the forest. Leaping up as agile as a panther, Led stomped on him as chaos again ran rampant while screaming people were grabbing, trampling, pushing their bodies against each other to get away from the fierce fight. One woman ran out to the porch calling out for help in a high-pitched voice laced with alarm. Screams from Aunt-T grew louder and more terrified as she was standing over her husband watching him bleeding to death. Terrified people fled through the front and back doors. In the melee, more fist fights broke out in the back yard. Then gunshots rang out and screams, thuds, groans and sounds of glass being broken. Someone was being beaten with a whiskey bottle, I think it was a woman, some drunken light-haired girl. Aunt-T had collapsed over Uncle Henry's chest, sobbing and half-screaming. His blood was soaking the floor by now. Led gave Mama one ugly look — she had backed up and was hovered against the wall as I myself had done, and then he staggered, exhausted, through the back door, stumbled out to the back yard and vanished into the night.

Now attention focused on Uncle Henry who was dying there on our shanty floor.

Most of the party goers had scattered and the chatter of their excitement crackled through the late night. Several people hovered around Aunt-T who had become hysterical and two older coal miners administered first aid. Petrified, I stood off in a corner of the kitchen a few feet from the excitement, my eyes wide with horror. What had been a good, friendly fish fry had turned into a nightmare from hell.

Suddenly Uncle Henry lost consciousness for he had lost a great deal of blood.

Mr. Hilton, a neighbor, who had run home to get his truck, pulled his Model-T Ford up to the front porch and yelled, "Get him in the truck! I'll rush him to Dr. Benjamin's place." Several men lifted Uncle Henry's limp body to the back of Mr. Hilton's truck and off they went in the early morning darkness.

A long painful silence gripped the shanty.

Mama sat on the bed crying into her pillow. Tears streamed down Aunt-T's cheeks. Several neighbor women stood in the kitchen crying inconsolably and trying to figure out what had gone wrong. No one knew whether Uncle Henry would live or die. As the night wore on, the discussions continued and the crying, and it appeared that the grownups had forgotten us kids. Marguerite lay sleeping on a floor pallet oblivious to the tumultuous happenings and I stood bewildered, staring at the kitchen floor where Uncle Henry's dark red blood had pooled.

The darkness of the night soon rushed away and the sun began to rise in the east. It was barely dawn on Sunday morning when the State Police and the County Coroner arrived at our shanty. The law people were milling around inside and outside our place. A tall, heavy police officer was in the back yard staring down at the sheet-draped body of a young man. Apparently he had been caught in the crossfire last night when the fighting broke out in the yard after Uncle Henry got slashed. I knew I'd heard gun shots, and screaming.

The State Police officer stood over the dead man shaking his head as his partner pulled back the sheet. He'd already seen the mutilated body of a light-haired young woman laying in the creek. I heard him say something about the usual effects of a bullet blowing apart the woman's skull from being fired at close range.

"Damn!" he mumbled, looking down at the man's smashed skull. "This poor son-of-a-bitch looks as messed up as those poor miners we hoisted outta that caved-in mine shaft only a few weeks ago. Remember? They was crushed nearly flat from falling slate comin' down on them." He shuddered with revulsion. "Well, so what the hell. Another nigger bites the dust. He'll never make any more trouble."

The other trooper re-covered the body and the two of them walked on into our kitchen.

I watched through the window as the Coroner and his assistant took the dead body away. They spoke to Mama and Aunt-T for a few minutes, and soon left.

Mama and her sister stood whispering about what had taken place during the course of the night. Mama was worried about Led. I heard that much. He was on the run now, a wanted man for slashing... or killing, Uncle Henry. I didn't think Uncle Henry was dead; Aunt-T would be screaming in grief if he was. But he could die in that hospital at any moment.

I watched again through the window as they took away the dead light-haired woman by the creek. Everything seemed to be happening in slow motion... as if it were a nightmare.

My eyes felt gritty from my being awake all hours. I was hungry, but I knew it was useless to expect Mama to fix food when all this had happened.

My sister Marguerite lay sleeping soundly. After being awake most of the night I was sleepy and tired too, and actually, I think I was in a semi state of shock. I stretched out on the pallet where rays from the still-rising sun lay heavy on my eyelids as they poked through the torn window shade. I remember

my last thoughts before I fell asleep:
I'm walking on the path of darkness... the path of darkness...
if I am not careful, it will swallow me into its deep shadows...

CHAPTER 16
Henry And Aunt-T Leave Leslie… "Ledbelly" Goes to Jail

The order was out from the Union Organizers: Get James Leadbetter for slashing Henry Sherrod. Henry was a strong union activist in the community. Enraged by Led's violence, the Superintendent of the mining camp had sent out the word and barred Led permanently from Nigger Bottom.

Several days later, at our shanty the grownups were saying they had arrested Led in another county. Then Mama heard that union members had caught Led, beat him badly and had thrown him into a dark room where he could neither stand, sit, nor lie down. He could only squat with his knees drawn up and his head bowed. One of the miners, a man who'd seen it and knew what he was talking about, described the place and Mama wept as she listened.

It was total darkness, he said. The still air made the room incredible hot and therefore Led would be drenched in sweat, as was appropriate, since this horrible punishing device they had him in was called a "sweat box." The air smelled foul, the miner said. It was always tinged with the stench of sewage from the nearby outhouses. Isolated in eerie quietness, Led would only hear his own long, angry breaths gulping air into his aching lungs.

Later we found out the miner was right. They had taken most of Led's senses away, except pain. The hard floor was wet, and he could not position himself away from the wetness. He tried getting on his hands and knees, but he slammed his head on the low roof of the little box and badly scraped an elbow. He crouched, hunched like an animal in a cage, sweltering in the blackness, swimming in his anger. Outside he could hear the union members yelling, "Lynch him! Lynch the bastard!" He tried to kill our union leader! Put his black neck in a noose!"

The doctor said that it was a miracle Uncle Henry survived Led's knife attack. It was lucky for Led, too, because if Uncle Henry had died, those union men would have lynched Led for sure. I do not recall hearing that any trial took place. Nevertheless, they sentenced Led to six months in the County Jail.

Now that Led was going to be gone for a long time now, I remember Mama crying day after day, telling her women friends that she was pregnant with his second child and moaning that he was not there for her. And above all, she had no one to provide food and to support the family.

Squalid poverty quickly became our way of life. Our shanty began to fall apart from neglect. The winds began to pick pieces of the roof away and we could see light through cracks in the walls. Food was hard to come by, so me and Mama and Marguerite picked wild green apples from trees and lugged baskets full of them home. She would sprinkle a thick, white Kayro syrup on top to give them a sweet taste and fry them in lard. That is what we would have as a meal.

Sometimes Mama got some pig mash and made bread. Lima beans and cornbread, if she had any corn meal, were treats for supper. Occasionally we had fried onions. Some days a neighbor would take pity on us, I guess, and give us a chicken. Then Mama would keep the chicken alive until she was ready to slaughter it for there was no refrigerators in the black community. Only a few neighbors could afford to own an ice box and pay for the five-cent ice blocks that kept food cold. Usually, we would have our chicken dinner — if we had one — on Sundays. Mama would use the other half of the bird to make a lunch pack and then off she'd go to the county jail to visit Led.

Two months passed with us living hand-to-mouth and Led still in the county jail. Uncle Henry recovered. He survived the deep cut that left an ugly scar down the left side of his face and his throat. Mama said that Uncle Henry felt he was indebted to God because he had been saved from the brink of death. Once Uncle Henry came back home from the hospital, he and Aunt-T professed a deep religion and they became active in the local church. He told Mama that he forgave Led, and prayed for him, and spoke of no hard feelings toward him.

On one bright Sunday morning, Uncle Henry and Aunt-T came to our shanty. They asked Mama to get on her knees and join them in prayer. I was playing outside, but I crept near the shabby screen door to listen to what was going on. I remember only the opening part of that long prayer, but it went something like this:

"In worship," Uncle Henry began, with folded hands and his face lifted toward Heaven, *"we count our blessings today. We give thanks for the power to grow, to serve, to conquer ourselves. We know we are God's people. We believe that Jesus will lift the burden of resentment and fear from our heart. We believe that Jesus,"* he sang out the word "Jesus, *"will let the gentle inflow of peace cleanse worries from our mind. We believe that with the help of Jesus, we can renew our dreams and our aspirations and rise above defeat, failures, discouragements and have another try at making most of our lives.*

Oh God, let this be a great day of beginnings. We know we brood too much over our failures. We hold on to disappointments too long. Heavenly Father, remind us that our souls cannot find a conviction to live by, until we begin to live by faith. Show us the way, Lord. Your way, and I will cease measuring myself."

With that, Uncle Henry and Aunt-T raised their heads, stood up from their kneeling position with tears in their eyes. They embraced Mama and each other and promised solemnly to live a good Christian life from that day forward. Later that afternoon, they packed their bags and moved away from Leslie.

Meanwhile, on a hot July morning in 1940 my new baby sister, Inez, was born. Marguerite and I were inquisitive. We wanted to know where she'd come from and how she'd managed to suddenly appear in our household. We asked Mama to explain the mystery, but she only smiled and told us that the family doctor had delivered Inez to our shanty.

Several weeks passed before Mama seemed willing to take baby Inez and us children to see Led in the county jail. It was a hot muggy Sunday morning when we boarded a bus. Mama held Inez, wrapped in a pink blanket, in one arm, and in her free hand she carried a basket of fried chicken, blackberry pie and slices of apple pie. As I remember, that ride was less than pleasant. We were forced to sit in the back of the Greyhound bus where we could feel every dip and gully along that rutted dirt road. To us children, it felt like sitting on a six-point earthquake.

Three hours later we reached the court house. The jail and court house were adjacent. It was the first time in my young life I'd ever seen a building so beautiful as that court house.

Usually, Mama said, when she had arrived at the jail with a food basket, a thorough search was made to ensure she was not violating security, and then she'd be rushed off to a large open room where prisoners were allowed to meet with their families.

This day, however, they allowed us to stand in awe as we studied the beautiful building.

It stood in the brilliant sunlight radiating newness and elegance like a grand lady in a new gown. The facade stood four stories tall, topped by a cupola of intricate design, and on its roof a final ornate crown of lacy ironwork. Double doors with elaborate filigree tops opened upon a high and narrow porch. Over the doors, twisting scrolls supported a cartouche shield on which was carved the words, "In God We Trust." They twined it with many tendrils around carved numerals that read "1890," the year it had been built.

Tall fluted columns rose to the roof. The high front steps were slate-gray wood, and down the middle ran a strip of red bricks flanked by pots of flowers. More flowers cascaded from window boxes and poured from iron urns along the curving walkway where Mama saw Led waiting. He had earned his jailers' trust by now, and had been given privileges to work around the courthouse yard, maintaining its manicured appearance. It was a quasi freedom they called being a "trustee."

Led greeted Mama with a passionate smile. I remember how his white teeth sparkled like pearls as he held his arms out to receive baby Inez. Looking back, I'm sure that Led knew Inez was not his child. And I'm certain he remembered that only a few months earlier he had threatened to cut that innocent child out of Mama's stomach. But then, with one dark finger he pulled the tip of the blanket from her sleeping eyes and kissed her cheek.

"So, Nora. You named her Inez?"

"Yes," Mama replied, not meeting his eyes. "Samantha named her after Henry Junior's fiance."

With that, Led seemed to chill toward the infant, but he did not comment. However, from that point on Mama noticed Led appeared disinterested in Inez's arrival, and I've always felt that she instinctively guessed, then and there, that Led already knew Inez was not his baby.

There was, of course, the suspicion that my baby sister Inez was that man Crooks' child... or she might have been Edward Sherrod's. Mama was always drawn to the handsome Sherrod family (remembering her first meeting with Edward when he wrestled the bear) and who knows where she went during her wanderings on those long, lonely nights when Led was off tramping around the county. She might have found comfort with Uncle Henry's young son, after all, she'd always had a kind of a yen for that handsome young man. Mama never discussed it, but from my own perspective I'd say it was probably Crooks — the big bowlegged man who'd come looking for her that night, bragging about her carrying his baby. We never will know for sure, unless someday Mama herself tells Inez who her daddy was.

Nevertheless, standing there in the court house grass and watching Led's chilled reception to Inez, Mama understood — as she always had — that there was a cold, detached part of Led which kept him from being overjoyed about anything. He was a hard man, and sometimes cold-hearted. Like his father Huddie, Led took pride in his nickname, Leadbelly. Everything in him was solitary, secretive, egotistical and rebellious and impenetrable as lead, the metal itself. He always seemed to have decided in advance not to commit himself to anything... or any one. But that day, even I could see he was trying his best to stir a caring feeling, and to strike a gallant pose... even though it was on the jail house lawn.

Led and Mama spent time talking about the unusual activity in and around the jail. It was activity going on three stories below that Led witnessed. From his cell, he could see when they brought in new prisoners. When multiple car doors slammed, most likely someone was about to be incarcerated, and Led told us how he'd jump up from his cot and rush to the small window and look to see if they were hauling in somebody he knew.

I sat there on the grass with Marguerite nearby and listened as Led told Mama his stories. I truly believe that he forgot us children were there, for some of the incidents he mentioned were not meant for children's ears. Perhaps he thought I'd never remember... much less understand. It's true I didn't understand all of it at that time... but after Led got out, I heard his jail stories again and again as he told them to different friends... half of whom couldn't believe he was telling the truth. I believed it then and I believe it now... and I came to understand all of it eventually.

"In the late evening at dusk," Led began, helping himself to some of Mama's fried chicken, "on Thursday, Friday and Saturday nights, there's some strange activity takin' place here in the jail house court yard." He went on to describe how the jailer would round up certain women and load them into police cars and cart them off. They would not return until in the wee hours of the morning after midnight.

One morning, Led said, while enjoying his freedom in trusteeship, he happened to meet a black woman who also was a trustee. She was responsible for interior cleaning — a position she liked because it gave her the opportunity to hear all the gossip — and the upkeep of the flower gardens around the court house. They called her Caldonia. She was a nice-looking, lighted-skinned lady with short hair, a shapely build and small feet. Caldonia told Led how she had suffered poverty, neglect and abuse from her coal mining husband, whom she had scalded with boiling water. The authorities arrested her and, among other things, charged her with attempted murder. She was serving time for that crime. Led recognized Caldonia as one the inmate ladies whom the jailers had driven off with the previous Saturday night. Curious about that excursion, Led asked Caldonia about it. She looked away, embarrassed at first to begin her sordid tale, but once she started, she got angry as she spoke and her anger helped her recall startling details as she told him, intimately, what went on when female inmates were lured from their jail cells on the pretext of temporary freedom for a good time. They were transported to some sleazy, deserted old house near the mining community of Kincaid. This dilapidated structure was owned by a close friend of one of the law enforcement authorities and it was used mostly for these rendezvous. These southern rednecks used a variety of coercions to persuade the young women to participate in this melee of sex orgies.

A beautiful 15-year-old black girl named Sybilla, one of the "persuaded" incarcerated female inmates, was their prime target. She was in temporary custody pending a transfer to reform school. Allegedly she was a runaway, and on that premise she'd been arrested. According to Caldonia, once they reached the house, a middle-aged police officer named Jim Pickens grabbed Sybilla by the arm and laughing, took her off to what he openly referred to as his "private fucking room." He was red-faced and fat, looked like a overweight ferret with a cigar hanging out of his loose mouth, Caldonia said, and she remembered seeing his belly shake and his face get all flushed when he jerked Sybilla into the room down the hall and closed the door. All the rest of the details Caldonia got afterward from young Sybilla herself.

Once inside the room the fat lawman began fondling Sybilla, a frightened but acquiescent female who had believed his coercive promise of freedom in exchange for sex. Loosening his pants he pulled them down until his organ sprang free from its confinement. In two harsh gestures he stripped off her clothes, leaving only her panties. The burley man began talking in a low voice, but although his tone was soft, his actions were savage.

"I want ya to treat me good, you understand? Really good, ya sweet lil' blackberry." His hands were moving all over her body as she stood nearly naked in front of him with lowered eyes and made no response.

Jim didn't like her stance. "What is you," he said with a snarl in his voice, "some uppity nigger gal? Don't you know you made to pleasure men like me?" He gripped her arm in a cruelly painful grasp. "Listen here. I'm sayin' I want ya t' be good to me, lil' gal. I wanna hear you holler for your mama! You got that?"

"Yes, sir! Yes, sir!" Sybilla said, trembling all over and trying to hold back tears. He was hurting her arm..

Grabbing her by the shoulders he moved his clammy hands down her young body where he began massaging her buttocks, making small grunting noises in his throat like he was thinking, "Oh, Lord, what a nice, soft ass; nice legs; hard, young breasts stickin' out with them rosy nipples goin' all tight." Again he gripped her breasts and pulled her toward him, tightening his hands on her tender flesh as if it were a death drip. She screamed in pain and begged the man for mercy, but he kept on grabbing and squeezing. He let his pants fall to the floor and kicked them away and his organ sprang out, dripping from his excitement.

Acting like a crazed maniac, Jim heaved Sybilla's slender black body onto the bed which was covered with a dirty white sheet. She lay there rigid with fear. Her legs parted slowly to let his fingers probe, separating and slipping them between the vaginal lips. He began to stroke her hair. Slowly, he moved his hands down Sybilla's neck, then across her collar bone. When he brought his face down to the middle portion of her body and cupped her breast in his mouth she relaxed, but she was still frightened.

Climbing on top of her, Jim went on his knees so as to pierce her. She was moaning, gyrating and throwing her hips from side to side, and all the time her heart banged against her chest like she was about to faint. Suddenly his hands caught her panties and he savagely tore them off like a wild man. Knowing what he wanted, and hoping to get it all over with quickly, she became aggressive. With her legs still spread wide, she bent forward, flinging her hands between her legs and captured Jim's penis. Pressing it between her vaginal lips, she started the gyrations again, while her hands caressed his taut testicles. She was raising him to heights of desire he'd never coped with before, and within moments she disappeared under his heavy body, pinned beneath him like a prisoner at his mercy.

They became drenched with her juice. Her mouth sought his and she sucked first on his lower lip, then his upper; moving from one to the other and using her tongue in a manner that set his blood on fire. His pale white skin became hot and his breathing was deep and rapid. All of his movements now were jerky and almost confused. She was giving him the ride of his life. Inspired, and probably believing he was superman, he raised her shapely legs over her head, forcing her into a jack-knife position, and began humping her with the force used to hammer in a railroad spike...bam! bam! bam! The bed rocked, banging the wall, with each thrust. Suddenly he yelled out like a howling wolf and she saw his wet skin turn waxy pale. Everything in him let go and his fat body rolled off the bed to the floor with the thud-crack! of a block of ice.

Sybilla sat up and stared down at the redneck policeman who'd talked so big and treated her so savagely. With his fat face buried in the filthy motel rug he was stone dead of a heart attack. She laughed for two whole minutes before she could put her clothes on and go tell somebody. All the time she was thinking, "Served him right, the goddam redneck fool!"

CHAPTER 17
Another Move And More Hard Times

With another visit behind her, Mama returned home unhappy and feeling sad. There was no food in the shack to feed Marguerite and me or little Inez. Aunt-T had left the Hollow, so there was no one she could turn to. We all were sad, for Mama's great vitality and passion — the very life blood she possessed that had always sustained us through all our hard times — seemed to have drained from her body. She began to cry, and I cried, too, not knowing how to do anything to help her.

Mama delegated me to watch Inez, who had begun to crawl early, while she went to the neighbors to beg or borrow something for us to eat. Inez was a peculiar child, with bowlegs, a flat-looking forehead and eyes that seemed too wide apart. She was not a very attractive little child and one of our neighbors, thinking it was funny, I guess, had taken one look at her just after she was born and promptly gave her the nickname of "Frog."

As the weeks went on, without Led to help provide, trying to stay alive in Leslie was a great challenge for Mama. All around us was turmoil and trouble and folks struggling to get by and empty bellies and sick children. The union organizing efforts were getting bloodier by the day as deadly battles between miners and company thugs became common. I remember hearing talk about how the coal company's hired goons were hunting down the coal miners, beating them near to death, or even lynching them on the spot. But unrelenting, the union members still fought on to bring unionization into the poverty stricken shanty communities. At that time work was so scarce that every family in the Hollow was suffering from hunger and disease, everything from scurvy to pellagra. With the impact of the Great Depression, and the lack of jobs and money taking such a heavy toll, white lightnin' soon became a

100

profitable business. The pure white whiskey was available in almost every shanty in Nigger Hollow.

Six months passed and our living conditions worsened. Mama heard they'd paroled Led from jail, but she knew he didn't dare return to Leslie. Led managed to get word to Mama for her to try to leave Nigger Bottom and travel to Kimberly, a small obscure riverside village about 24 miles southwest of Montgomery and 12 miles west of Deep Water where Uncle Henry and Aunt-T lived.

Talking about my Aunt-T, Mama asked me why I always called Samantha's name that way, like Aunt-TEE. I told about my saying "Bunchie" that time in the kitchen and the knife-waving incident over a year ago.. everything except about me pissing my pants.

"Was she drinkin'?" Mama asked.

"Yeah, she was. She fell down outside and Uncle Henry brought her over in the wheelbarrow that time, remember?"

Mama smiled. "Well, then that's why. She was just meanin' for you to say "Auntie." Not Aunt TEE, like the letter in the alphabet, Charles."

I grinned and felt like a fool, but I never referred to my aunt as "Aunt-T" again.

Like most families in the community, people would leave one shanty town and head for another mountain community in search of new jobs and a better life. Mama was no exception; she was ready to leave that poverty-ridden place. For several days she gathered up what she perceived to be the most important items we owned — which wasn't much — and bundled the items up in a bedspread. Then we sat around waiting for Uncle Henry and Aunt Samantha to arrive.

Somehow Mama had sent word to them, and they agreed to motor down to Leslie and help us move. They owned a Model-T Ford truck — one of the most popular means of transportation at the time — and it was exactly what was needed to move me, Mama, Marguerite and baby Inez out of the poverty-ridden hills of Leslie Hollow.

It was late on a Sunday evening when Aunt Samantha and Uncle Henry arrived in Nigger Bottom. I had only seen my Uncle Henry once or twice after he'd gotten cut by Led, and I was curious about his scars. The first thing I did was look at his face and neck. Sure enough, a big discolored scar mark ran straight down the side of his face and across his neck. He caught me staring at him and frowned. I looked away, but I couldn't help wondering how in the world his poor old head had stayed on after getting a gash like that.

As we got ready to go, it began to rain and this gave the grownups time chit-chat about past events and the trip to Kimberly.

The rain stopped just as the daylight slipped away into darkness. Uncle Henry heaved the bundled bedspread to the back of the truck. We all loaded into the cab of the Model-T truck and were on our way, hopefully leaving Nigger Bottom forever.

Soon we were on the narrow, one-lane road leading to Kimberly. First we traveled south to Route 60, then west toward Smithers. The highway was partly dirt and partly paved, but some places along the way were just a muddy trail that laced through the tall mountains. As we drove along, the crowded truck clattered on the bumpy road. Margaret and I were jammed into a small space behind the front seat where Uncle Henry and Aunt Samantha and Mama, with Inez in her arms, were bouncing along.

As the truck rambled through the foothills above the river, amid the sprawling darkness of the forest and the giant oaks, our headlights revealed deer browsing here and there along the rutted ridge that flanked the road. Uncle Henry swung the truck in wide turns, dodging the muddy trenches created by the monsoon-like rains which had dredged the deep furrows in the road. The wide turns kicked up awesome clouds of soft, sticky mud, showering the windshield and the cab of the truck. On we went, the tires hungrily grabbing at the gravel and dropping down into gut-wrenching gullies that marked this craggy road. In some places, the heavy rains had entirely washed out the road leading to our destination and Uncle Henry had to back up and find a detour to Montgomery.

Occasionally, ghostly headlights of an approaching motorist would appear. When that occurred, Uncle Henry and the other driver had to pull off to the side of the road so that each would have room to pass. In spite of my cramped position in the cab I drifted off into a dozing sleep, but the thought of getting stranded out there on that desolate roadway frightened me.

It was a foggy morning when we reached Montgomery, a sleepy-looking town at that time of day. We could hear the raging Kanawha River and as we drove near its roar, a misty haze of moisture filled the air. By the road side, frost-bitten yellow leaves still hung from trees as if they were emulating the holidays. Heavy headed chrysanthemums were beaded thick with water, and from the red hips of the roses, tree spiders stretched their great wheels of pale silver, jeweled with cloudy opals of dew.

Aunt Samantha complained of being hungry, as were we all. Uncle Henry agreed to drive to a local 24-hour café he remembered during his past travels around Montgomery. We pulled into some lonely-looking street, hoping to find the café Uncle Henry spoke of. I waited anxiously to get out of the truck having been crammed in the rear for several hours, and every part of me was sore. Uncle Henry found the small café.

Looking through the windows we saw maroon booths and jukebox-selectors on the tables. Uncle Henry heaved himself from the truck and walked to the front door. A toothless waitress stared as though Uncle Henry were a unicorn. Apparently she ordered him to the back door, because that was where he headed.

In a little while Uncle Henry came back to the truck with a brown cardboard box that smelled of food. He handed the box to Aunt Samantha and then heaved himself back into the truck and started the motor.

"Henry, where you going?" auntie asked.

"There's a little park down the street a ways. We all can get out and eat there."

"Okay," Auntie groaned, "but let's go. I'm hungry."

We parked across the street from the park which I saw had several benches and tables. This early in the morning nobody else was there. There were three toilets: one for men, one for women, and the sign on the third toilet read, "For Niggers." Beside them stood two drinking fountains. A stream jetted up from the white folks' fountain; the water fountain for "Niggers" barely dripped. I was stunned to see such blatant examples of open racial hatred. Even at my young age I had to wonder aloud how any black person could survive a life time without murdering a few white folks who had taken such pains to humiliate us.

We sat at a table in the lower end of the park. I believe Uncle Henry picked that table so that we would appear obscure. Mama opened the brown cardboard box and we saw that the café had given Uncle Henry a quantity of scraps and food leftovers. Fortunately, it was a place that practiced generosity toward transients, and I figured that my Uncle had gone there before during his travels around West Virginia.

After we finished eating, Mama and Aunt Samantha began discussing our living options for the next several days. Auntie said she knew of a Christian lady who lived on a mountainside called Stanford, who might take us in. Again we all crowded into the cab of uncle's truck.

At 8:30 in the morning, we reached the side road leading to an old, two story, drab-green house. Blackberry bushes were surrounded by a stand of oak, maple and walnut trees. Further up the mountain was a clump of wild apple and cherry trees. A mountain breeze blew through the valley where the Kanawha River appeared and meandered quietly. This landscape was a relieving contrast to the muddy road we had traveled. The wind felt cool on my skin. Here and there on the mountainsides I could see log cabins connected by thread-like paths that followed an old hunter's trail.

Auntie climbed down from the truck and walked up the wooden steps leading to the back door of a white house which looked ominous to me. The wide porch lead around to the front which was bedded on tall stilts, and the anchor of the porch hung on the second floor of the house. Nearby were other small homes, all decaying with age and the inability of the residents to maintain them. Auntie knocked. A little, short, ugly woman opened the door and stared out at Samantha with confused and heavily-painted eyes.

"Hi, Bertha," auntie said loudly, putting on a big, friendly smile.

"Samantha? My God! Come on in."

Bertha's home proudly displayed a tattered, green front lawn and a scroungy rose garden on either side of the badly battered wood steps. Uncle Henry stood at the bottom of the steps and surveyed the house without comment. We could hear the roar of the rush-hour traffic on the nearby one-lane roadway, and standing in her yard the smell of river water was unpleasant. Nevertheless, the warm demeanor of the house transcended the neglect and blight around the place. Auntie emerged with a broad smile. "Sherry!" she called. "Bring Elnora and the kids up here to meet Bertha Brown." Uncle Henry helped Marguerite out of the truck. Cuddling Inez in her arms, Mama took my hand and up the steps we went. On the porch Mrs. Bertha said, "Come on in."

The furnishings were ancient, and on the surface the house appeared clean and orderly, yet there was something tainted and odd about it. Auntie introduced Uncle Henry, Mama and us children. Up close I saw that Mrs. Bertha was older than I had first thought. Her graying hair was tied in a tight knot behind her head. Her body was heavy, her breast sagged like an empty purse, and when she tried to smile, I noticed most of her teeth were missing.

Mrs. Bertha led the six of us through a large roomy kitchen where an old coal stove sat in the middle of the room along the wall. On the other side sat an empty icebox. A large wooden table, with a cheerful pot of wildflowers on top, sat smack in the middle of the room and was surrounded by four chairs. We followed her up the stairs and into a small room. Nothing in that room was newer than ten years old, but beyond that, I felt a terrific swelling of joy because there was a real bed were I could sleep. This was a welcome relief after having slept in a crowded truck all night.

I understood that Mrs. Bertha was giving us temporary lodging until Mama could get word to Led that we had arrived in Kimberly. And her house, as compared to our previous shanty in Nigger Bottom, was certainly a sanctuary of comfort and relief. Yet, for some reason I felt eerie standing in that upstairs room, looking out the one small window to the river. It felt suddenly like the old walls were folding in on me… as if it were haunted… it smelled dusty and dry. I knew it would be difficult for me to sleep there, and as Aunt Samantha and Uncle Henry made ready to leave I cried to go with them, but Mama would not permit it.

We all stayed in the room most of that day. Through the window I could see the steamboats pulling barges of coal down the river. The swooshing roar of noise from the two-lane highway easily penetrated the walls of the building. It was like a prison for us children, for we were not allowed to venture outside the small room. There was no water or toilet. The outhouse was located a distance from the dwelling up a slight incline.

On close inspection I saw roaches crawling about even in the daylight. Rats — huge ones I imagined — squeaked and scampered in the walls and one ran across the room. I shuddered, dreading the oncoming night. All was not well and Mama appeared very unhappy, sitting on the bed or pacing the floor and gazing out the window, hoping to see Led coming. She'd heard that he was living across the river in a company shack and that he had obtained a job working the smelting ovens.

Finally, Mama learned from Mrs. Bertha that at the bottom of the hill across the railroad tracks, there was a large-framed, flat-faced white man who operated a rowboat business. For 15 cents he would row people, or messages, across the river. Desperate now, Mama hastily wrote a note, ordered us to stay in the room and watch Inez, took it down the hill and across the railroad tracks. After a brief discussion, she gave the note to the man with her instructions. The note was to be delivered to James Leadbetter working at smelting ovens Number 14 and 15. The white man took the note and, giving no change to Mama's quarter, rowed across the river. Two hours later the white man came on to Mrs. Bertha's place bringing word that Led would arrive late that evening with groceries.

Now that we were looking forward to Led's arrival, the day seemed to creep along. We were all hungry. Mama breast-fed Inez, and then, although Marguerite had been weaned long ago, she nursed her too since there was no other nourishment available. Unexpectedly, Mrs. Bertha knocked at our door, asking Mama to bring us kids down to the kitchen and have something to eat. This was welcomed news because as I recall I was starving, but I didn't want Mama to know. Anyway, we all went down stairs to the kitchen and, for the first time, we met Mrs. Bertha's daughter, Trudy.

CHAPTER 18
My First Crush… A Harsh Lesson In Love

Trudy was a thirteen-year-old, light-brown-skinned girl. She had a pretty face, a mature woman's bust line, shapely legs, and was well built. She had just arrived from school and seemed to be happy to meet us. We all sat at the table where Mrs. Bertha placed several glasses, a gallon of fresh buttermilk and a large pan of hot, buttered cornbread. This was the best meal I had seen in days.

I began to eat piggishly and Mama caution me to watch my manners. I was only seven years old but I started getting a very strange, compelling feeling about Trudy. Suddenly I began to like the place. Maybe my perceptions were wrong, but sitting there at the table it seemed to me that Mrs. Bertha was verbally and physically abusive to Trudy, smacking her leg one time when she didn't pass the buttermilk as quickly as Mrs. Bertha wanted, and looking mean glances at her. Every word she spoke to young Trudy seemed to be in anger.

It was about five o'clock when Led finally arrived. He had two bags of groceries which I remember to this day included candy and peanuts and powered milk, cheese, bread and canned meat. Led appeared happy to see his family, but he was less than cordial toward baby Inez, ignoring her almost completely. However, Led was not an easy man to read. Hardly any of his true emotions showed in his face and it was hard to know his happiness from his anger. We all felt happy, though, and Mama and Led chatted a while. From what I overheard, we would be moving to an oddly-named place called "Sink Clear" in about two weeks. At dusk, Led made his way down to the river and the white man's rowboat, needing to cross before dark. He kissed us all on the cheek and took off.

107

The night drifted away and I was filled with uncertainty and unease. For whatever reason I could not sleep in that strange house, though I was close to my family, huddled all in one small bed with Mama, Marguerite and baby Inez. We were all awake at dawn as sunlight seeped through the thin window curtains. Even up in our tiny room the aroma of fresh coffee filled the air. We could hear, off in the distance, morning doves cooing and birds singing in the trees. On this shining Saturday morning, with all the glory of April blossoms, Trudy came to call us to come downstairs.

When I saw Trudy, my whole world became glowing and happy. It was like the air, the skies, and earth were conspiring to intoxicate me... to enrapture me with the joy of everything that lived. I was only seven, but my heart sang at the sight of her and I thought the world of beautiful Trudy. Inside myself I knew I had suddenly obtained some here-to-fore unreachable level of understanding... some new sense of maturity and realization... not expected, or guessed, by the adults around me. Up till now, my love for the opposite sex had gone unnoticed and unrecognized. But that morning I felt a deep stirring, a kind of an awakening, so strong and so thrilling I instinctively knew not to say anything to anybody about it.

"Good morning all," Mrs. Bertha greeted us.

"Mornin'!" Mama and I responded.

Surprisingly, Mrs. Bertha had prepared breakfast for us. There were homemade pancakes, thick slices of bacon, oatmeal and buttered hot biscuits. My sister Marguerite played with her food. I never knew her to eat very much. Inez scrambled down from Mama's arms while the conversation went on between Mama and Mrs. Bertha about coming events of the day.

Chewing my food slowly, I eyed Trudy furtively with sly, hidden glances in her direction. She was so beautiful I forgot how good the food tasted... and to a boy with my appetite, that meant something.

After breakfast, Mama sent us children outside to play in the grass and sand. The warm sun shone down upon us as we played and a gentle wind ruffled the branches of the eucalyptus and the sprawling pepper trees. Plumes of lilac bowed on delicately-foliaged branches that grew over the porch and shadows lay blue against the whiteness, and the peace and order, of the house. There were chickens, ruffling and clucking in the yard, pigeons cooing in the branches overhead and a mean old cat lay, eyeing us suspiciously, her furry belly to the sun. As I played in the sunshine, my heart was calling out like a song for Trudy to come out and play with us.

Mrs. Bertha had a job in Montgomery, the grubby little town we had visited a few days earlier. She worked there as a house cleaner for some white people. This morning, she asked Mama to come along with her and help with the cleaning chores. Trudy would stay home and babysit the children. Without hesitation, Mama agreed. Shortly, the two ladies had made their preparation and left for town. In Mama's position, she could do little other than to agree to go with Mrs. Bertha. Anyway, I was just happy that beautiful Trudy would be left alone with us.

My happiness did not last long.

As soon as the grownups had gone, a young man from next door emerged from his house and pretended he was feeding the pigeons. He was a handsome young fellow who looked to be about the same age as Trudy. They waved at each other and Trudy called out, "Hi, Melvin."

"Hi, Trudy." he answered.

Suddenly Trudy rushes over to him and, just like that, they were leaning on the wire fence that separated the two properties. They were soon involved in a flirtatious conversation. It was obvious they knew each other well. I felt left out, because all of Trudy's attention was now focused on Melvin. I had been just waiting for Mama and Mrs. Bertha to leave, because I wanted all of Trudy's attention for myself. I was so angry at her in that moment, I'm sure that if I'd been older — and grown-up like they were — I would have made an ugly scene. I could just see myself storming over to her by the fence and saying, "Get away from that kid, Trudy. I don't want you foolin' around with anyone else but me." Of course, all that was only in my imagination.

After a while Melvin climbed over the fence, Trudy took his hand passionately and they walked to where we children were playing. "Charles, you watch your sisters now. Melvin is coming with me. He's gonna help me move my furniture and decorate my room."

"Okay," I announced. There again was a situation where my newly-gained insight and perceptions were not recognized. Just because I was seven years old, they believed they'd pulled the wool over my young eyes. But I could smell something fishy was going on. I climbed quietly up the steps behind them and saw them walk through the kitchen, with Trudy leading the way, and on into her bedroom. Feeling suddenly flushed and anxious, I had to see what was going to happen in there. Waiting a while, I walked around the porch, very quietly, to the window of her room, flattening myself along the porch siding I listened to their conversation.

"Don't be afraid, Trudy. It will feel good, I promise you." Melvin said.

The window curtains were drawn shut, but holes in the dilapidated window shade gave me just enough room to look through. I saw it all.

Trudy rested her chin on his neck just above his shoulder as he softly caressed her buttocks. Both of them were breathing like they had just run the hundred-yard dash and Melvin moved his hand down to cup her young, tender breast.

"Oh, yes," she almost moaned. "Yes."

Trudy's face was very flushed and she seemed excited, but relaxed. I could even see the pulse in her throat throbbing and she was smiling a mysterious smile, all soft and starry-eyed, like she wasn't focusing her eyes. Shocked, I stepped away for a moment. I'd never seen anything like that before. I could feel something rising inside me, making my blood run hot in my veins. I felt my own heart-beat accelerate, and somehow I was scared by the excitement of my own feelings. Drawn like a magnet, I returned to my peep hole in the shade.

Trudy was giving herself over to Melvin completely. His hands were all over her now. As he backed her against the wall, she allowed him to touch her wherever he wished. He pulled her dress from her shoulder and they firmly cupped her nude breasts in his hands. As he lowered the garment past her small waist and over her rounded hips, Trudy reached down and helped him. Melvin stopped, surprised at her sudden enthusiasm.

"Why did you take so long?" he asked in a hoarse whisper, not expecting any answer. Then he smiled into her eyes. "Now that you got the idea, baby, why don't you lay on the bed?"

Trudy just smiled vacantly and nodded as she stepped out of her dress, then dropped her silken panties down and stepped out of them. Completely naked, she stood in front of the hard- breathing Melvin and waited.

"Oh, yeah... fantastic!" Melvin mumbled repeatedly as he tore off his own clothes. When he was nude, Trudy glanced down at his long, hard penis. The length of it flabbergasted me, but Trudy seemed not all that impressed. The quietness of the room eased as they touched and breathed together in the stillness. I coughed, but they didn't even hear me. At that point I knew I could be standing right there inside the room and they wouldn't notice. They were totally oblivious to everything except the excitement that was happening between them at the moment.

Melvin took Trudy into his arms and kissed her passionately. He was breathing hard and his movements were stiff and unsure, but Trudy — so loose and pliant — seemed to melt into each gesture he made. In a moment they were on the bed. Trudy lay spread-eagle beneath Melvin. At first it appeared they were engaged in some kind of wrestling, or a fight, and I began to worry about how could I help her. But just as I was ready to scream out, I saw Trudy put her silky arms around his neck.

"Oh, Trudy! Oh, Trudy!" Melvin said repeatedly, as he plunged his long penis deep into Trudy's tight vagina. Melvin was sweating profusely, and he was gripping the sides of the bed, appearing to struggle and his face was squenched up in a frown of deep concentration. His efforts, along with her cooperative rocking motions, caused him to make small groaning sounds. After only a few more strokes, he moaned loudly and collapsed on top of Trudy's beautiful light-brown body. Frustrated and confused, I ran. I could hear the hammering of my heart. It pumped frantically as if it were flooding with blood, thumping and pounding behind my ribs like a caged animal. My face felt hot and my eyes were gritty, like I had a fever. I was frightened... and angry... and disgusted at what I had seen... and yet wildly frustrated all at the same time.

When I reached the play box where I'd left Marguerite and Inez, I found Marguerite asleep and Inez playing with a three-foot garter snake. I ran to Inez, screaming, and the snake swiftly slithered away. It is a good thing it did, because I was so upset, so savagely angry about what I'd watched Trudy do with Melvin, I could only see through the bright red haze of my fury, and in my blinding rage I would have grabbed that snake and bit his damn head clean off.

The day passed slowly, and as I sat under the pepper trees lost in sad contemplation, I knew I never wanted to see Trudy again. If she were in my presence, I would look the opposite way. If I had to meet her in passing, then my eyes would be down cast. Although, I must admit, in my childish jealousy and pain, I actually thought about blackmailing her in order to win some sort of concession — something on the order of Melvin's rewards — and I thought about telling all I had seen to her mother, knowing she would be severely beaten for her sin. I never did, but maybe that's what my seven-year-old pride wanted in order to be satisfied.

Eight days passed before Led returned to Mrs. Bertha's. to help get us moved away. He had borrowed a friend's truck to haul our few belongings.

Trudy was away that day, and I knew I would never see her again. Part of me was glad, but part of me — struggling with some deep hidden yearning — felt like I was crying inside.

CHAPTER 19
To "Sink Clear"... A Piano... And The Power Of Music

Sink Clear was a sorry-looking housing settlement two miles west of Kimberly. A tacky strip of land stretching between the river and the railroad tracks running above the river, it was about six-hundred yards long and sixty-yards wide where the flimsy houses had been built. The front of our house was no more than twenty yards from the railroad tracks, the back was about the same distance, slanting down to the river bank. It was an old, abandoned railroad community like some place out West, but here the rundown, dilapidated houses had been cast off to poor black folks. Some white family lived in the last house at the south end of the strip, but they were worse off than the poorest black family I knew. There was a saloon and a grocery store situated across the tracks and up the hill a ways. Several more houses for white people were sprinkled along the paved highway.

They called it "Stink Clear" rather than Sink Clear because of the enormous waste being dumped into the river, waste which originated from the smelting ovens and coal mines. Sink Clear was a literal sink, because the septic Kanawha River flowed swiftly to the South, bringing with it all the impurities from the north. The old railroad community was a very dangerous place for anyone to live, especially children.

We moved into an old building which had once been a railroad boarding house where workers would gather to eat their meals and collect lunch sacks, water and other nourishments. This nourishment would sustain them while they worked the railroad miles away. Old pictures hung on the walls throughout the house. Mostly they were pictures of small, fat children and there was usually a large shaggy dog guarding them who resembled "Tags" in the Dogwood comics. A dreary front room faced the railroad tracks where the windows caught the path of the sun. The living room carried the stiff image of a formal parlor meant for visitors or clergy. A large stove, wearing the trademark *Kalamazoo,* provided heat, and the furniture consisted of uncomfortable hardwood chairs and a few unpadded benches.

Right away I discovered that the previous tenants had left an old upright piano standing in one of the barren corners. Like most energetic little boys, I hammered down several white-ivory keys at random. The resonance sounded so pleasing to me it instantly triggered an interest that has endured from that day on. Music, and the piano in particular, proved to be an intrinsic and inborn calling, fulfilling a need that helped to satisfy my hungry soul.

On cool days, the big old house was heated by fireplaces fueled by coal. Bedrooms were situated upstairs and down. The only comfortable downstairs room — reached by walking through the dining room via a hallway — was the kitchen where we generally ate our meals. The kitchen faced the river and held a large, coal-burning stove. Attached to the kitchen-side of the dwelling was a medium-size porch where a wooden shelf and a granite washbasin had been placed. This was where the railroad workers washed their hands before meals. Through our kitchen window we could see the community outhouse that sat on the edge of the hillside with its backside turned toward the river.

Led and Mama were still fussing around in the kitchen and Marguerite and I were wandering around outside. I was under heavy admonition not to go near the railroad tracks. It was late afternoon now and the sun, sinking behind gray clouds in the west, made the sky look bruised. As I watched, the river, formerly gray, began taking on the colors of the sky above. I could hear the barge's paddles dipping into areas of welts and wounds. As the light began to fail, red-orange water rapidly faded into puddles of black and blue. The barge's lights glittered on the water creating specters of wonder.

After we had lived there a while, I enjoyed wandering down to the water to watch the barges go past. I marveled at the river boats, bright with candlelight and oil lamps. The paddle wheels churned the water, and smoke swirled from the tall stack. I wondered what it would be like to be aboard one of them, knowing the boats steamed all the way to Charleston. To me that town seemed a world away, but I liked dreaming about it anyway.

Looking across the river I could see Led's place of work. At night the smelting ovens glowed in the dark and created a spectacular view. In this community, even as it had been in Nigger Bottom, white lightnin' was plentiful, and again Led and Mama started to have Saturday night parties. It seemed like everyone in Sink Clear drank white lightnin'.

Every day I would bang on the piano, making sounds and listening to them. I learned to pick out little melodies and musical phrases I'd heard on the radio. Sometimes I played bits of my own invention. When I created a tune that I liked I would play it over repeatedly until my fingers got tired. Occasionally, I played the same four or five notes in sequence for an hour or longer, as if I were afraid to stop. Soon I could imitate the sound of the freight train's locomotive that constantly roared past our house. It wasn't long before I had composed a tune I called "Chu-Chu Boogie-Woogie." Music, any kind of music, seemed strangely soothing to me. The daily practice helped develop my thin hands, forearms and elbows. Sometimes I shouted wildly at the top of my lungs into the cacophony I was creating, but I would always return to the more interesting business of repeating melodic notes that sounded pleasing to me. Then I discovered octaves, and the key of C, which I played hour after hour, entranced by its marvelous symmetry.

On one stormy day, while I was busy practice the piano, I head a strange voice. Instantly I knew it was the speech of some intoxicated person. It turned out to be a man folks around there called Mr. Hut. He was an alcoholic migrant who loitered daily around the community. When he was deeply into his whiskey he would walk around singing cadences like the Army drill squads. "Hut-two-three-four; Hut-two-three-four." He repeated that marching cadence over and over, thus earning his name.

The day I met Mr. Hut he was intoxicated and smelled of hard whiskey. A lot of folks considered him the neighborhood drunk who, unfortunately, liked to sit on the railroad tracks when inebriated. I say "unfortunately," because it was his favorite perch there that did him in.

Homeless, Mr. Hut was a classy, red-eyed man with gray, nappy hair and a long, ragged beard, somewhere between fifty and sixty years old. One chilly morning I arose to find Mr. Hut. asleep behind our house. That morning I saw Mr. Hut had buried himself deep in an old greenish-colored army blanket. It stunk acridly of urine and decayed food, as did the once-cinnamon-colored overcoat he was using as a pillow. Old Mr. Hut had a weather-beaten face and it was equally dirty. When he turned onto his hip, the sacky blanket opened revealing his red plaid shirt caked with the mud and grime. He was lying in a shallow gully that had been beaten-out by rain, and when I stumbled upon him he yawned. Realizing I meant no harm, he painfully crawled out of his sleeping blanket. With an unsteady gait, he walked over to the corner of the house and relieved himself. Mr. Hut's pants were so caked with muck that I could not tell whether they had started out being blue jeans or brown pants.

Later that day, around ten o'clock, word in the community circulated that a fast freight train had killed Mr. Hut. The locomotive was going so fast when it hit him it ripped his body into several bloody pieces... and the engineer never stopped the train. The word was that when news reached the engineer that he'd run over and killed a black man in Sink Clear, he just shrugged and said, "Aw, what the hell. That's just another nigger bitin' the dust."

The railroad company claimed that Mr. Hut was trespassing on their land and had failed to yield the right of way. "Couldn't hit him if he weren't standin' on the tracks, an' that's our property," they said. "He coulda just got off, couldn't he?" Everybody felt bad about old Mr. Hut being run over and killed, and it didn't matter whose fault it was.

As I came to learn, trains in Sink Clear had already killed several children. Even the slow freights did not try to stop when they spotted a black child on the tracks, no matter how young. I recall one Sunday afternoon a two-year-old baby had managed to toddle onto the tracks. They said that the locomotive's engineer ran over the child with sadistic pride.

On the other side of the tracks from where we lived was an old graveyard. They buried people of all races and backgrounds there. Slaves, gun slingers and Chinese railroad workers were there. One old brown grave marker set toward the back of the graveyard displayed its sad epitaph: "Here lies my slaveboy George, born 1815, died of a whipping 1844." Weeds grew tall in the graveyard, and every once in a while some old white man would cut the grass. I was hoping that's where they'd bury Mr. Hut... but I heard later there wasn't enough of him left to be worth diggin a grave for.

CHAPTER 20
Racing With Death… A Near Miss!

It was mid summer. Mama and Led had suddenly stopped attending church and they'd begun drinking more frequently. As a result, they got into arguments more frequently also. When Mama drank alcohol she was not herself. She turned mean, abusive and indifferent toward us children. Often I wanted to say, "Mama, I love you, but go away!"

Part of the time Mama was warm and loving. Other times she was rejecting and hostile. When she sobered up, she'd tell us kids that she loved us. It was hard for a child to know what to believe while observing her duality. Frequently, she seemed absorbed in solitude and she often became so despondent she couldn't express any passion… it was as if nothing at all mattered. This inconsistent behavior made me confused about what so-called "love" really was. I perceived it to mean that when a person "loved" you, you could be adored one day and painfully attacked the next.

As days passed in Sink Clear, Mama became even more depressed and despondent. She was frequently sick, especially in the mornings, throwing up and complaining of headaches and stomach pain. Secretly, I became suspicious, and worried, that Mama's illness was the bad effect caused by her consumption of such enormous amounts of alcoholic spirits. She always referred to the morning-after effects of her drinking as a "hangover." I saw that her alcoholic habits were constantly repeated cycles. I did not know it then, but my mama was an alcoholic.

Finally Mama decided she was feeling so ill she would visit the company doctor who had an office in Montgomery several miles south of Sink Clear. After a physical examination and a health history review, the doctor told

116

Mama to stop consuming alcohol because she was pregnant. Shocked and dismayed, Mama was not happy to hear this, as she did not want any more children.

Led came home late that night and Mama told him she was pregnant. He seemed happy to hear the news, but a little bewildered. As always, it was difficult to judge whether Led was happy or unhappy. Ledbelly was known to laugh when he was angry, and to appear angry when he was content.

As time went on, it was evident that Led was beginning to have difficulties at work. The smelting ovens provided only three workdays per week for the black employees. They claimed that they didn't need unskilled workers for six days. A three-day week for black miners was common in those days.

By now, most grownups were talking about the war in Europe. Hitler, the German Dictator, was becoming infamous. Rumors prevailed that he was systematically destroying the Jewish race across the continent of Europe. In Sink Clear, the same old trouble was going on between the unions and the companies. In spite of the fact that companies hired men to beat up union organizers, hoping to keep them from forming the union, some miners stopped work anyway and walked out on strike against the coal operators.

At night, the striking miners roamed about, stealing anything they could get their hands on belonging to the coal company. They would then sell the commodity for money to buy food.

People who lived in Sink Clear shopped the community store which was up the hill across the tracks along Highway 61. They called it the "Hunky" store because a Hungarian family owned it.

On my way home from the Hunky store one evening, I heard the freight train hooting its warning horn. I glanced across the road and saw that this one had a long procession of coal cars and boxcars and it was heading south toward Charleston. On occasions, the train would stop for ten or fifteen minutes, stretching out across the road, and anyone trying to cross to the other side would have to wait till the train moved on. Lately, whenever Mama sent me to the store, my main objective was to try to beat the train to the point where pedestrians usually crossed the tracks. This day was no exception.

Looking out of the front door in the twilight, Mama saw me start running and realized what was going on. She rushed out of the house to the edge of the porch and shouted, "No, Charles! Charles! No!"

I heard her, but my mind was made up and my feet started pickin' up even faster. I was intending to beat that approaching train to the crossing point. Holding on tightly to my brown grocery bag I raced it, and to me that locomotive gained speed with every step I took. I could hear my own heart banging against my ribs, my breath roaring in and out of my lungs. It seemed to me, as my bare feet slammed along next to that screaming freight, that a different form of sight took over my senses. Not a different focusing of the eyes, but some great feeling of alertness was spreading all over my body, a shifting of my senses, as if I could suddenly see with my skin… hear with my skin… I felt I could see the slightest sound. I opened my mouth to listen, and my mouth, too, seemed to see and to hear. My hair felt electrified, my skin tingled, and all the time I was watching the giant wheels of that train rolling, rolling, faster… faster.

How can I ever forget that night? I was alert in every fiber; all my senses were wide awake; I was prepared for anything, and utterly without fear. As I ran, pumping the elbow of my left arm like a piston and squeezing that heavy bag to my thin chest, I felt as though I was doing something more than racing a train… In my mind I was crossing a bridge from one side of my life to the other. I knew that the bridge would fade away behind me, like a dream world, to which I would never return, for I knew I was passing from reason to feeling, from security to adventure, from rationality to dream. I loved the rush of feeling, the thrill, the challenge. Faster and faster I ran, utterly alone in the cool-rush of night air, but this time my solitude was not a torment; there was something mystical about it.

My wide-open eyes flashed to the train and again the engineer seemed to be in actual pursuit, aware of the chase and grinning as if about to bag a prize. His eyes were staring at the track ahead and he hunched his upper body forward and backward, vigorously, as if he could urge the train forward and help it to catch up to me.

The locomotive's screeching horn, Mama shouting my name, the sound of my own feet smacking the dirt, my heart pounding, all came together in one harmonious symphony as I reached the intersection and leaped across the track. By a hair I won. The locomotive's cattle-catcher missed me by a fraction of an inch. It was so close the engineer believed he'd hit me. When he reached Montgomery, he was bragging that he'd finally picked off the little nigger who liked to race his train, and he was laughing. They chagrined him the next day when he learned he'd missed me.

Upon reaching the other side of the tracks safely, I ran to Mama's arms, elated, feeling ten feet tall. She embraced me, but then she began to beat on me for taking such a terrible risk and racing with the freight. She shouted over and over, banging on my head with every word, "Don't you ever do that again!"

I didn't tell Mama, but I had done it because other boys my age were always boasting about how they had beaten the train, and they'd called me "chicken" because I hadn't done it. I didn't see my foolish risk-taking as a dangerous trick. To me it was just a means of gaining a little status with my peers, as other boys did. Now, of course, I realize why those trains killed so many youngsters on the railroad tracks. They were little daredevils, not unlike myself, who were racing with death and got caught.

The train incident upset Mama tremendously. She must have known there was always the threat of me being killed on those tracks and she was ready to move away from Sink Clear.

I knew Led was ready to leave also because the operators of the smelting ovens were out on strike in support of the striking miners. Led supported the miners, so consequently he was on the coal mine owners' hit list. Owners hired gun-carrying thugs, under the auspices of the police officer called the High Sheriff, to hunt down dissenting miners. They especially enjoyed hiring men who were known to be tough and gangster-like in all their dealings. They gave these thugs guns to carry and paid them well to beat miners down; to use fear and threats to keep men from joining the union. This trouble had convinced Led to leave Sink Clear. One evening, Led slipped away with the promise to Mama that he would be back for us soon as he found new work and another place for us to live.

CHAPTER 21
Hold It Right There, Nigger, or I'll Blast Your Black Ass Off!"

In Sink Clear hired thugs were running rampant. Several men had already been killed. These goons swarmed over the hills, raiding the miners' homes, and if a union sympathizer was found they'd take him up the mountain for killing. Families reported their loved ones had been taken away and never seen again. Human bones were regularly found on mountain trails.

Union organizers and striking miners were in hiding everywhere. Usually the best places to hide out were in the thickly treed forest, the hollers and the overgrown cemeteries.

One man, Tom Meade, came to our house saying he was a friend of Led's. He was hobbling along, could hardly walk, and his back was a bloody pulp. After taking off his shirt to show Mama his wounds, he drank some water and then walked across the railroad tracks to hide out in the old cemetery. He stayed hidden there for several days and Mama sent me out at night to bring him food and water.

On one Saturday evening, several burly white men came to our house looking for James Leadbetter. They pushed on into our house over Mama's claims that Led wasn't there and looked everywhere, poking under the beds, searching through our dirty clothes basket, through our folded clean clothes, in the kitchen drawers and cabinets. They said they were looking for guns and certain literature or papers to prove Led was tied in with what they called the "International Workers of the World." They claimed James Leadbetter was a communist. Of course, they branded anyone involved in any kind of union organizing as a communist.

Things were not looking good for us. At that point, knowing how hard they were searching for Led, we didn't know whether he was dead or alive.

Mama was getting big with her pregnancy, but she worried so about Led she couldn't hold off and she began drinking white lightnin' again.

Three weeks later, about two o'clock in the morning, Led slipped into the house, woke us all up, and said we were going to a place called Minden.

It was dark. The clouds hid the moonlight. Led guided the family west, along the railroad tracks. Silently, we all struggled down a hillside and into a waiting rowboat. A tall, stiff-necked white man was the pilot. We loaded into the boat, and were on our way across the river. Usually a trip across that river is a simple exercise.

"Led! Hey, Led!" I called out as quietly as possible, but my voice held some urgency.

"What?" he snapped from the front of the boat.

"I think that barge is going to run us over."

Mama turned and saw the oncoming barge, pushing up a rolling trough in the dark water, its lights gleaming like little red torches. "Oh, Lord!" Mama gasped.

"It's gonna miss us by a mile," announced our pilot facetiously. "Don't worry about it."

For the next few minutes, I peered into the darkness, listening to the cascading water as the paddles dipped into the river, bringing the barge closer. As I watched, feeling my heart tripping with fear, I was sure that if our direction did not change we would most certainly collide.

Again I called out to Led, but his mind seemed to be off somewhere in the mists, and he paid no attention to my whining about such mundane events. "Don't worry about it," he said. Somehow our pilot got us beyond the prow of that oncoming barge in time.

When we reached the other side of the river, we exited the boat silently and the pilot pulled away from shore, heading back. Inez, my baby sister, was in Mama's arms, wrapped in a large blanket and safe from the cool, soft wind. We walked along the river bank and suddenly some man appeared out of the dark. He was a one-armed thug on the hunt for striking miners. He wore dark coveralls and a wide brim hat. There was a squawk of alarm from him, and he had a shotgun in his hands.

"Hold it right there, nigger, or I'll blast your black ass off!" he said to Led. "Just make one move, and I'll splatter your backside all around this river, along with the rest of your little niggers." Then he called out, "Hey, Billy Bill. Over here. I caught us some niggers."

Another man appeared from his hiding place and ran down to the river bank where we were being held captive. A tall, muscular white man appeared wearing a denim jacket and horn-rimmed glasses. He was holding what looked to be a thick rope and a baseball bat. He spoke.

"What's your name, boy?"

"James Leadbetter," Led said crisply.

"Well, well. We got us a prize. Ledbelly, huh? Our company will pay good money for your dead ass, black boy." The thug raised his fist in what was supposed to be the first blow of a beating for Led.

Quick as a cat, Led kicked him low and drove him back against a makeshift boat pier which cracked apart and fell to the water below. The second man swung wildly with the baseball bat and grunted as if any blow to the body would have killed Led instantly.

Led grabbed the bat somehow, and as they struggled he kept hold of part of it with his left hand. A flash of silver in the moonlight and Led ripped twice across the man's face with his straight razor. Blood spurted. The man dropped the bat and grabbed for his face. Led grabbed the bat and smashed the man's head and body several times. I remember seeing broken teeth come flipping out and how blood poured from his nose and mouth. That was just what they were planning to do to Led... and maybe us, too.

Now the man Led had knocked into the river started climbing out of the water. Rushing at him with the razor in his hand, Led slashed him one time across the neck. More blood spurted and the man fell into the water, only this time, face down, his body floated on down the river.

"Watch out, Led!" Mama screamed.

Led was a split-second late for the warning and he caught a blow across his back.

The other man had picked himself up and was wielding his baseball bat. As he swung, he lost his footing, stumbled, went down, and slammed into the water.

"You fuckin' black son-of-a-bitch! I'm going to kill you!" Lunging out of the dark water he swung the bat again.

Led wheeled and with lightning speed managed to get one leg up and he caught the flying attacker smack in the belly, knocking the wind out of him. The man's legs buckled and he went down. The baseball bat lay a few feet away. Led picked it up, rammed it hard into his opponent's torso. I heard the last bellowing air leaving the man's body. The thug tumbled to the ground in a tight ball, groaning and holding his gut.

"Let's get outta here!" Led yelled. He grabbed Marguerite and all of us rushed toward the paved road where he had parked a borrowed black two-door Ford with a rumble seat. Led opened the rumble-seat and lifted me and then Marguerite.

"Charles, wrap the blanket around you and hold it tight to keep warm," Mama said. With Inez in her arms, Mama made her way to the front seat. Led jumped in, started the engine, and off we went, leaving one dead white man floating down the river and another one smashed up enough to slow him down for a day or so.

Led drove steadily, taking us swiftly through the growing darkness. Once on a curve, the tires squealed, and he slowed automatically, but by the grim look on his face I knew he was thinking that one way or another he was going to get us to Minden. We were now on a main causeway, built over and through dank-smelling swamp-grass. "Goddamit, this is a lousy stretch of road," Led said loudly over the noise of the engine. "Especially at night. Fuckin' state troopers are out lookin' for bootleggers." He slowed to forty. Mama didn't answer. She was exhausted and had dozed off. to sleep.

From my perch on the driver's side of the rumble seat I could see there was a long curve up ahead. Led probably knew this road by heart, for he edged the car a little closer to the shoulder. A long tongue of lights licked toward him as an oncoming car rounded the curve and poured straight down the stretch. Led, dazzled by the light, stomped on his dimmer button and his headlights dropped low to the road ahead. The oncoming car did not dip its lights, and Led did a sharp pat-pat with his foot on the dimmer button, signaling the other car, but the driver paid no attention.

"All right, goddamn it. You want some, have some!" Led stomped viciously on the dimmer switch, our headlights lifted and reached straight over the blackout in front of him, rebounding off the unlit rear end of an old truck which was barely crawling along at the beginning of the curve. Within a fraction of a second Led was on top of it. Half-blinded by the blazing lights of the other car now passing on the left, Led jerked the wheel to avoid running smack into the rear of the creeping junk heap that had appeared elephant-like in the road. I heard the wheels scream and felt the rear end sway as the car swerved straight into the path of the oncoming car. Again Led jerked furiously at the steering wheel, this time to the right, and missed the approaching car by inches. Tilted up on two wheels, Led twisted again to the right. I heard a loud BANG! as the right front tire blew out. Skirmishing desperately with the steering wheel of the careening car with his left hand, his right arm went out to brace Mama's shoulder. The car skidded violently off the road and stopped right in front of an embankment.

Stunned, we sat there on the edge of that steep cliff in silence for a minute, catching our breath and hardly believing we were alive. We'd missed the shadow of death by a whisker. After a while, Led got out to see what he could do about the tire.

CHAPTER 22
To Minden... Another Coal Mining Camp

Morning came and a warm wind cleared the dawn sky. The welcome glow of the sun rose over the deep mountain canyons, brightening the ribbon of road that lay ahead as we drove on toward Minden, West Virginia. It was ten o'clock in the morning when we reached our destination. Minden is another coal mining camp sprawled in a valley below the small town of Oak Hill. A mountain breeze constantly blew through the narrow, rolling valley floor where a shallow creek meandered quietly. The dark green of the underbrush and the plentiful number of tall oaks was a pleasant relief from the ghostly appearance of Sink Clear.

Here and there on the mountainsides were company houses, connected by a spider web of pathways and white fence rails that followed the old foot-trails. Led drove the car along the winding roads, searching for the black neighborhood.

Minden was a large, scraggly-looking community surrounding by tall mountains. The black folks lived on the northern end, and the white folks lived on southern side. The white neighborhoods were plush with manicured yards, lush plants and trees and paved roads. They enjoyed a large company store, a dental office, a doctor's office, a library, a large school house and a recreation center, all centrally located for the convenience of the whites.

Contrasting with the spiffy white neighborhood, the roads in the black neighborhood were unpaved, merely sprinkled with red cinders and slate-rock to prevent vehicle wheels from sinking into the deep mud. The difference between the two areas was like night and day. Clearly, the black folks' habitat was a living, breathing, palpable image of what I had come to think of as the paths of darkness. There were no stores, no medical facilities or recreation area to be seen, but there were two school buildings. Obviously, Mama remarked as we drove by, the white folks in Minden had no intention of sharing their school buildings with blacks. One school was for black children grades first through fourth; the second served grades fifth through eighth.

After an hour or so, Led pulled the car up to a newly painted house with a white picket fence around it. The house had an enormous back yard that dwarfed the skimpy front yard where a large pile of coal sat inappropriately. Wooded steps led to the front door. Inside, the house was clean and it had hardwood floors. There were two bedrooms and a dinning room, each with its own fireplace. The roomy kitchen housed a huge, black, cast iron stove where a large bucket filled with coal sat on one side and a pile of wood on the other. Upon first sight of the stove, Mama fell in love with it, anticipating the pleasure of baking and cooking on it.

The first night in the new house I did not sleep much. I was very tired, but I kept waking up. Night pressed thickly into the little room where my sisters and I lay. I kept hearing unfamiliar sounds in this new house, and from outside. I finally half-dozed off, but then I dreamed of running… running away from the river where the dead white man was floating… running and being pursued by a wild, red-eyed man who had a razor… It was a nightmare and I screamed in terror. Led rushed in.

"What's wrong, boy? Can't you sleep?"

"No," I answered. "There's a red-eyed man looking in the window."

Led pulled up his trousers, slid out his infamous razor, and hurried to the front door. Cautiously he opened it and looked around outside the window. Closing the door he growled, "There's nothing there, boy. Go to sleep. I gotta work in the mornin'."

I lay back down, feeling somewhat reassured, but still frightened by my dream. I closed my eyes, waiting for sleep, but a small corner of my mind was wide awake, trying to figure out how to escape the nightmare.

Before the dawning light the next morning, Mama was up preparing breakfast and a lunch bucket for Led. His lunch bucket was round and consisted of two compartments. The bottom was for a half gallon of water, the top part for a sandwich. Some lunch buckets had a third compartment where miners kept their personal amenities.

In the dark of morning, when miners went to work, you could see the kerosene lamps they wore on their hats. To me they looked like fireflies, all steering about in the dark. The men would load onto coal cars which were about five-feet wide, ten-feet long, and three-feet high. Each coal car rested on four iron wheels and moved on rails much like railroad cars. One coal car could carry twelve to fifteen men. An enormous, heavy, electric machine resembling an iron box — called a "motor" — sat on the rails and it would pull an average of 25 to 30 coal cars loaded with miners, transporting them through the shafts five to ten miles under mountains. Miners would work under the mountain every day, never knowing whether they would come out dead or alive. Almost every day a coal car would bring out a dead miner, and sometimes, there'd be several dead miners being hauled out... the same men who'd come in laughing and joking along with all the others early that same morning.

Just outside the mine, the noise from the gigantic "tipple" was overpowering and injurious to a person's hearing. The tipple was a tall, sprawling monster-like machine that sorted the coal fed to it by endless loops of conveyor belts. It gobbled up the chunks of coal, separating the best from the lesser according to sizes. Then, spewing the churned material from its belly, it spread the sorted coal into railroad cars by other conveyer belts.

At the end of the work day, the coal cars, pulled by the "motor," would transport men from under the mountain. Their face and clothes would be jet black with coal dust. Going in, you could tell whites from blacks. Coming out, you couldn't, until they'd hustled off to the bath house which, in most mining camps, was located out near the tipple. There they would scrub down, and the water from the baths would run black from the drains.

It wasn't long before Led was making what was considered to be high wages for the time. They paid miners by the tonnage of coal they loaded, or by the number of coal cars they filled. Each car could hold approximately three tons. For the first time in many long months, we were living well and had plenty to eat. My sister and I had better clothes and better toys to play with.

I remember one night Mama and Led invited some friends of theirs to our house for dinner. That night Mama outdid herself displaying her extraordinary cooking ability. She began preparing that dinner the night before by making some of her famous light rolls. She let the dough wait overnight, then she'd roll small pieces of it into little balls, put them into a pan greased with butter, and leave them to rise for several hours before sliding them into a hot oven. They were delicious and so light Led teased saying he'd have to tie them to the dinner table or they'd float away. The rest of that sumptuous meal consisted of brown gravy, ham, roast chicken, Bar-B-Que ribs, collard greens with okra, cornbread and potato salad. Desert was mounds of home made ice cream, pound cake and blackberry cobbler. With some variations, Mama would prepare this kind of dinner every Sunday and holiday. All the guests who ate dinner at our house bragged for months on how good the meal was.

It was a warm night in May 1941, when my baby brother was born. He was a dark- skinned baby with curly black hair. Led was very proud of his son. He named him simply "TC." For the first few months, Mama breast-fed TC. Later she weaned him to feeding from a milk bottle. After coming home from work, Led would prepare the baby formula, then cradle TC in one arm and hold the milk bottle in the other. Him feeding his infant son like that was as close as I ever saw Led act in a tender-hearted way to anyone. Maybe he was different when he was alone with Mama, but in front of us kids, and company, he just didn't like having people know what he was thinking, or showing his emotions. Still, he had his good sides, and often went out of his way to be friendly to someone down on their luck.

One late Friday night, all of us were awakened by someone knocking at the front door. Led pulled on his trousers and went to see. Turned out to be a friend of his who had hitch-hiked from North Carolina to Minden, hoping to land a job in the coal mines. His name was Sam, and of course, Led invited him to stay at our house, since all the local hotels were Jim Crowed and did not serve blacks. They even had signs saying, "No Colored People Allowed" or "Whites Only."

Naturally, then, our friends, or friends of a friend, were welcomed at our place, and Sam lived with us for several days.

On about the third day of his visit, Led and Mama went off to shop and Sam agreed to babysit. At some point during my parents' absence, Sam pulled out his penis and dangled it in front of Marguerite and me. Marguerite was frightened. She thought it was a frog, and being afraid of those dark, wet-looking things, she screamed, "Frog! Frog!" and ducked around behind me. For a second I thought she was referring to Inez, since "Frog" was her nickname, but Inez was barely walking and had no idea what was going on. Although I was only seven, I had seen a hanging penis back in Kimberly where Trudy and Melvin were engaged in sex, and I knew what Sam was doing. Sam paraded around the house for several minutes with his frog-looking penis dangling out of his pants. Every few minutes he would grab it with one hand and rub on it till he'd ejaculate. Stung by what he was doing in front of my sister, I said, "Hey, Mr. Sam, what are you doing?"

"I… I is playin' with my frog," he faltered, and went right on doing it.

At two o'clock Led and Mama returned from shopping. Marguerite rushed over to Mama screaming, "Mama, Mama, Mr. Sam got a frog in his pants."

"What?" Mama responded.

"A frog," Marguerite insisted. "He got a frog in his pants. Big, ugly ol' frog."

Led heard her and immediately figured out what she was talking about and two seconds flat he was on his way to the bedroom where he kept his straight razor. He retrieved the razor from under his pillow and headed back down the hall swearing under his breath. Sensing danger, Sam took off running and Led chased after him. Mama stood in the doorway, beginning to cry, calling out as they disappeared across the tracks and into the trees, "Don't kill him! Please don't kill him!"

Led didn't return home till late in the evening, still furious, and with his clothes heavily stained with dried blood. "Teach that son-on-a-bitch!" he muttered, "messin' with my daughter." He gathered up the few belongings Sam had left behind, took them outside, and buried them in the back yard. I never did learn what happened to Mr. Sam.

TC was an active baby, and as he grew older, he quickly began crawling around the house. He had a mighty curiosity, and he was into everything, tasting and testing by putting whatever he got his hands on into his mouth. I think the problem started when Led began bringing home a white, flaky candy made out of coconut. Like most babies of that age, TC loved sweet food, but most especially he prized that white candy.

Late one evening, we were all sitting around the fireplace listening to the pleasant clink of the dishes as Mama washed them at the sink. Led had Marguerite and me intrigued by his ability to do drumming on an old, empty cigar box with his fingers while singing the Ham Bone song. He never missed a beat. We had just finished eating what Led called a "down home" supper. To him, that meant fried chicken, green beans laced with ham, buttered cornbread, mashed potatoes, brown gravy and Kool-Aid. Mama had weaned TC by now and he drank milk and ate small pieces of that sweet white coconut.

We were all having fun while TC was crawling about, and before we noticed, he had crawled to the kitchen on his hands and knees. Busy washing dishes, Mama did not notice him as he inched open the storage cabinet under the sink. Somehow TC managed to remove the top from a can of lye, a dangerous dry chemical Mama used for washing and general cleaning. In his usual tasting and testing way, the baby took a handful of the white stuff and put it into his mouth. Instantaneously, he screamed as if a murder was taking place. Glancing down and realizing what was happening, Mama screamed at the top of her voice, "Help! Help, Led. Oh, God!"

Led jumped up from his chair and rushed to the kitchen. "What's wrong, Nora? What the hell's goin' on?"

"The baby," she screamed. "TC put lye in his mouth."

Led scooped TC off the floor and cradled him in his arms. Tilting the child's head back as gently as possible, he got a good look at his son's mouth and assessed the injury. TC was kicking and screaming at the top of his lungs. Led used fresh water and his own fingers to wash out TC's mouth. Then grabbing a blanket, he wrapped it around TC and ran next door to the Young's because they owned a Dodge sedan. Mama was right behind him.

In a minute or so, Mr. Young, Led and Mama, with TC kicking and screaming, rushed off to a local hospital. Mrs. Young came over to our house to sit with us kids, knowing it might be quite some while before our parents could return. She stayed throughout the night.

That whole incident with TC and the lye was a very disturbing tragedy to me. I began to sense that things could happen, terrible unforeseen things, hurtful things… all part of trying to get through this life. I could not sleep that night. I lay awake thinking back in my own younger days, remembering the threatening experiences I had lived through… experiences that might have snatched my own life away from me just as TC's young life had been threatened just earlier. Some, like racing the train, had been my own doing… and some had just happened, like the car swerving on the road behind that junky old slow-moving truck that night. Staring up at the ceiling with my eyes wide open, afraid to dream, I felt I was on some long, mystifying journey… traveling down a dangerous road all during this growing up time, and once again I saw it as a path of darkness.

They hospitalized TC for several weeks. He became a favorite baby at the hospital. All the nurses and doctors spoiled him. Their caressing him and giving him so much attention seemed to awaken his senses and helped reconnect him to the world he wanted to reject for it had treated him so painfully and been so cruel to him. One nurse gave TC a soft, loving massage every day. It was her loving touch — when his infant mind needed reassurance that all around him was not hurtful as the lye had been — that encouraged him, helped him over his fears, and gave him confidence in his surroundings again.

When TC was released from the hospital, it was like a grand home-coming. We were all very glad to see him. He was well now and on seeing us he presented one of the most charming smiles that anyone could ever see. But that was not the end of this tragic incident. The friction between Led and Mama grew worse each day. Led couldn't stop blaming Mama, accusing her of being neglectful for leaving that open can of lye which nearly cost TC his life. I felt sorry for Mama, knowing how badly she felt about it herself, and I hated to see her quarreling with Led, knowing the alcoholic bout they would end up in. But all I could do about it was to pull Marguerite with me and go off into the back bedroom to play, trying to stay out of the way.

CHAPTER 23
Led's In Jail, Mama's Drunk, and I Nearly Kill Billy Drumbrew

It was December 1941.

Dark winter skies clouded the short days and the nights had grown cold. Snow had already begun to fall and it piled high that year. People were shoveling in order to get in or out of their houses. Lucky for us, Led was still working in the mines.

Christmas was in the air and people were bustling about with the Christmas spirit. Led and Mama enthusiastically announced plans to go Christmas shopping. They planned to ride the coal company's bus to nearby Oak Hill, two miles southeast of Minden. Then catch a Greyhound bus to a small town called Beckley, eighteen miles further south of Oak Hill.

They hired our neighbor's daughter to baby-sit TC, Inez, Marguerite and me. The baby sitter's name was Loretta. Loretta was a beautiful young woman, 13 years old, and very attentive to us, especially TC who seemed to adore her. I remember every detail of that day for suddenly the news splashed everywhere: *"Japanese Attack Pearl Harbor!"*

My secure little world seemed to turn upside down as I saw grownups appearing to panic and be confused, fearful that the Japanese might attack America's mainland. I didn't have much of a grasp of geography at the time and had no idea that Japan was only a tiny island across the sea. We were suddenly at war and it shook my world. Within what only seemed like days, men from local families in Minden were getting draft notices for duty in the U.S. Army. The tragedy of Pearl Harbor destroyed everyone's Christmas spirit.

Led received his notice by special delivery mail. Like all the other men, he went off on a bus to Beckley to complete the initial examination for induction into the Army. He told us all goodbye and hugged Mama, fully expecting to be in uniform the next time we saw him. Unfortunately things didn't work out that way.

On examination, they found Led's hearing was not acceptable. Consequently, he was designated as "4-F" and exempted from serving in the Army. However, the state police had distributed lists of "wanted" men to the induction centers, knowing they'd catch a few hard-to-find law breakers that way, and Led was arrested and held in custody. He was accused of killing a man back in Sink Clear; one of the hired thugs who had gone for him with a baseball bat the night we slipped away.

Again Led was in jail, this time for murder of a white man. This meant double trouble for Led, because when a black man killed a white, the black community knew the whites expected revenge and usually a lynching took place. Deeply upset and sick with anxiety, Mama feared for her husband's life as he awaited arraignment. She visited the wives of other union members, seeking support and a solution for Led. She did manage to get a little help for the family. For several weeks, union members delivered food to our house and sometimes the neighbors donated money or food for us. Still, it was never enough. Food and money were in short supply for everyone. The miners and the union members sympathized with Led's situation and understood his dilemma, but there wasn't much they could do for him. Hired company thugs had inflicted similar hardships for many families and caused the "disappearance" of many coal miners throughout the Appalachian region.

On the arraignment day, the main "eyewitness" to the murder, which Led allegedly committed, did not appear. However, strong anti-union advocates were there and demanded Led remain in jail — despite the unusual hardship on his family without his income — until the witness could be found.

The judge agreed and a semi-man hunt began to track down Alvin Zimmerman, who was not too eager, I later discerned, to come forward to the witness stand and lie about what he himself was doing waiting on the riverbank that night with a baseball bat.

Meanwhile, the authorities held Led in confinement causing serious problems for us at home. With no money coming in, there was never enough food in the house, and night after night we children went to bed hungry, got up hungry, and spent most of the day trying to get something to eat.

Depressed now, Mama still managed to find a way to get her alcohol and she was drinking heavily all the time. I think in her drunken stupors she was not even aware of us children, crying and waiting for her to feed us.

Our neighbors, the Drumbrews, who lived on the north side of our house, had several apple trees in their yard. Just looking across at their apples made my hunger worsen. Their son, Billy Drumbrew, frequently sat in his yard casually tossing red apples around just to entertain himself. Subsequently, he scattered luscious-looking big, red apples all around his yard. One dusky evening around sundown, Billy was lingering in his yard, just fooling around doing one thing or another.

"Hey, Billy!" I called to him from my yard. "How 'bout givin' me an apple, please?"

"You can have an apple," he responded, "but first you gotta do somethin' for me."

"Okay. What you want me to do?" I was so hungry I would do most anything to get something to eat. In my young mind I could imagine having to do something out of the ordinary for him, something he was too lazy to do for himself.

"Come on over here and I'll show you," Billy called out.

"My Mama told me never to come in your yard."

"Your Mama is a drunk. She'll never know about it." Billy was fifteen years old, nearly eight years beyond my seven-and-a-half-years of existence. He seemed honest, so I trusted his judgement. Quietly, I slipped out of my yard, walked past the fence that separated the two proprieties, pushed through his gate and found him under an apple tree.

"Follow me," Billy said, with a funny-looking grin on his face as he ambled toward the outhouse.

Reluctantly I lagged behind, puzzled. "What I have to do?"

"Hurry up. Come on." he said.

"Tell me what I have to do," I insisted, beginning to feel uneasy as he reached the small wooden outhouse.

Billy opened the door to the outhouse. "Here. I'll show you." He stepped inside.

The smell was repellant and overwhelming, but I was long accustomed to the rank odor of outhouses. Cautious, yet naive, I peeped into the darkened toilet shed.

Suddenly Billy yanked me into the small space. Holding me with one hand on my neck, he quickly undid his pants and pulled out his penis. Grabbing me by the head with both of his hands he forcefully shoved my head down toward his body. I struggled and called out in fear and disgust. Billy's grip on my head tightened as he held me against him and hissed, "Shut up! If you don't be quiet I will kill you!"

He crammed his hard penis deeply into my mouth. It was long and wet and I could feel it hitting the back of my throat. I gagged. He shoved it harder. I was choking and could not breathe. He seemed to be pushing the entire weight of his body into my mouth. From that point on, all I remember is biting down on his penis as hard as I could. It was a natural reflex action because I was near to passing out, seeing stars and I could not catch my breath.

Billy screamed and backed off, letting go of my head and grabbing for his genitals. As he did, I dashed out of the outhouse, running as fast as I could. I glanced back to see if he was running after me, but he wasn't. I could still hear him screaming out his pain. I was terrified that he'd come after me. I rushed home, up the stairs, into the house and went to the room where Mama lay intoxicated. I was trembling all over and wiping my mouth on my arm, trying to get rid of the bad taste in my mouth, but instinct told me it would be no use to wake Mama and tell her what had happened to me. I left her laying there and went to the kitchen. My heart was still thudding in my chest and my breath was coming hard, not so much from running as from my emotions. There on the table lay an ice pick. As my eyes focused on it, a terrible urge to kill Billy came over me. I had never felt such a murderous rage before. Motionless, I stood there, thinking about plunging the ice pick through his heart, and then watch him thrash to his death like a chicken without a head. A sudden rush of elation filled me at the idea… yet I was terrified. My hands trembled violently, so I locked them together behind my back while my unleashed imagination ran wild. I finally was able to calm down and I put the ice pick away in one of the drawers where I wouldn't see it and be tempted.

However, from that time on I carried an intense hatred for Billy Drumbrew, and I remember vowing to myself as I stood looking out the window at those damn apples, feeling my gut growling with hunger and feeling the flush of humiliation and hot tears on my face, that someday, when I grew up, I would kill that sonofabitch if it was the last thing I did.

That nasty experience with Billy was hard for me to get past. I felt such heavy shame because somehow I thought I should have suspected, or known what he was up to. What really got me down was my own stupidity, allowing myself to get lured into that outhouse with Billy. Of course, there was no one I could talk to about it, no one to explain or reassure me that I wasn't to blame. Lying in the darkness that night in bed, I felt the grip of despair and self disgust.

Weeks passed, yet that incident with Billy stayed in my mind, embittering my soul and souring my peace of mind. The hatred I felt for him didn't recede, and I found I was carrying it with me every day, turning it over in my mind, dwelling on my pain, and my hunger for revenge on him. Finally I came to realize, young as I was, that dwelling on that horrible memory was turning me into something I didn't like. I felt that I was only a few steps away from becoming a raging monster who might actually pick up that ice pick and do a killing. In my mind then, feeling that way, I was no better than any of the wild-acting grownups around me whom I sometimes hated for their unruly drunken behavior, and for getting into bloody knife fights. In the deepest part of my being I knew I did not want to be like that, so I began to try harder to fight down the hatred and my yearning to slide that pick into his flesh. It took time, a long time, but slowly I gained control and was able to get past it, but I never told anyone about it… and I never discussed it… until now.

CHAPTER 24
Mama Writes A Poem

Within a few weeks of the attack on Pearl Harbor, men were being sent off to war, causing much grief and worry throughout the community. The government permitted only those men who did not qualify for military service to return home and continue working in the coal mines, even through it was obvious they would need more coal to fire the great factory furnaces in the northern cities to build war materials.

It was a strange and difficult time for a young, impressionable child. Knowing that our country was at war — and my imagination played up that word "war" to great heights of anxiety which I told no one about — I was scared, for I didn't fully understand what might happen next. I kept wondering if we would be bombed like they'd bombed Pearl Harbor, or if the Japanese soldiers would invade our land.

It was a time of terrible confusion for me and I was trying to hold all that fear inside myself, for there was no one I could turn to. It seemed like my world was falling apart. All of a sudden, Led — the only source of food and shelter I knew — had been put in jail, my mama was crying and drinking all the time, all us kids were hungry, and I didn't know what to do about it.

All around me, neighbors and people who stopped by our shanty, were talking about the war, worried and concerned about their loved ones who had been sent overseas.

It was scary talk to me, listening with rapt attention, and hearing folks say things like, "Oh, I'm prayin' for him all the time he come back in one piece."

On hearing words like that, my imagination went wild and mentally I pictured long, long rows of dead men... and pieces of dead men... arms and legs and heads... and all type of horror like that, just like they draw in horror comic books.

Sometimes I'd go off to the back bedroom and stand there by myself, looking out the one small window at the trees and the mountainside, at the sky and the clouds and the birds, just standing there trying to get myself grounded in reality again. And then, when I'd come back to the kitchen and the visitor had left there'd be my mama, with the whiskey glass still in her hand, sitting at the table, staring off into space with the look on her face that said as clearly as if she spoken the words: "Don't talk to me... don't come near me... I can't deal with children right now... I can't deal with anything..." and I'd know there'd be no food on the table unless I could find something in the cupboard or get something from the neighbors.

That was one of the hardest times for me, for as I watched all that was going on around me — my mama's constant dependency on the drinking, her increasingly abusive behavior toward us kids, the fact that there was hardly ever any food in the house — I began to lose my sense of self-worth, my self-respect and my pride. I wanted to *do* something, to scream and rage until somebody *saw* our despair, to force Mama out of her drunkenness and make her *see* what she was doing to us... but I was just another child, powerless to change the world I lived in.

Mama continued to be lost in her alcoholic haze, drinking every day, getting mad over the slightest thing and slapping us around. She would beat on me especially, smacking me on the side of the face with her open hand or suddenly whirling around and whacking me with whatever she had hold of — a wooden spoon or a metal pot lid — knocking me flat to the floor because I would nag her to do something about TC's incessant crying, or Inez needing her smelly diapers changed, and she would lash out at me in her hatefulness and aggression from the whiskey. With week after week of that abusive, drunken behavior, I began to lose all trust and respect for Mama. I never got to the point where I actually thought I hated her, but there were so many times when she'd smack me and my own anger would rise and I'd want to hit back because it was wrong... it was just *wrong* what she was doing. But my even *thinking* about doing a thing like that made me feel like the biggest sinner on Earth. I must be a terrible boy, I thought, having such dark and angry thoughts. But the inner conflict went on and on, and it got worse as Mama's drinking went on and on, and my life seemed to be nothing but chaos, fending off blows and constant hunger. Just when I thought I couldn't stand it any longer, some friends of Mama's, an older couple named Leona and Novello, came to live with us. Both of them were disabled, but Novello was active enough to be a participant in the "Work Project Administration," — the WPA — which brought a little financial assistance into the house.

Novello and Leona both helped Mama caring for us children, especially when Mama would go off to visit Led in the county jail. Leona did the washing and ironing while Novello took odd jobs around Minden and other nearby communities wherever work was available. With Novello working, I figured there'd be a little money and I expected there'd be some food in the house. Then I discovered that both Leona and Novello were heavy drinkers.

Again my world came crashing down, for by then I understood only too well what having other drinkers around all the time would do to Mama, and I was right. Food became scarce because the little money we did have was mostly used to purchase liquor.

I was extremely sad to see my mama drinking whiskey and becoming intoxicated day after horrible day. She was not herself when she drank like that. Half the time she acted cold to us kids, uncaring and withdrawn, like she had no responsibility for us and we could shift for ourselves. The rest of the time she became wildly abusive, screaming terrible words, damning us all to hell, cursing us for bothering her, slashing out with her hands and saying anything hurtful she could think of. I knew then that Mama was a habitual alcoholic, but there was no way I could keep liquor out of her hands.

Of course, on the rare times she was sober — or even not quite so drunk — she was loving and warm, repeatedly telling me I was her little man and that she loved me. But those words seemed empty to me, for after a few drinks she became so absorbed with worry and so irritable as to become unapproachable, and no matter what words she had spoken I did not feel loved. There was no consistency in my life, nothing I could count on. Alcohol turned Mama into a totally unpredictable person, and I was too young to know how to deal with it. Seeing her warm and loving one minute and totally rejecting and mean-acting the next only made my confusion worse.

One day when Mama was sober, she went to the kitchen and spent some time sitting at the table, writing down some words on a tablet. She seemed to be in a sad, melancholy mood, so I kept Marguerite and Inez busy in the other room not to disturb her. I couldn't read then, but later in the week, when Mama was really drunk, stumbling around the house mumbling to herself and crying, a neighbor must have heard her carrying on and called Mrs. Bertha, for somehow she arrived to care for us children. Mrs. Bertha found the writing tablet on the kitchen counter where Mama had left it. I had followed her to the kitchen, hoping she'd fix us something to eat, and I watched her read what Mama'd written. She read it in silence, while tears flowed from her eyes. I was bewildered to see her cry and I ran out of the kitchen. Then suddenly she called out, "Come in here, Charles. You, too, Marguerite. Let me read what your mother wrote." She picked up the tablet and read us a poem.

I LOVED YOU ENOUGH
by
Elnora Martin Leadbetter

Someday, when my children are old enough to understand
the logic that motivates a parent, I will tell them:
I loved you enough, more than you will ever know.
Enough to ask with whom, and what time you will be home?
I loved you enough to insist that you save your money
and buy a bike for yourself.
Even through we could afford to buy one for you.
I loved you enough to be silent and let you discover
that your new best friend was a creep.
I loved you enough to make you take a MilkyWay
back to the drugstore (with a bite out of it)
and tell the clerk, "I stole this yesterday and want to pay for it."
I loved you enough to stand over you
for two hours while you cleaned your room,
A job that would have taken me fifteen minutes.
I loved you enough to let you see anger,
disappointment and tears in my eyes.
Children must learn that their parents aren't perfect.
I loved you enough to let you assume the responsibility
for your actions, even when the penalties were so harsh
they almost broke my heart.
But most of all, I loved you enough to say "No"
when I knew you would hate me for it.
Those were the most difficult battles of all.
I'm glad I won them,
because in the end
you won, too.

I was almost eight years old, and as Mrs. Bertha read Mama's words to me, something touched me deep inside. By hearing her poem, I understood what my mother was saying to me... saying to us... and I knew that deep in her heart she did love me... but because of her alcoholism she was not capable of living out the words she had written so eloquently.

CHAPTER 25
Heartbreak, Starvation, and Stealing Lunch Buckets

The war raged on throughout the world. Every day, people were talking about someone having lost their life in Germany or in Asia. Our next door neighbor received word that her son was missing in action. I'll never forget the sound of the heart-breaking moan that escaped her lips as she stood on the porch of her shanty, listening as another neighbor woman read aloud — since she couldn't read — that yellow piece of paper from the government. I could not identify it then, but I knew it was a sound like no other sound on Earth. Now I know it was the sound of loss, and of hope against that loss; a sound of belief, and yet the fear of failure of that belief; it was the sound of love and a prayer, all breathed out at once.

Many a time, I heard people talking about the mangled bodies being sent home in closed coffins which could not be opened. Half the people I knew were in mourning for their loved ones.

Everybody kept saying bad things about the Japanese, depicted them in comic books and in the newspaper comic strips as ugly, round-faced yellow people with little slit-eyes that were nearly closed and with excessively long front teeth. Tojo, Hitler, and Tokyo Rose were the major topics of conversation in the community.

But little by little I became oblivious of the suffering of the community, for there was too much suffering going on at home for me to deal with.

Every day I could feel the hunger gnawing like a starving beast within me. My stomach growled loudly, became swollen and painful, and I was weak and always on the verge of nausea. Frustration plagued me every living day for I had no idea how to find food that was not in the cupboard, especially when surrounded by intoxicated grownups who sat sprawled in their chairs,

142

stupefied and staring at me with blank eyes or snoring like a buzz saw.

They didn't hear Marguerite's crying, ignored Inez's whining and TC's pathetic sobs... they didn't hear me yelling at the top of my lungs that we were hungry. *"WE'RE HUNGRY!"* I'd scream, torn up inside at the sight of my mama slumped over at the barren kitchen table. Nobody moved. Nobody heard me. Novello would sometimes grin some sick-looking, gummy grin that made me feel like smashing him in the mouth... or weeping.

Liquor was not all that cheap, and even the grownups had to eat sometimes, so Novello devised a plan to steal food. His scheme was to visit the miner's bath house situated around the entry/exit of the mines — a spot referred to as the "drift mouth." The drift mouth was usually found near the tipple, that enormous, coal-sorting machine I've mentioned before. Miners who worked around the tipple usually stored their aluminum lunch buckets in the bath house.

Novello's plan was to take me along with him to act as a decoy. I did not understand the circumstances, but the word "food" brought joy to me as it would to any starving child. Whatever it was, if it meant getting something to eat, I was all for it.

For several weeks, Novello stole an average of two lunch buckets per night. Finally we had accumulated so many lunch buckets at our house that in order to get rid of them Novello had to wait for night fall and bury them in the back yard. I knew Novello was doing wrong, but I could not prevent myself from gulping down my share of those lunches as I told myself that whoever they belonged to, at least they were going home for supper. That stolen lunch was all us kids had the whole day.

On occasions, miners would leave billfolds or money in their lunch buckets. The "money" was usually the mining company's "script" money. When Novello found one of these, it was like he had discovered a gold mine. Right away, Mama would scribble a grocery list including pinto beans, lard, flour, oats, canned milk, and fat-back, and send me to the company store.

The Minden store was the mining company's marketplace and it was located far at the southern end of the Minden community. Before they'd put Led in jail, I had reluctantly gone with him to that store many times. It took at least forty minutes to walk there, as it was a little more than one mile away over rough terrain. We got there by one of three routes. The best way was by the narrow black-top highway, but that route ran though a hostile white community. Another way was a less traveled dirt path, mostly used as a driveway for cars, situated between the back of the shanties and the east side of a mucky creek, but it also wound through the edges of the white folks neighborhood. The third way was the longest way, but it was a route that followed along the railroad tracks and lay between alpine mountains and the creek and hardly anyone used that.

This was the first time I was to go to the company store alone and Mama instructed me to go by way of the dirt path as she felt that was the quickest way and would be reasonably safe.

It was mid-morning when Mama sent me on my way. As I hiked along the path, skirting the edge of the white community, I encountered several white boys who were about my age. They began calling out, "Hey, nigger, what you doin' in our neighborhood?"

I didn't answer; just kept walking on as fast as I could. I could feel anger rising up in my throat and I wanted to shout back, but there were several of them and I was alone.

They kept on yelling insults at me and then, not satisfied, they started throwing rocks.

One hit me on the arm near the shoulder, delivering a bruise and a sharp pain. I started to run, scared now that they'd hit me in the head and bring me down like a hunted animal.

Their shouts brought older white kids out into their yards and they joined the melee of name-calling and rock-throwing. I could feel their hatred boiling in the air around me as the rocks whizzed past my ears. It was like a shark's feeding frenzy and I was the prey. Hurrying past them as fast as my thin legs would carry me, they continued shouting curse words and dirty names, throwing rocks with all their strength as if they truly meant to kill me, and then I saw their white parents looking on with grins of approval.

"Get 'im, boys," one shouted. "Two on one nigger's fun." Those goading words rang in my ears. That was what they always said when they saw more than two white kids beating up a black kid. I raced along, dodging the rocks and stumbling down that dirt path, trying get past them and then one boy sicced his vicious-looking dogs on me. When they started after me, barking and showing their teeth, I screamed out in fear and ran for my life. Those dogs were right on my heels when, gasping and panting for breath, I ducked into the company store. I heard their owner laugh and then he whistled for them to come back.

Trembling, I stood inside the store, totally exhausted, crying with relief. Those dogs would gladly have torn my throat out. Searching my pockets, I discovered I'd lost the money Mama had given me. Again my heart thudded with a jolt of fear as I realized that I had two problems: first, getting back home, and second, telling Mama I had lost the money.

If Mama was drinking whiskey, and was in one of her snarly moods, I knew there was no way I could reason with her or get her to listen to what had happened. She'd just start beating on me, screaming curses, until she got too tired to lift her arms, and I'd have to keep out of her sight half the day till she forgot about it in her drunkenness. And on top of that, there'd be nothing to eat.

After a short rest, I still hesitated over what to do as I stood near the entrance of the company store wiping away my tears — I was scared to stay in the store without buying something and scared to go home to Mama without the food. I finally decided to chance going back home, but I wasn't going on that dirt path behind the white folks' houses again. I'd follow the railroad tracks this time and keep out of sight, hoping the white kids wouldn't come after me. I made it home safely. When I got up my courage and went on inside I found Mama passed out drunk and sleeping. I was glad I wasn't going to get a beating, but I was sorry to see her so drunk again... and sorrier still to know that there was no food in our house.

CHAPTER 26
School In Minden

One morning a truant officer came to our shanty door. He was polite in a rather stiff and formal way, but he didn't waste any words as he asked Mama why she had not enrolled me in grade school at Minden. Mama tried to explain that I was being home-schooled, and that she was my teacher, but the truant officer was not convinced. I think he noticed that Mama had already been drinking at that early hour — he probably smelled the whiskey — and he cited Mama for not enrolling me in the local elementary for black children. He didn't say anything about Marguerite who was peeking around Mama's skirts. She had turned six that spring, but she was short for her age and so frail he must have thought she was younger. Mama apologized and started to tell him that she really was giving me lessons, but she stumbled a little over her words, and that seemed to antagonize the officer. He drew himself up with his chest all puffed out and his eyes snapping like a mean-minded turtle.

"You tellin' me you educatin' this boy?" he barked. "I don't believe you teachin' him 'bout anythin' except how to get hissef whiskied up before breakfast." He snorted a contemptuous laugh and took out his notebook and a pen from his pocket. "I'm writin' down that I tol' you, see?" He wrote in his book. "An' I'm comin' back to arrest you if I don't see this boy's name on the enrollment list they give me next Tuesday." He stepped back and adjusted his hat more firmly on his head. "Okay, now. You get him in school, hear?"

"Yessir, I'll do that," Mama said, and her voice sounded meek unless you were listening real hard for the angry overtones. She yanked me away from the door and closed it a little bit too hard as he went on down the steps. "Damn you fat ol' black bastard," she muttered, and I could see her mouth pulled down in anger and her eyes flashing. I didn't say anything. I knew that face. I went into the other room and listened. Sure enough, I heard the kitchen cupboard bang like I knew it would when she went for the whiskey on the top shelf.

Actually, what Mama was telling the officer was true, more or less, because when she was sober, she did try to teach me some fundamentals as early as my second birthday, and she was trying with Marguerite too. Mama taught me how to say my ABC's and how to count from one to one-hundred. Later I learned some basic arithmetic, some reading and writing, and how to read music, as she was fond of music. But her explanation didn't satisfy the mining camp's truant officer and the local laws on school attendance.

In Appalachia, it was popular for black folks to begin teaching the basics of education, social skills and social values when their children were around two years of age. "If children are not taught to behave, they will run over you," she'd say. When Mama wasn't drinking, she liked to use praise and encouragement to elicit proper behavior in us kids, but if that didn't get the expected results, she believed in punishing children effectively — including spankings — as a means of producing lasting memories. A well-aimed swat on the bottom made a child pay attention, she'd say, but first children had to learn to control their own narcissistic impulses. Then a parent could guide the child with praise or appropriate punishment to keep control. But that's only what she *said*. What she *did* was mostly different.

Unfortunately, in spite of all her correct beliefs and theories, and her good intentions — intentions which I'd heard her discussing many times with her sister Samantha when she was sober — Mama was very inconsistent with her methods of child rearing because of her alcoholism. I could never fully grasp how she differentiated between my earning praise or my earning punishment, but I learned early on that there was always a discomforting price to be paid whenever Mama was intoxicated, no matter what I did.

That Monday morning Mama dressed me in blue-jeans and a pullover shirt, prepared a peanut butter and jelly sandwich for me to carry, and off we went to Minden elementary school.

Not knowing what to expect, I was nervous, but part of me was looking forward to being with other children my own age. Also, even at the age of eight in that spring of 1942, I had a natural curiosity about the world and was interested in learning.

We arrived at the school house just before the first period began. The teacher, Mrs. Watson, smiled at me and Mama, and introduced herself. Mama did the same and introduced me.

"This is my son, Charles, and this is his first day in school."

"Hi, Charles," Mrs. Watson responded. "I'm sure you will like it here."

I was very shy and tried my best to hide behind Mama.

After the introductions, Mrs. Watson and Mama talked for a few moments, but then Mama was ready to go. "You be a good boy," Mama said, letting go of my hand, and I wanted to cry as she walked away for that was the first time I had ever been left alone with a group of strange children. I swallowed back my tears, too embarrassed to show my emotions, and waited for Mrs. Watson to tell me what to do. I wasn't really afraid, for she had made me feel welcome, but I was still nervous, especially about getting home from school. I knew Mama had asked one of the older kids who lived nearby to walk me home, but I didn't feel confident about him showing up or protecting me.

Mrs. Watson pointed out a seat at one of the empty desks and I claimed it. It was in the center of the room, two rows away from Mrs. Watson's desk, and directly behind a young girl whose body twitched continuously, her head and shoulders being the most violent, as if from some kind of crippling palsy.

At recess time, children of all sizes flowed into the school grounds to mingle in the play yard, their sharp cries bouncing off the walls of the school house. The girls played hopscotch and bounced up and down on the see-saw, while the boys played leap-frog, jumping over each other in a sea of constant motion. Staying close to the wall, I made my way to the front steps at the main door just in case I had to run back inside to Mrs. Watson. I considered her my caretaker now. I sat on the steps with my skinny arms wrapped around my knobby knees and watched the other kids play games.

Surreptitiously, I noticed a group of tough-looking and aggressive boys pushing one-another and joking around, and then they kind of clustered around in a little group, talking intently while looking at me. Terror struck deep in my heart at that moment, for I was in mortal fear of the school-yard bullies whom I had already heard talk of. From where I sat on the steps, I could actually feel the hateful, hurtful energy they radiated as they glared in my direction and it bewildered me. I wanted to hide my frail body from their cruel teasing and brutal violence, but there was nowhere to go.

As it turned out, my fears on that first day — a day full of terrible anxieties and heart-pounding worries about the bullies I saw surrounding me — proved fatefully accurate in the days to come. I clearly remember standing in that Minden school yard, waiting for the classmate Mama had asked to watch over me. It was two o'clock and the afternoon classes were over. Suddenly a boy I did not know began walking toward me with what I saw as an angry look on his face. *Oh, God,* I thought. *It's starting now!* My heart pounded in my chest as he came closer and all I could think of was that I was about to be mashed to a pulp. I didn't wait to find out if I was right about his angry look, I just took off running. I ran till I couldn't run any more; till I was purely winded and felt like my legs had turned to iron stumps. But by then I could see my own shanty and I sagged, dizzy and light-headed, against a tree, waiting to catch my breath before walking in the front door. I didn't want to have to tell Mama that I was chased home on my very first day. I just didn't want to tell her how afraid I was.

After a while, I became immune to the bullies' verbal threats. I acted like I didn't even hear them and never raised an eyebrow no matter what they called me. But in spite of my put-on bravado, I was still terrified of being beaten up, and I knew the other kids enjoyed watching a fight and would do nothing to help me. I quickly developed a strategy for remaining safe, and that was to make myself as invisible as possible, and, if that was impossible, to cleverly befriend and seduce my tormentors with offers of academic assistance that Mama had taught me. Also, when feeling threatened, which was often, I'd offer them my peanut-butter and jelly sandwich during lunch breaks, sucking-up to them any way I could in order to protect myself.

God, how I hated having to do that; hated myself for allowing them to terrorize me; hated what it told me about myself and my frailty and my uncontrollable fears. Those early encounters — dealing with deep-seated fears that forced me to bow and scrape and put on my phony act of friendship to win them over, all the while hating their guts — were the beginning of my realization of the truth about the dark and hidden underbelly of all masculine power. Those damaging school day experiences etched painful psychic scars in my soul that I will never forget.

One summer morning, before class started, I was sitting on the front steps of the school dreaming about my teacher, Mrs. Watson, and in my mind I was comparing her to my Mama. When the bell rang, I went directly inside before the others. As usual, I was the first one in the classroom. Sitting very still at my desk, I found myself staring at Mrs. Watson who was calling the roll. I was lost in my daydream and didn't hear my name called the first time. Mrs. Watson called my name again, somewhat louder, and I blinked and came out of my fantasy long enough to respond. My face flushed, but she could not guess that I had been star-fixed on her attractive good looks, or she would not have been so sweetly apologetic for calling my name so softly. Sitting there at my desk, my day-dream began again. To my eight-year-old mind, slim Mrs. Watson was a very pretty woman. She was very kind, and so good looking my eyes were fixed on her most of the time.

This developed into a new situation for me, and I didn't know how to deal with my feelings. All I knew was that I admired everything about Mrs. Watson. She was the first grown woman of my own race I'd ever known who was actually living a life of what I knew even then was upright and strongly moral behavior. She seemed to have order in her life, instead of impulsively jumping one way or another like my Mama tended to do sometimes. When she spoke to us children about our misbehavior, she spoke kindly, but with authority and knowledge. Even when she scolded, or spanked children for misbehavior, her reasons were clearly justifiable; the same when praise was appropriately deserved. However, she also demonstrated that although using reasoning and praise to control boisterous children was good, those two methods would never fully substitute when meaningful punishment was called for. Mrs. Watson's firm-handed teaching methods and her no-nonsense attitude certainly kept my narcissistic tendencies in check, for I feared (correctly so, I'm sure) the consequences, had I told her of my secret feelings.

Part of my admiration for this teacher stemmed from the fact that she seemed to be a person who could predict, with reasonable certainty, what tomorrow would bring. That was so unlike anything I'd ever known in my life. I never knew when disaster would strike at my house, never knew when I'd find myself packing up to move again, never knew from one day to the next whether or not we'd be eating supper that night, or if my mama would be home with us kids or out drinking again, or if Led was coming back or taking off someplace new, and a million other questions that never got answered or resolved. Mrs. Watson didn't surround herself with chaos and unsolvable problems. She had an aura of peace and steadiness about her that was so appealing to my young soul, I couldn't help but wish that my mama could be like her. I loved my mama, but seeing Mrs. Watson, and watching her example, I knew for the first time how badly my mama's drinking had hurt all of us

CHAPTER 27
"Even If They Knock You Down..."

School was out at two o'clock, and once more I had my eye out for the bullies I feared. There was one bully named Lorenzo Payne, the leader of the pack, a boy I knew could be maliciously aggressive for I had already witnessed his rough assertiveness, and I was terribly afraid of having any kind of confrontation with him. I felt they'd all been watching me for the last few days, waiting their chance, and that afternoon I sensed that Lorenzo and his gang were poised to attack me... the "new kid." I didn't wait around to find out. As soon as the final bell rang I took off running. Sure enough, they took off running behind me; all of them. I could hear their panting, and the slap-slap-slapping of their running feet getting closer by the second. Across the school yard I galloped, remembering the nasty, big red rooster that chased me back in Leslie Hollow.

My heart began pounding, adrenaline pumped in my veins, but I didn't get far for I was not strong enough to outrun them. Overtaking me quickly, with Lorenzo leading the pack, they all started punching me relentlessly, striking anyplace on my body they could land a blow. While I was ducking and trying to ward off punches with my arms, I did not notice one kid who bent down on his hands and knees behind my legs. Lorenzo pushed me over the kneeling kid's body and another boy simultaneously landed a punch that knocked me off my feet. I fell, striking my head against the curbstone so hard that I almost lost consciousness, but I was so intimidated I almost welcomed the blow, thinking "Now you won't have to go to school and get beat-up any more." I was only half conscious, but I remained lying there a few moments longer than was strictly necessary, just to scare him into thinking he'd really hurt me badly. Then a few of the other kids picked me up and urged me on.

"Get 'im, Charles! Fight him, you fuckin' chicken!"

But my flailing arms were ineffective and I was down again in a flash. Lorenzo flopped his big butt down on my head, deliberately pushing my face into the dirt and sand. In a frenzy, the other boys attacked me with punches and kicks. Again I flashed back to the rooster, leaping on my skull, attacking me with such vengeance. I screamed with all the force I could muster, crying out loudly, and making as big a ruckus as I could. My desperate shouts must have frightened them for they stopped their attack, leaped away from me and, with guilty looks toward the schoolhouse, ran away. Slowly I picked myself up. Bruised and with a badly bloodied nose, I looked like I'd fallen into some pig sty. I sniffled and cried all the way home.

Mama was horrified at my appearance. Still crying and sniffing, I told her about the beating Lorenzo had given me as she stood over my chair in the kitchen, weaving unsteadily with her whiskey glass still in her hand. To this day I do not know why I did not tell her the truth; that it was not only Lorenzo who had beaten me, but him and several other boys. Maybe because it was Lorenzo himself I feared most, or maybe because I was afraid to say several boys were beating on me for fear it might engender a greater outburst of drunken anger. I never knew what Mama would do, or which way to jump to please her.

In any case, after I told her, she seemed upset, and angry, but not wildly so. She stepped back and stared into my face, holding up my chin with her hand. "You listen to me, now," she said, and her voice was low in her throat like it was when she was dead serious. "From now on you will stand and fight back. You hear me?"

"But Mama, I..."

She smacked my face with the flat of her hand, but not hard... just to shut me up and get my attention. "Even if they knock you down, you must get back up and fight."

Tears filled my eyes because I couldn't imagine myself standing up to five or six of those bigger kids... but I didn't want Mama to hit on me anymore either. "Yes, ma'am," I said, but I couldn't bring my eyes to look at her.

She had slopped most of her whiskey on the floor when she smacked me, so she turned away to find the bottle. Then, seeming to remember something, she put her glass down on the table, came back to my chair and looked me over, her eyes unfocused and distant. Assuring herself that I had no serious cuts or broken bones she embraced me with some compassion. I didn't know what to think, with her smacking me one minute and hugging me the next.

But I did know she meant what she said about my fighting.

During the next few days, Mama insisted on escorting me to school. Occasionally, when she came to the school to escort me home, her loud and quarrelsome attitude, and her obvious drunkenness, embarrassed me, and alerted the entire student body to my dilemma. This brought humiliating and endless teasing by all the kids about me being a "mama's boy" and a few other hurtful remarks about my mother being a drunk.

After that I begged Mama not to go with me to school any longer. The teasing I was getting was worse than the physical beatings I would surely be in for from Lorenzo and his buddies. In order to avoid another beating from them, I devised another strategy. When school was out I made sure I was the first one out the door and I hit the steps running. Several times Lorenzo and his friends tried to catch up to me, but it was useless since I had a good head start. However, they soon caught on to what I was doing and stopped chasing after me, preferring a new plan of their own.

One rainy Friday afternoon while on my way home from school I notice none of Lorenzo's bullies were around. This was unusual, and highly suspicious, and I sensed that they were up to some ploy to ambush me. Cautiously I trotted down the path, then I slowed till I was just sort of skipping along, keeping my eyes ever watchful and my body on full alert. Surveying the dirt road ahead of me, I knew there was only one possible place they could jump me, and that was from under the bridge I had to cross. It was the only spot where they could be hiding. Approaching the bridge cautiously, my sixth sense told me they were waiting in the dark places under the planks. I paused at the edge of the bridge momentarily, and then with all my might I dashed across it faster than I had ever run. Sure enough, out came Lorenzo and two other bullies.

"Get him! Catch him!" they screamed, stumbling after me.

I ran with all the energy I could muster. The other two boys quickly gave up the chase, but Lorenzo continued the pursuit and he was catching up to me.

The landscape whizzed past and in what seemed like moments, I reached the wooden gate to my home. Frantic now, for Lorenzo was still coming on, I didn't take time to fool with the balky latch on the gate, I squeezed through a gaping hole left by rotted wood. Just as I slithered my body inside the gate I felt Lorenzo touch my back. Fortunately I was inside the gate in the nick of time. I glanced at the house and there stood Mama in the doorway.

Suddenly I remembered what she had said: *"Even if they knock you down, you must get back up and fight!"* Without hesitation then I swirled around and faced Lorenzo just as he was trying to squeeze himself through the hole in the gate. His body was larger than mine and was only half-way inside, making him vulnerable. Luck was with me. I doubled up my bony fist and caught him with a good, solid punch right on his nose, then another and another. Blood began to pour. He yelled and backed himself out of the hole in the gate, stumbled, and fell to the ground. As quick as lightning I jumped on top of him and began to throw punches to his head and face. I was unstoppable, blind with rage, a rabid bulldog. Now it was Lorenzo who began to scream and cry, but there was no let-up to the savageness of my attack. I could hear Mama's voice in the background screaming, "Stop it, Charles! Stop it now!" But I had too many stored up hurts, too many grievances, too much venom boiling inside me to listen.

Being stronger than I, Lorenzo heaved my light frame off his body, got to his feet and ran, but like a sicced hound I stayed on his tail in hot pursuit. Blood dripped from his nose as I chased him back up the road where he'd chased me. Still crying, Lorenzo was now running home.

I couldn't believe what was happening as I pounded after him, shouting taunts as he had taunted me. All the other children from school, still on their way home, saw me chasing Lorenzo and stared in amazement, for to them, me chasing Lorenzo home, was purely an impossibility. But Lorenzo, taller and with longer legs, finally outdistanced me. In frustration, I picked up pebbles from the road and threw them at him to emphasize my victory.

All the way back home I was flushed with a sense of pride and self-confidence. And when the memory of that big old red-feathered rooster flashed across my mind again, I thought, "I just wish I could see him now. Man, I would kick his red ass and whip the livin' hell outta him."

The glory of my victory faded when I saw Mama walking toward me. She stopped in the middle of the path, her hands on her hips, and said, "Why didn't you stop fighting when I told you to, boy?"

"I didn't hear you," I lied, but I wasn't hanging my head.

Mama sounded angry, but her eyes radiated a sense of pride in me. She grabbed my upper arm and gave a couple of slaps to my behind and said, "Now you get on home." But I could tell she was holding back a big smile and her anger had evaporated.

CHAPTER 28
I'm The Bully Now

The victory over Lorenzo changed my life.

Now, I could walk to school without fear of being attacked by him and his bullies. In fact, as the days passed and word of my victory got around, I became the school bully... a somewhat less-aggressive version of one, but a bully just the same. But it felt good to have other kids be in awe of me and my prowess. It felt good not to be shoved around and hit on. It felt good that when I said something the other kids listened. Suddenly I had freedom and authority I'd never enjoyed before.

Now, for the first time, I could visit the school's recreation room and play little tunes on the piano without fear of being beaten-up. I was thrilled to see that whenever I did play the piano, children would gather around to listen. Even Lorenzo, who had made peace with me and was now my best friend, came to listen to me play.

As time went on, being in school turned out to be the best part of my day, especially at lunch time. At home recently we had hardly any food in the house — Mama was drinking up our groceries, I guess — and I no longer brought a sandwich. Hungry, I sat in class listening to my empty stomach growl and wishing it would hurry up and be lunch time, for I knew a good, free lunch would be in the offering. In front of my friends I always acted like, oh yeah, a free lunch, big deal... for I was too embarrassed to let on that I was starving and looking forward intently to lunch time.

One Friday, I was summoned to the principal's office. It seems that Mr. Chiles had gotten word that I was bullying children on the school grounds, particularly a young girl named Gwendolyn Smith — the disabled child who sat directly in front of me in class. Gwendolyn was a very smart young girl whom polio had left with badly deformed arms and legs and a crippling walk and whose head and shoulders remained in constant jerking motion. This poor little child was a sweet-faced ten-year-old who had finally told her parents she was being tormented at school, and the first kid they blamed was me.

Although I had nothing to do with teasing her, I did witness other children regularly picking on Gwendolyn because of her unfortunate condition. As a result, she always left school after everyone else, hoping to escape being subjected to such humiliation. I recall seeing as many as ten youths gathered outside on the playground during recess time, relentlessly attacking her, calling her ugly names and throwing dirt and mud on her while shouting abusive language. I did not take part in those assaults. Those same kids laughed as they poured salt in her school lunch or took her sweater and dumped it into the garbage can. Gwendolyn was abused not only in the school yard but in her neighborhood too where classmates pelted her house first with stones and finally with smelly grease and rotten eggs.

Being called to Mr. Chile's office was not good news, and I got very anxious. I knew whenever they called any student to the principal's office it meant a whipping was going to take place. As I found out, having heard of my vengeful, blood-letting scuffle with Lorenzo — for some reason he seemed unaware of the torments visited upon me which began that battle — Mr. Chiles prejudged me and assumed I was the individual causing, and leading others into, this troubling behavior in the school yard. Giving me no time to explain, he accused me outright. "I hear you have been bullying Gwendolyn Smith, Charles. Shame upon you, tormenting that poor crippled child." He picked up the wooden punishment paddle he kept in his office. "God will deal with the pain she is suffering from your ugly bullying, boy... and in His name *I* shall deal with *you*."

After bending me over the chair, he began to strike me with the paddle. His blows were very hard and came fast, smarting badly through the thin material of my pants. Over and over again he struck me and I began to cry and struggle. Finally he let me go saying "Let this be a lesson you will never forget, Charles Williams. God hates a bully!" I left his office in tears of humiliation, hurt more by the false accusation than from the blows to my burning bottom.

What I never forgot was Mr. Chiles.

Every Friday he spoke to the student body, and his stringent words on the Friday following my paddling still ring in my memory. "Be a solid citizen," he encouraged. "Work hard and be respectable." Then he paused and paced a few steps toward the front of the podium. "Being a monster is not hard… but being an Angel is very hard." And he looked at us, face by face, sitting before him. "I believe you can all be Angels. Yes! Angels. You can all be Angels," he repeated. "But first you must learn to be a good student, you must learn to be kind to one another…" He paused again and looked almost directly at me I thought. "Learn to respect each other," he continued meaningfully, "and put aside the evil temptation to make fun of other's shortcomings, their errors, and… their differentness. Give up your wicked prejudices." Here he opened his arms wide as if evoking a blessing and finished. "Learning to accept others, as they *are*, is true beauty. Remember, God does not like ugliness."

That was a strongly impressive moment for me, sitting there in that classroom. In a way, I saw Mr. Chiles as a sadist whom I hated passionately because of the unjust paddling he'd given me a few days earlier. But at the same time I knew that while standing up there on that stage, if Mr. Chiles could read my secret thoughts at that very moment, he would know me as the monster of depravity I thought I truly was. The odd part was, even as I thought it, I realized that thought had neatly captured a profound truth about my nature. That realization stunned me and I blinked my eyes with surprise, asking myself questions like, "Was I the only one who had such dark secret thoughts? The only one who felt himself a monster?"

I looked searchingly around the classroom, studying the innocent-looking faces of my classmates, and was suddenly terrified that I was different than they. How could I know that most of them carried, like I carried, dark secret thoughts, daydreams, and fantasies which they sternly suppressed, had to suppress, struggled to suppress? Was I the only boy with strange and partially-buried feelings, terrible drives, and inexpressible longings? The only one whose feelings had turned him into some ugly monster afraid of revealing his true self?

I shivered with agonizing fear. Oh, how I wanted to believe that the other children were like me; that they, too, harbored dark fears, and given certain provocation, their inner selves might, in some moment of weakness, reveal their monstrousness to other children around them. I gripped my own hands tightly in my lap for at that moment I wanted to cry, to scream, to flail about wildly like a madman in terror of being different from all of them… in terror of my secret monstrousness… of my shame… of my guilt. Only with the greatest of effort was I able to hold back every sound, struggling with all my might to contain even my breath, but I could not hold back the hot tears that rolled silently down my cheeks.

CHAPTER 29
"This is Mr. Charles Ayers, Son. Say Hello To Your Daddy."

Life at home was worse than it had ever been. Mama was drinking more every day and seemed to be trying to keep herself drunk nearly all the time. Leona's husband Novello was finally caught stealing one of the miner's lunch buckets. Discovered eating the evidence behind the bath house, Novello was quickly hauled into court, convicted, and tossed into the county jail. Disgusted and disenchanted, Leona didn't want to stay in Minden with Mama being drunk all the time and all us kids to take care of, so she packed up and moved away.

During that period, the whole camp community seemed to have lost respect for Mama because of her drinking. Drunk and loud-talking, she'd stumble around the company store and forget what she'd walked down there for. She was argumentative at the least little thing, spouting angry words at people who aggravated her, and everybody aggravated her. It was the alcohol talking, and making her act that way, but she couldn't leave the stuff alone. Every penny she got her hands on went for bootleg white lightnin'.

To make matters even worse, Mrs. Myrtle, a neighbor woman whose husband had just been drafted into the army, was now left alone, so she and Mama became good friends. Unfortunately both of them were boozers, drinking some form of alcohol every day. It got so Mama spent most of her time over at Mrs. Myrtle's house, letting us kids fend for ourselves.

With Leona and Novello gone, Mama let herself fall to ruin, forgetting about the house, the laundry, the cleaning, and the necessity of feeding her four children. All she thought about was getting her hands on the next jug of white lightnin'. I never had clean clothes to wear to school anymore, there was no way for us all to bathe or for Marguerite to wash her hair. There was no food at all in the house and no one to care for us kids or clean up TC's diapers, while Mama lay intoxicated or recovering from a hangover.. which meant we dared not go near her.

Unable to bear hearing Marguerite and Inez and TC all crying from hunger, laying on the floor on a blanket, weak and starving under my eyes — and my own belly empty so long I had forgotten what food tasted like — I took matters into my own hands and did the only thing I knew to do. While Mama lay on her bed in a drunken stupor, I found a paper bag in one of the kitchen cupboards and went walking around the community, knocking on peoples' door and begging them for what ever scraps of food they could spare for me and my sisters and for milk for my baby brother. Some gave, some didn't, but all clucked their tongues about me coming out begging like that, and I heard them saying to each other after the door was closed, "That woman ain't fit to rear them kids, lettin' 'em go hungry that way. Drunken ol' bitch, boozin' all day. Ought somebody to do somethin'. I feel sorry for them poor chil'ren."

My face would flush with shame, but my belly's message was louder and stronger... so I'd go on to the next house, hoping somebody would give us food..."There's four of us," I'd say, ashamed to be begging like that, but too hungry not to.

Late in June, 1942 — I had turned eight that March — Charles Ayers, Mama's ex-husband and my biological father, unexpectedly showed up at our house one afternoon. I learned later that he'd heard about how poorly we were living, how neglected we children were, and how neighbors were bad-mouthing Mama because of her addicted drinking, and he'd come to take me away.

This was the first time I'd ever heard that this man was my father.

Since my name was Williams, I had always assumed that Virgil Williams — the man who had shot Mama in the leg just after I was born — was my father. But now I was being introduced to some tall, clean-cut, handsome-looking stranger — some kind-faced gentleman in a nice suit and shiny shoes — and being told *he* was my daddy.

"Charles, come here, son," I heard Mama call. "I want you to meet your father."

I came out of the bedroom. She was standing at the front door, holding it open for this nice-looking man who had just walked in our filthy shanty.

With him standing there, it made everything in the house look ugly and even worse than the mess it was. Clothes on the floor, stuff laying around, dirty glasses in the kitchen, and all like that. Mama hadn't done any house cleaning for weeks.

"This is Mr. Charles Ayers, son," Mama said, pushing me toward him, for I was hanging back nervously. "Say hello to your daddy." He reached for my hand, but I held back, eyeing him cautiously. "He is your *real* father, Charles," Mama explained. "Your blood father, you understand?"

I knew what she was saying, but I couldn't quite grasp the reality of it all. We looked at each other, he and I, just standing there; him really giving me a long inspection and me lowering my eyes, too shy to stare back at him.

"Hello, son," he said. With a shock I realized his voice sounded just like mine, only a little deeper and more gentle. "He's a fine-lookin' boy, Elnora," Mr. Ayers said. "Too skinny, though." And then he laughed. Again my heart leapt up in my throat. I sounded just like that when I laughed. "But maybe we can fix that."

The two of them began to talk and I walked away. *What the hell,* I thought. *I don't know him. He walks in here and he suddenly becomes my father. Where the hell's he been all this time then, if he's my dad?* My heart was breaking with all kinds of questions I couldn't ask and wasn't even sure I wanted to know the answers to.

He called out to me once or twice, "Charles, come on in here, boy…" but I didn't go. I felt like saying, "Go to hell! You ain't nothin' to me." Marguerite came over to where I was standing by the window and put her arm around me. "Mama says that man's your daddy, Char," she said softly. Marguerite always called my name as "Char" since she was a tiny baby.

"Go on away from me," I said, nearly snarling. "I ain't in no mood for you right now."

It was hard, suddenly finding out you had a daddy who looked like that, dressed fine like that, and talked like that. Frightened and ill-at-ease, I resisted all Mr. Ayers' attempts to befriend me, avoiding him in every way I knew how, stopping short of actual rudeness. Not out of respect, but out of fear of my mama's smacking me for being impolite.

Still, as I listened to them talking in the other room, I felt allied to him in a strange, new way… as if he were part of me and I was part of him. His voice, the way he held himself, his gentlemanly manner, all of that appealed to something inside me; something deep within that recognized a sameness (or a would-be sameness) that was just busting to be acknowledged. Suddenly,

161

I saw myself in him, a self I wanted to be, and something in me yielded and I felt tears flood my eyes. This man was my father... *my father*... I was flesh of his flesh. I wiped away my tears and went into the other room, ready to learn everything I could about this man.

After that, our bonding seemed to take hold rapidly and without any effort at all, once I had opened myself to the opportunity. It was a kind of intrinsic kinship that is beyond explanation. Before long Mr. Ayers had convinced me — and Mama, who was anxiously eyeing the whisky glass she'd left in the kitchen — that since I was living in misery, I'd be better off living with him.

I didn't need much convincing. I knew we were all barely surviving; living on the edge of darkness, a kind of madness, really... a jumbled daily chaos so "normal" it had become everyday life. I craved order and the security of a planned path. The only consistency I knew was inconsistency. The only predictability I had was the lack of predictability. I had been living my childhood on an emotional roller coaster. That is all I understood. Now here was my dad, a man who appeared to have some order in his life, much like my first teacher, Mrs. Watson, and I was yearning for that very quality; grateful to meet anyone who exhibited consistency and level-headedness. Instinctively, I knew it would be a better way of life for me.

After much crying, and wavering back and forth about it, Mama reluctantly gave permission for me to travel back to Buckingham, Virginia with my father. Marguerite burst into tears when she realized I was going away, but Mama held her close and soothed her and said everything would be all right. I tried to feel sorry about going away and leaving my mama and my sisters and baby brother behind, but I just couldn't. I wasn't sorry at all. I was glad. I was actually bursting with ill-concealed joy that this was happening to me, hardly trusting to my good luck that it should come about. I was going to Virginia with my dad. With *my dad!*

There was nothing to pack — all my clothes were dirty or nearly worn out — and nothing I really wanted to take with me, so I was ready as soon as I finished washing my face and hands.

As we walked away from the house, I could hear Mama crying, and the sound of her sad sobbing has lived with me until this day. But despite her moaning tears, my dad revved up the car engine and we motored away. In the distance, the sound of Mama's weeping soon died away.

My dad drove a three-year-old 1939 Packard car, and he kept it like new. Buckingham County, Virginia, was our destination. By the time we got underway, it was late evening. The sun had dropped low in the sky and a light rain was falling. The rhythm of the windshield wipers and the steady purring of the motor soon put me to sleep.

I quickly slipped into a dream. The smooth-riding car provided a feeling that I was floating across smoky mountains and over muddy rivers. In a deep sleep, I saw myself running away from the brutality of the path of darkness I had been traveling. From the darkness, I entered a different world; a make-believe world where I had often fled to escape my drunken parents; a world where I didn't have to deal with fears. This beautiful dream world was my refuge.

In my need to escape the ugliness of my reality, I often made up many different worlds to live in, and I was always the central figure in those dreams. Sometimes I was myself, Charles Williams, to whom wonderful things happened. Sometimes I was an altogether different person, Dick Tracy the comic book hero, perhaps, but I was always someone powerful, someone upright and respected.

Recently, however — with everything at home falling apart and Mama going crazy for her white lightnin' — those old dreams failed to nourish me and gradually I'd worked out a new one. In my new dream, I was always patient and sad and understanding. In spite of the dysfunctions and cruelties of my family life — a family who did not appreciate me and whom I selflessly tolerated with saint-like acceptance — no one guessed the grief in my heart because, to everyone else, it looked as though I had a life of ease. They said to me, "You seem happy, Charles." And I would smile my slow, sad smile. Nevertheless, secretly I longed to trade my life for a better one, especially for the good images I saw in the comic books and in the Sears Roebuck catalog.

CHAPTER 30
Carter G. Woodson... People And Politics

Just when I was beginning to sleep well, my Dad stopped in Montgomery. It was apparent he had arranged to pick up another passenger. Dad gently picked me up so as not to disturb my sleep — I kept my eyes closed, but I wasn't really sleeping — and laid me down on the back seat of the car. His passenger, Carter G. Woodson, obviously an old family friend, sat on the front seat. Like my dad, Buckingham, Virginia, was birth place and home to Mr. Woodson. Soon, Dad and Mr. Woodson were deeply involved in friendly conversation, and it was apparent the two of them had much in common.

As I listened to their lengthy discussion I only grasped part of all they were saying, but I was so revved up from the thrill of being with my father all my senses must have been on red-alert. From the back seat I was taking in the heady, polish-and-oil smell of the well-kept car, the set of my dad's broad shoulders as he sat behind the wheel, the sound of the motor, the feel of the plush upholstery under my cheek, filing sensory data a mile a minute, and I still remember a goodly amount of what was said.

It was immediately clear that Mr. Woodson was profoundly concerned with what could be done to fix the wrongs in America; especially the wrongs done to African-Americans. Dad and Woodson began talking about the Civil Rights Act — called the Freedmen's Bureau Act — that was supposed to help slaves exercise their rights and adjust to freedom. Dad maintained that it was the failure of the reconstruction era in the South that had caused such hard times and so many problems for black folks.

"But never mind all that," he said, dismissing the government's role. "Mainly, the problems affecting black Americans today are," and he ticked them off on his fingers as he drove, "low self-esteem, depression, loss of identity and values, dysfunctional families and lack of trust. Now I know lots of white people have these problems too, but I believe they are much more devastating to our people.

"It was slavery stripped away our personal identity, and our ability to assimilate," Dad went on, "and as far as I can see we haven't gotten either one of those back yet. There's been no real healing process in that area, Carter, and I think there's a real need for that healing process."

Mr. Woodson nodded.

"After those slavery years," Dad said, "and I mean long after — when blacks were supposed to be free — my grandmother still couldn't relieve herself in a public restroom unless it said 'Colored Only' on the door. Of course it still rankles us; of course it still burns. How could it not? Yet, somehow we've got to get past all that and deal with the opportunities presented in the here and now. Am I right, Carter?"

"Yes, that would be a good thing," Mr. Woodson agreed. "We need to get our emotions past all that, but it is *not* a good thing to forget. We must remember our slavery years. We…"

But Dad interrupted eagerly. "Look at us blacks! We've tried so damn hard to assimilate into the Eurocentric culture of the whites, we've practically forsaken the identity of our own ancestors."

"True," Mr. Woodson said, and then he went on about how he was trying to incorporate the black experience into American history as a whole. Dad made Woodson laugh when he said that someday we would know him as the "Father of Black History." But in spite of his modest chuckle, Woodson *was* an authority on African-Americans in America, and he spoke eloquently about his dream of having a Black History Week recognized throughout the country.

"It's important," he said, "for black Americans, for *all* Americans, to honor the achievements of *our* great orators, our writers and poets, our great athletes, our black men who have been such forceful leaders, and such inspirational voices, and changed the direction of our lives. We, as a people, need to honor them. I was thinking that the second week of February, which coincides with Abraham Lincoln's birthday, would be a fine week for us to celebrate our own black pride. If we could achieve that," Woodson went on, "think how it would uplift our black brethren and replenish their well of hope."

Mr. Woodson gazed out the car window for a moment, taking a long, hard look at the Virginia landscape moving past his eyes, lost in his deep thoughts. Then he turned back to my dad who had been driving in meditative silence. "Like you say, Charles, those ugly memories are still there, still hidden in

My dad, CHARLES AYERS and CARTER G. WOODSON
taken sometime in 1934

our hearts, and we need a healing. Most of the black folks I know carry emotional scars and psychological chains resulting from their parents', or their grandparents' brutal slavery experiences, plus the blatant prejudice we all encounter every day of our lives just trying to get through this world and be treated like decent human beings."

Mr. Woodson paused for a moment and then continued. "I still get incensed at those racist politicians who are preaching that blacks are inferior people who have contributed nothing of substance to society." His voice rose slightly with his anger. "But, you know, Charles, it's not just the politicians talking like that. It's in the colleges, the universities. I pray I'll live long enough to eradicate the obscenity of the racist remarks being made in white academia today. Those prejudiced ignoramuses are still perpetuating those myths, spreading them and inducing others to believe them. Very damaging," he said, shaking his head. "Very damaging."

To this day I remember Carter G. Woodson's emotional conversation with my dad in the front seat of that '39 Packard, and I will never forget that wonderful man who was such a revered educator and an inspiration to his people. I was in awe that such a great man, with such a great mind, was a friend of my family.

I must admit I was proud of my dad, too, for I discovered he had a great range of knowledge about a number of subjects. Mainly, he had some strong ideas about what he referred to as "liberal dependency" — his tag for the government's pre-war handouts. Dad seemed to have a profound dislike for people who spouted what he called "the politics of compassion"; meaning those folks who encouraged governmental financial assistance in return for no effort on the part of the receiver, and for free services or "free rides" of any kind.

"Work for it, earn it, build your pride by attaining it," he said forcefully. "Set an example by your achievement. If I had any message at all, it would be for blacks to wake up and stop letting some sleazy, white politician undermine the very structure of the black community by taking away their industry, their hard work and their pride by handing them some "free" dole money or "welfare" in return." His voice was rising as he warmed to his topic. "Free rides always sound good… Hey! Jump on the bandwagon!.. but I believe that is devastating for blacks! It blows the foundation of self-respect right out from under them. It's definitely a fraudulent transfer of money — something for nothing always is fraudulent — and it does far more harm than good."

I sat up to listen. This was interesting and he was just getting started. "You know, Carter," he went on, "I've heard politicians use that fraudulently language, and all sorts of high-sounding rhetoric, to disguise these damaging policies which in my mind — and in reality — are only another form of slavery!"

"Slavery?" questioned Mr. Woodson, turning to raise his graying eyebrows at my dad.

"Yes, slavery!" Dad insisted, banging his hand on the steering wheel. "If a man is totally dependent on you, is he not your slave? If the food he eats and the clothes on his back come from you, do you not effectively 'own' him? You can't tell me that *that* kind of mental and emotional dependency is not slavery! It's just called a different name."

Mr. Woodson nodded.

"All those whites who are always talking about 'compassion' for the blacks; who are trying to change the rules and make things 'easier for the struggling black man,' are basing their political appeal on the black man's struggles... using those very struggles as a step-ladder to serve their own damn political ambitions. Are they really helping the black community?" he asked. "No! They are nothing but the slimiest of political snakes, using black folks and their problems as a springboard to power for themselves."

Woodson agreed with a smile.

"What do they care," Dad continued, "if they encourage black men to get used to getting something for nothing? What do they care if they take away his pride and nail his heart and soul to the cross of some spirit-bustin' 'free ride' just to get his vote?" I could tell he was getting emotional, but I thought it was interesting, and it excited me. "What does it matter to those white politicians if they teach a black woman to rely on welfare money to feed her six children instead of helping her find a way to learn, and lift herself out of the mire of dependency! A *hand out* is what they're giving. And what we need is a *hand up!* It's not right, Carter. As long as liberal dependency is the politic of the south, there will be no real emancipation for the blacks. All their compassionate give always can only be likened to the image of the same old 'Benevolent Great White Father' on a plantation."

Woodson laughed. "Great White Father," he repeated, scornfully. "You got that right."

"I'm saying that so-called 'helpful' behavior is paralyzing to blacks, and the whites know it. All it does is insulate people from the normal striving necessary to achieve a solid, family life, and from the system of incentives and rewards essential to a man's independence. Am I wrong?"

I was impressed with my dad's knowledge, but as we drove along toward Buckingham, I grew too tired to listen any longer so I curled up on the velvety upholstery and went to sleep.

CHAPTER 31
Grandpa And Grandma Ayers

It was early morning when we reached Buckingham and I got the first glimpse of my father's family farm, a sprawling, one-level home constructed of logs and sawed lumber, surrounded by eighty-some-odd acres of land which was owned outright by his father and him and his brothers and sisters. I think my dad said that thirty acres of it was his. Thirty acres! And my dad *owned* it!

As we drove up, corn fields stretched as far as I could see off into the distance in one direction and bush beans, tomatoes and other kitchen crops spread out in the other. Trees sheltered the dwelling, especially the left side, where a giant oak draped its leafy branches protectively over what turned out to be the kitchen roof. On the ground under that oak someone had stored crocks of butter and jugs of buttermilk, half buried in the earth, to keep cool in that deep, breezy shade. The porch was wide, with comfortable-looking chairs, a two-person wooden swing, and it had several rounded pillars holding up the overhanging roof.

Dad pulled over to the side in a cleared area and we all piled out of the car and hurried up the three steps to the big front door. There were many glad shouts of welcome and I received a warm, open-arms-greeting from my Grandpa and Grandma, Daniel and Elizabeth Ayers. It was strange meeting my dad's ten brothers and sisters, all of whom lived in that rambling homestead and whom I'd never seen before. All of a sudden I had five uncles — Uncle Edward, Uncle John, Uncle William, Uncle George and Uncle Harry, and five new aunties, Aunt Nancy, Aunt Edna, Aunt Cora, Aunt Florence and Aunt Sally (one of Mama's sisters was named Sally, too.)

Grandma Ayers was on the quiet side, with a kind face and the brightest, dark eyes I'd ever seen, flashing everywhere at once, not missing a twitch. Her hands were always busy at something and from the day I met her I don't remember ever seeing her sitting down and just plain resting. She, and my girl-cousins, too, would all be knitting something, or sewing something, or darning socks or overalls, shelling peas, stringing beans, whatever. You never saw them sitting still.

My dad had already told me that my grandma's maiden name was Elisabeth Fields and that she'd been born in 1872, the child of an ex-slave and a white father. Grandma had been raised by her white family, he said, and in 1890, at the age of eighteen, she eloped with the handsome, young Daniel Ayers and they'd gotten married. She and my grandpa had been together there on the farm for over fifty years.

I quickly saw that Grandpa Ayers, a tall, muscular, slightly-stooped man with graying, nappy hair, was also different from my dad. He was quiet-natured, steady, and firm-voiced, and he seemed to set himself apart, sort of, from all the excited talk and the rambunctious goings on of our greeting.

It was breakfast time when we arrived and coming from the poverty I'd left behind, I was round-eyed with wonder to see the food Grandma Ayers laid out on the hand-made plank-table in the dining area just beside the kitchen. I'll never forget the delicious aroma wafting from that laden table and how my stomach ached with eagerness to swallow it all down. There was hot biscuits in a basket covered over with a cloth napkin to keep them warm, fresh churned butter, blackberry jam, peach preserves, all the cold buttermilk I wanted, platters of fried eggs and other plates full of crisp, thick bacon slices that water my mouth even now thinking about them. Of course, I dove into my plateful like the half-starved little pig I was, and only stopped when everybody laughed at the lightning speed of my busy fork.

My dad laid a gentle hand on my arm saying, "Son, you don't need to be in such a hurry. The food won't disappear. There's plenty here and you can eat all you want." I was embarrassed, and I did slow down on cramming those hot buttered biscuits into my mouth, but only slightly. Before I left the table that morning, I shoved two biscuits with bacon into my pockets. Bitter experience had taught me not to depend on what was promised for tomorrow. I was not taking any chances.

After the meal, everybody scattered off to do chores and I got to sit out on the porch and talk to my grandpa. They made it clear that I'd get this day off, but I'd be given a fair share of work to do starting tomorrow. I didn't mind. Being in this beautiful place was worth working for. But right then the sun was blazing in the clear sky and the shady front porch beckoned. My stomach was bursting full for the first time in months, and I wanted nothing more than to sit on the porch swing in the shade with my grandfather.

As we talked, Grandpa Ayers told me about his family history — well, it was *my* family history, too, I realized — and I tried hard to remember what all he was saying. He saw my face wrinkle up with concentration as he spoke the names and he grinned. "Aw, don't bother trying to remember all the names, boy. Gramma's got it all written down on some pages of the bible. You can copy it out someday for yourself.." It was hard, but I did copy it out, with some help from my Grandma Ayers later when she was giving me my school lessons.

I found out that my Grandpa Ayers was born in 1870 and he was the son of two slaves from North Africa. Of course, that made me remember that my mama's mother, Malissie Martin, had been the child of slaves, too, and I mentioned that. Grandpa Ayers said yes, he knew that because Charles, my daddy, had told him long ago when my mama had lived there before I was born, and then he went on with his story. His slave parents came from a small village called Ounianga Kebir, a spot where Libya, Chad, Sudan and Egypt border. His family's African name was Ounianga (Oh-nee-ANG-ah) after the village from which they came. His parents' ancestors had come from the ancient Black Kingdom of Nubia, a Kingdom that is now a part of Egypt and the Sudan. Like my mother's father, Grandpa Charlie Martin, Grandpa Ayers' father had been forced to take his master's name also. Grandpa Ayers joked about his heritage by telling me, "I am a black-skinned Egyptian with a black Jewish heart."

I didn't understand about the Jewish part. I had never known any black Jewish kids at school, and though I had heard of the Jewish religion, I had never actually known any Jews. Grandpa Ayers leaned back in his porch rocker and explained that growing up right there on the farm as a boy, he had made friends with his white neighbors … who happened to be people of the Jewish faith. Over time, and after many, many hours of discussions on the subject and study, he'd come to feel that the Jewish faith — their beliefs, their traditions, the Torah they used for their holy teachings, their philosophy and their morality — was a good, upstanding, moral path to follow; one that seemed on much firmer ground, and made more real sense to him, than the Baptist preaching he'd been brought up on most of his life. So he became a Jew, converting to the Jewish religion as a young man, and was still semi-active in the Jewish faith.

I thought it strange, but Grandpa told me he had always been welcomed by the Jews in Buckingham, and other nearby counties, and frequently attended their synagogues. "Oh, yes," he said, when I asked if he knew about being a Baptist, as I had been taught — in spite of my mama's reluctance to listen to the preachers — "I'm well aware that the churches here are the cultural base of our black community." He rocked awhile and then added. "They have lots of good activities. Always something going on there. Lots of young talent — music and drama and singing — comes to light during the entertainment part of the socials and the pot-luck dinners. You'll go sometime with one of your cousins, maybe."

Later I learned that Grandpa Ayers was a World-War I Veteran. He served in the United States Army, and was very proud of his military service to America. While we talked about that he asked me if I knew why my dad wasn't in uniform. It hadn't crossed my mind. I was aware of the war going on, but I hadn't connected it with my dad. Grandpa explained that my dad had voluntarily gone for the physical, but had failed the eye test. "Never did have 20/20 vision," Grandpa said, "even when he was a kid. Got one weak eye an' that's what's keeping him out of the military."

As we talked, I was curious as to how Grandpa had been able to own all this land and the house. Ever since I was five years old I'd heard Led talking about how a black man can't ever own any property, and how no matter how hard he tries the whites find a way to take it all away from him either with owing taxes or claiming unpaid debts. I didn't understand how life could have been so different for my grandparents.

Grandpa said that he believed that who ever told me that — I didn't mention my step-daddy's name — was dead wrong. "It all has to do with attitude," Grandpa said. "It's what you *believe* you can do, and what you set your sites on." He told me that his father had worked first as a sharecropper, like hundreds of other black families in the south, but he set a goal for himself to own his own place someday. It took a long struggle, but he worked hard, and educated himself as best he could, and finally succeeded in buying 30 acres of land and two mules from his Jewish neighbors.

He leaned forward in his rocking chair and pointed out a section of land, covered with tall corn stalks. "Right over there, Charles," he said. "That, and this plot where the house stands, was the start of it. My daddy always had a good size spread with a few head of cows, some hogs, and most of the acreage in corn. Of course, he raised soybeans, wheat, and cotton like almost everybody else around here. And we had a beautiful peach orchard back then, too. Some of the old trees still bearing out behind the barn. And we always had a kitchen garden," he said. "Okra, peas, greens, butter beans, two kinds of squash, three kinds of cucumbers, some for pickles, and sweet potatoes. Just like we have now," he said, gazing around at the rolling land.

"Then, as time went on, and we kids grew up, after my daddy died he left what he had to all of us. Through the years, I negotiated now and again with my Jewish neighbors, and with a combination of bartered labor and services, and some cash, we bought more land. Still got those old handwritten deeds of sale, too. They add up to us owning this eighty acre spread now." His brown hand swept around in a big half-circle and pride shown brighter than the sunlight in his eyes.

"Now, you know, son," he said, "one of the basic differences between us and other black families in this community — aside from my being Jewish —" and he laughed, "is that one word: ownership. That gives us the edge, see? That gives us a little advantage over the next guy. Ownership, Charles. One of the most important things a black man can do is own property. That's something you don't ever want to forget."

That evening, we all sat around the dinner table, eating a feast of fried chicken, hot biscuits and brown gravy, ham with peach preserves, sliced tomatoes, collard greens, sweet potatoes, and the best-tasting blackberry cobbler I ever had. Grandma Ayers put big spoonsful of cream on top of the crust and I ate till I had to unfasten my pants.

As the grownups talked I learned that Grandpa Ayers and Carter Woodson were long-time friends. My grandpa had not attended school like Carter had, since they needed Grandpa to help out on the farm. Although the school year for blacks at that time was only five months long, Grandpa could not be spared from the farm chores to regularly attend the local school for black children.

Buckingham County, like many other counties in the south, had an established education system for white people only. Consequently, Grandpa Ayers never obtained a college education. Carter Woodson moved to West Virginia, where he continued his education and became a world renowned educator. Grandpa Ayers remained in Buckingham where, as time went by, he became skilled at performing many local farming services. Although not certified, he was able to handle — and was frequently called on to perform — various minor veterinarian procedures such as castration, pulling needle-teeth from hogs, nipping tails and assisting sows.

I was thrilled to discover that Grandpa was a poet. I had already begun making up little songs when I played the piano, and now I knew where that unexplained inner-ability I had come from. It made me feel proud, as I glanced around that dinner table, to know that all these people… these nice-talking, intelligent, educated people were part of me and I was part of them.

They talked about poetry for a while and Grandpa mentioned Langston Hughes, saying how his poetry related to the struggles of blacks in America. "There is not any medicine in the world that can be matched with poetry," Grandpa said. "Poetry is the true healer of the soul."

Carter Woodson took over the conversation then, and when Grandma and the girls started to clear the table after desert, the three of them, along with several of my uncles and aunts took their coffee cups and went into the living room to continue talking together long into the night. As for me, I could hardly keep my eyes open.

I gratefully followed Grandma Ayers down the hall to one of the back bedrooms and discovered I was to share a featherbed, my very first experience with that kind of bedding, with my dad's brother, Uncle Harry. He was the one with the widest smile and the whitest teeth I'd ever seen.

I slid out of my pants and Grandma took them saying she'd wash them for me since they were almost stiff with over week's worth of wearing. She must have felt a lump in the pocket for she reached in a pulled out the two bacon-biscuits I'd pushed in there right after breakfast and forgotten about. She didn't say a word. She just put the crumbled mess back into the pocket, not wanting to get crumbs on the bedroom floor, and came over to me, putting her thin arms around my shoulders.

For some reason, tears came up in my eyes and I thought my heart was going to break as she pressed my face into her warm body. I could just feel the love pouring out of her, and I was ashamed that my first thought had been that she was going to smack me like my mama would have done.

All she said was, "You don't have to hide food anymore, Charles." She hugged me tight and patted my shoulder. "There'll always be food here, honey. I promise." Then she took my pants and my sweaty undershirt and went out to the kitchen and I started washing my face and hands in the big basin she'd filled on the dresser. When she came back she showed me how to use the small step-stool to climb up onto the high, feathered mattress. It was like climbing onto a cloud. Amazed, I sank into the clean-smelling fluffiness and drew up the warm quilt. I was asleep so fast I don't even remember closing my eyes.

Three months passed, and I was happy on the Ayers' farm.

My dad took off again with the family's beat-up old work truck, like he did every week or so since I'd come there, to go strip mining coal, which he'd barter for produce or cash payment. Then he'd sell the farm commodities off the tailgate of his truck to the families living in the rural coal mining camps.

On the farm, the cool September dawns brought the sweet smell of wild flowers that clung to the warm dew and kissed the Virginia air. I seemed to be the only one who appreciated that wonderful morning perfume, except my grandma. She'd go out on the back porch off the kitchen and stand under the shade of that old oak for a minute or so every morning, looking about at the hen house and the barn and the corn fields, taking deep breaths and setting her mind, it looked to me, to the work of the day ahead. The scented air surely went unnoticed by Grandpa who stayed busy with his tractor and other farm equipment, tilling the dark soil, feeding livestock and carrying out other chores before the hot sun could cast its glow over the tall oak trees.

Grandma Ayers kept busy too, and right away she was seeing to my serious lack of wardrobe. In those lean years while the war was going on, farm people didn't squander cash money on store-bought clothes. In the Ayers family, all the clothes were homemade. My aunts, along with Grandma Ayers help, quickly stitched up two pairs of denim overalls for me just like the farmers wore —with bibs across the chest and wide straps that came up over my shoulders and crossed in the back — and two or three short-sleeved cotton shirts made out of twice-washed flour sacking (the large, cotton bags that flour used to come in) or sugar bags. That bleached-out white cotton made nice, soft underwear, too.

I was enjoying myself at the farm. Sure, I had chores to do. Grandma Ayers didn't tolerate loafers, and she kept me, and everybody else, hopping for the best part of the long, hot days, but it was a good feeling to work on the farm; a good feeling to hoe the weeds out of the tomatoes and pull them, like Grandma showed me, from the seedlings she was nursing along. It made me feel useful, and like I was worth something... not just a dumb kid with no brains who couldn't do anything right. I discovered I could do a lot of things right. And I got to feeling pretty good about myself.

That was a strange new feeling for me, since after living with Mama for all those long, alcoholic years I'd got so I thought I was pretty near the bottom of the heap when it came to being worth something. But there on the farm, I did my jobs just like the rest, and it felt good.

I think what I was beginning to feel was self respect, but I just didn't know the name of the feeling at the time. I only knew I felt happy when I got up in the morning; I knew there was going to be food on the table; I knew my grandma loved me, and I had a hunch Grandpa did too, only he didn't show it as much as Grandma did with her hugs and her sweet voice to me and the way she'd smile and put an extra spoonful of ice cream on my peach pie. I didn't go to bed hungry anymore, I didn't have to listen to loud arguments with ugly language while a couple of intoxicated adults, who were supposed to be my parents, staggered around the house screaming at each other and paying no attention to all us kids crying with empty bellies.

Of course, I was yet to discover the jubilation the family would enjoy after harvesting a bumper crop from the fields or the exhilaration shared after the successful sale of a prize-winning hog or a cow. On the Ayers' place everybody worked, everybody had a job, and everybody knew that it was family cooperation that kept the farm doing so well. Grandpa Ayers was a shrewd businessman. He kept a close eye on which farm foods were most needed in Buckingham and nearby counties, studying the markets well in order to know what was best to plant so that he'd get the best price for his produce.

After school and on weekends, I, and all the other Ayers children, cleaned the animal stalls and fed the animals their afternoon rations. Once chores were completed, my cousins spent long hours grooming and priming the sleek calves and the fattest of the hogs, washing them and combing them and even tying a ribbon on the pig's tale, to get them ready to compete in the annual Buckingham fair. Each year the Ayers family won an impressive collection of ribbons, trophies and cash prizes.

Hard work was the family motto, and along with them I learned to toil all day long in the scorching heat preparing food for canning or drying or pickling or dry storage; washing clothes; caring for the younger children. I saw their determination with my own young eyes and knew that they would do whatever it took to make a living. I wanted to be like them. I wanted to be proud like them. I wanted to achieve as they did. Their lifestyle was a wondrous revelation to me.

CHAPTER 32
My Education Begins… And Grandma Speaks Her Mind

Summer was winding down and suddenly it was time for me to go back to school. I had already discovered that in Buckingham, black kids attended school only on Mondays, Wednesdays and Thursdays. They brought their lunches and stayed at the school all day. This was very different than my school life in Minden where I'd started the second grade. Grandma said the reason school was only three days a week was because the children were needed to work on their family farms, and the reason they had to stay at the school all day was because the school was so far away from where the children lived they usually had to be brought by horse and wagon on the day of school.

Buckingham County school system was racially segregated as was common throughout the nation in those days. The oldest black children attended a public school built specifically for "colored" and located many miles away from their homes. One of my aunts had driven over to the school house and registered me, so my name was on the roster and I was expected.

Dressed in a new pair of overalls and a clean shirt, I waited while Grandma packed up two sandwiches and some peach pie for my lunch. Then I stood on the front porch and watched Grandpa hitch the horse's wagon to the rear of his yellow John Deere tractor. He helped me scramble up and off we went down the dirt road.

House by house we stopped to pick up the neighbor's children and then, with almost a full wagon-load of little kids, we kept on driving down that back-country road. On and on we went, passing several "White's Only" schools — I counted three — and still we went on. It didn't seem right to me that the school for us blacks had to be so far away and so difficult to get to. Those that didn't have transportation just plain didn't get to go, and had to rely on learning through self-education and home study. It wasn't right, I thought, because there were all those closer schools. Why couldn't we share one of them? Or have one of them for our own use, if those white kids didn't want to sit with us?

I was only eight, but I didn't need to be told that the situation was unfair and unequal. I could see for myself as we slowly passed by, that the white children's schools were equipped with stuff I'd never seen in a school yard. They had slides and swings and baseball diamonds, and green lawns to play on. Their schools were close by their white communities so they didn't have to travel miles and miles away for an education as we blacks did. "How come they stickin' us so far off like this, Grandpa?" I asked.

"Because nobody in the black community is actively protesting," he replied in his firm voice as he shoved the clutch into a lower gear on the steep downgrade.

"I don't get it. Protesting what?" I asked.

"The situation. Nobody's objecting to the fact that there are separate schools for the blacks. Why do you suppose that is, Charles? Why don't the black folks make a big fuss about that?" That was Grandpa's way, asking questions instead of just answering. He liked to make people think for themselves.

"Maybe they don't mind because…" I racked my brain for a reason and finally came up with one. "Maybe they *like* having their own schools better. Maybe they don't like all the stuff the white schools teach, and, like Grandma says, how they're always sayin' black folks don't have any history or… or culture." I stumbled over that word, but I knew what it meant.

Grampa laughed. "I can't believe I heard that from you, boy. You're getting pretty smart, aren't you! Well, I'd say you're right. Black folks have learned that the white schools, especially here in the South, have a prejudiced perspective about what's to be taught; a perspective conducive only to white folks' heritage and… well… they're completely dispassionate about black culture, ritual's, traditions and customs."

I let it go at that. I understood what he was saying. The white schools weren't going to teach anything about our black history and such; nothing about our achievements or help us to make progress with our rights. Maybe it was just as well that we did have separate schools. But it still didn't seem right that ours had to be so far away.

We arrived at the schoolhouse and I was surprised at how well-kept and clean it was. There was no trash blowing around in the school yard like there'd always been back in Minden and there was even a big sand-box for the little kids. I didn't see any baseball diamond, but there was a beat-up looking, wire-mesh back-stop so I knew there'd be ball games. I loved all sports, running especially, and I knew I had some real ability in that department.

I entered the classroom, found my teacher and was assigned a desk. Right away I noticed that the kids behaved differently there in Buckingham. They weren't running back and forth like wild animals and banging the desks around and falling over the chairs and making a general ruckus while waiting for class to start. They were all clean looking for one thing, with neatly combed hair. Some of the girls wore bright hair-ribbons on their braids. They all were just sitting around, talking together quietly and I noticed a few kids smiling shyly at me — the new boy — but with a welcoming kind of smile, not the sly, threatening look I was expecting.

I began to feel good inside, instead of scared. I began to look around the room, at the words on the blackboard, at the books stacked on the teacher's desk, at the pictures hung up around the room — pictures of famous black men and women my dad had mentioned to me — and I began to think that maybe... just maybe I could settle down and learn something here. Maybe I could get educated and make something of myself. And for the first time in my life, I felt like I might have a future.

Looking back now, I realize it was a turning point for me that day, being in that better-kept, better-run, better-equipped school. It was a black school, but it was a good black school. Up until that time, I didn't know there *were* schools like that for black kids. I had never imagined anything different than the run-down, dilapidated school buildings I'd seen in the coal mining camps where I lived.

In all my life I'd only had two, maybe three, books in my hand; none of which had been mine to carry home and study. Just being there in that clean and orderly room — God, how I remember loving the orderliness of that school room — made a difference to my life. It opened my eyes. It showed me there was a way; there was a brighter path... and I had a chance.

When the teacher walked in that morning she wore a nice-looking dress, polished low-heeled shoes and a light blue sweater over her slim shoulders. Her voice was pleasant and she smiled a lot as she called the roll and acknowledged every new student, including me. She passed around the books which had been stacked on her desk

I got mine in my hands and didn't even open it for five minutes, just sat there smelling it, feeling it, touching the thick cover and reading the dark printing. "*Third Grade Reader*" it said. From that moment on I was in love with books.

The teacher instructed us to turn to the first story.

I fingered the pages carefully. There were pictures. A white boy and girl were walking down a road. It was a country road because I could see cows in a pasture behind the fence and the children were swinging pails — lunch pails like the miners used to carry to the coal mines. I still remember the pink dress the little white girl wore and the denim pants of the young boy and his blue shirt and his blond hair.

As that memory comes flooding back to me now, I realize how important it was for me to be in that place, at that time, in my young life. It's a fact that random, indiscriminate punishment and the lack of consistency can drive laboratory rats into madness. That same chaotic life can also affect children and drive them into a kind of madness too.

That evening, after Grandpa picked up all us kids with the wagon/tractor, my home study period began. Grandma Ayers had been a grade school teacher herself, and what I didn't grasp in school, she explained and worked on with me. She taught me spelling and much more about arithmetic, slowly explaining long division and writing down problems for me to solve. As I worked at the kitchen table with my grandma, I paused sometimes just to listen to the quiet house and remember my life in the coal mining camp of Minden. Our coal-company, broken-down shanty. My two sisters, Marguerite and Inez. My baby brother TC. Mama. And school.

I recalled the times I was running scared, worried about getting roughed up and having to give up my lunch just to befriend some bully so he'd lay off me. It had been difficult for me to concentrate on learning anything. When Mama was drunk, which was most of the time, she never wanted to hear anything about my homework.

In Minden there had been at least 40 kids in our class and one teacher trying to keep order in the room and teach something at the same time. It was next to impossible. The only things I ever did right in that school was my arithmetic and my music. I had a natural understanding of numbers — they made sense and they were dependable. If two and two equaled four, it equaled four every single time with no exceptions. Two and two were never three sometimes, and five if you turned one upside down. It didn't matter. Two and two was *always* four. And if you did twice twelve it was always twenty-four. Nothing less. Nothing more. It was always the same answer. Reliable. Once you learned it, you had it, that one time and for always.

And with music, I had a natural ear for it. I could always pick out tunes on the piano by just listening to the melody in my head and then finding the corresponding notes on the keyboard. But now, with my Grandma Ayers, I was learning more than just playing tunes by ear. She was teaching me how to play scales, teaching me how to play a melody by reading the notes off the sheet music like you'd read a printed page of a book. It was fascinating to me, for again, it was sensible and logical and always the same. Middle C was always Middle C. There were signs like flats and sharps and key signatures, and they never lied to you. Once you learned it, it was yours. It was a wondrous new world to me.

More than a teacher, my Grandma Ayers played piano herself and she was fond of the black composer, Scott Joplin, a well-known ragtime pianist, as I was. She allowed one-hour session every other day for my music lessons, and under her tutelage, my piano playing and music reading progressed steadily. Every once in a while she would fold her hands in her lap as we sat together on the bench of the old upright in the living room and quiz me.

"What is the relative key to G minor?"

"B-flat major," I'd say.

"Why?"

"Because the flatted notes in the B-flat major scale and in the G-minor scale are the same: E-flat and B-flat."

"Good. Now what is the relative key of E-minor?"

"G-major."

"Why?"

"Because the G-major scale has one sharp, F-sharp, and so does the E-minor scale.

"Relative major of C-minor?"

"E-flat."

"Why?"

"Because they both have A-flat, E-flat and B-flat in their scale.

"That's fine, Charles. I'm proud of you."

Grandma was the best music teacher I ever had. As I said, it was at first a shock to me to realize the beautiful orderliness of the keyboard and the mathematical relativity of harmony. I soon saw that my previous learning was haphazard and had no foundation. My playing had been all emotion and instinctive. Fun to listen to, but not based on knowledge ... more accidentally right than precise. Now I felt I was at one with the very soul of music and at last I was beginning to truly understand the marvel of its construction.

Family discussions were a tradition in the Ayers household.

Sometimes they went on at the dinner table, sometimes out on the porch at twilight, sometimes it would just be Grandpa and Grandma and me sitting around the kitchen table on a Sunday afternoon. Grandma always had her sewing or her knitting in her hands, Grandpa had his pipe or a book of poetry. As we sat together, me with my new *"Reader,"* they liked to discuss the problems within the black community in Buckingham.

This time Grandma was talking about how puzzled she was over the careless way some of the black women, single mothers mostly, she said, were living in the community, and she named a few and Grandpa nodded his head. "What's the matter with them, Daniel?" she asked, calling Grandpa by his given name. "Letting their children run wild like they do, not bothering to teach them manners or keep their clothes clean, not taking responsibility for them. Don't they know how important it is to spend time with a child when they're young? To teach them how to behave by *example?*" She bent her head to her knitting, not expecting an answer. "You know, I think too many black women — the young ones especially — are preoccupied with insignificant matters... like how their hair looks, or where they're goin' on the weekend, and they're spending time with religious rituals and such, and just letting their lives run on automatic drive."

"Maybe its because all those things are easy, Bethy. They don't require any deep, self-examination. You know, it's hard to sit down and look into your own soul, and test your own feelings, and ask yourself if you're doin' the right thing." Grandpa lit his pipe. I loved the smell of the burnished tobacco he used.

"Why do you think those women are like that?" I asked, trying, in my childish, inquisitive way to find an answer as to why my mama lived like she did — carelessly, and seemingly without the sense of direction and purpose, or the calmness I'd observed in my first school teacher, the attractive Mrs. Watson.

"Well," Grandma said, and she took her time thinking for a while, "maybe black women need a vision that's more worldly. You know, not just a local group of housewives and mothers getting together at church and trying to impress each other. I mean, a little group meeting here and there is fine, but it isn't enough to do the hard work that's needed; it isn't enough to pull a struggling young black woman out of the... the *squalor* some of them have come to *accept* as a way of life."

As she talked, her dark eyes blazed with her own vision as she stared out the kitchen window, looking off across the fields. "Maybe black women today need a unified group across the nation," she said, "maybe even *bigger*; across the *world,* maybe. A group with an uplifting togetherness of purpose. Maybe black women need to be shown good examples by honoring those among us who have struggled and won... those who have educated themselves... like you did, Daniel. There are plenty of decent black women who have escaped poverty and oppression, who have walked away from drunkeness and worldly living, who have made hard choices and lifted themselves out of... of the downward spiral of low self-esteem..." she paused, but she wasn't finished, "and the terrible, self-de*struc*tion of *acceptance* that pushes so many young black girls down to the depths of depression."

It was a long speech.

Grandpa had put down his pipe and was giving her his full attention.

She sighed. "You know, honey, I think these young girls need a new vision of hope, a *change* in their expectations of life. Someday maybe there'll be a new upsurge of determination that will move them... *move them hard*," she said, and her small fist came down on the table making me jump, "until they see how to avoid the lazy path of just *going along* the white man's megalomania. They need to know their Africanism, their own proud black history, and where they came from."

Grandpa smiled. "I never heard you go on like that, Bethy. You must have been thinkin' on that for a long time."

"Yes. A long time. It worries me, Dan'el... seeing these young families suffering and not working at doing something about it; seeing how these young children are coming up in the world... like our Charles here. His mama..." She stopped when Grandpa frowned and shook his head.

"Well, it's hard," she concluded. "It's terribly hard."

CHAPTER 33
Goin' Fishin' With Grandpa

One Saturday morning in October Grandpa Ayers and I set off at dawn in a shivering mist. It was a meandering sojourn across green pastures laden with thorny blackberry bushes, along mossy creek banks and into the thick forest. We took fishing poles with us just in case we found a spot in the creek where the fish were biting. I trudged along energetically beside him as he carried his fishing gear in one hand and his long, 12-gauge shot gun slung over his shoulder. As we walked beside the creek bank, about a mile away from our farm house, there on a rock near the creek sat an ancient, wrinkled white man.

"Hi you, Nick!" Grandpa called out.

"How are you, Dan?" the old man answered.

Grandpa Ayers fished in his pocket and tossed him a fat plug of apple tobacco. The old man could not chew very well because most of his teeth were gone, however, he gummed the wad enthusiastically. When he shifted the tobacco in his cheek, his jaw action reminded me of the steel handles on freight train wheels working up, down, and sideways.

Continuing our way, we walked a half-mile further before Grandpa found a wide space in the creek that looked promising. It was an old, abandoned beaver pond and it was just the kind of spot he was looking for. He unloaded his fishing gear, braced his shot gun against a tree, and glanced around for a suitable place to sit. One of the large flat rocks looked good, so he placed a wiggling earthworm on his hook, cast his line into the creek and settled back to wait for some unlucky fish to bite and send his bobber dipping under surface of the water.

I climbed up a buff and sat with my head cocked like a pistol hammer, staring up into the morning mist so heavy it was almost hiding the bare hickory and walnut trees that sculpted the landscape halfway up the hillside and along the creek. I had settled myself directly under one giant oak which towered so tall it must look out over the entire forest and into the surrounding meadows. It's brown, gnarled toes dug far into the slope beneath where it stood firm, facing the north winds. Thick and dense, the giant oak had the look of a tree that intended to stay right where it was. Gazing up, I searched for its majestic crown... a point still reaching for the sky.

I finally did what a tree of such magnificent height seemed to demand of the child in me. I lay down with my head on its extended roots and my body pillowed in its fallen leaves. Daydreaming, fantasizing, I drifted off into a little boy's wonderland while my eyes inched up the full length of that dark timber. Lying still, I studied the amazing pattern of converging lines that created an odd feeling of depth and perspective where swooping limbs branched out from the straight trunk. Closing my eyes, within moments I had slipped off to sleep.

My dream was suddenly shattered by Grandpa calling my name. Awaking, I yawned, stretched out my arms and enjoyed the uplifting feeling.

We left the creek bank and climbed up a ravine. As we walked along the top of the moraine, a black bear and her two cubs came within perhaps thirty feet of us. They saw, or scented, us and quickly ran off while Grandpa and I stood frozen in our tracks. We walked on then, but after a few yards Grandpa coaxed me up a pine tree to see if I could spot the bears. They spotted me before I saw them, and again, snorting in a snuffling sound of anger, the mother bear and her cubs ran deeper into the trees.

I'll never forget walking through the woods that day with my grandfather. He didn't hold my hand, but just being beside him in that quiet forest gave me a deep feeling of security and joy. I always think of it as a treasured, peaceful moment through my paths of darkness.

CHAPTER 34
"You've Got To Go Home, Son… Your Mama's Dyin'."

After our fishing trip, we came home to find the long, wooden table set for dinner. I still hadn't gotten used to having such plenty and I took great interest in what was to me an exciting menu. This time it was a feast that included fried fish rolled in corn-meal, collard greens, baked pheasants one of my uncles had bagged, pork and beef Bar-B-Que ribs, fresh lemonade, blackberry cobbler and pound cake. The homemade ice-cream was already in the ice-cream maker and ready to churn. Old ice-cream makers were wooden buckets that held a steel canister in the middle. Inside the steel canister was a curved agitator, also steel, which turned in a circle, mixing up the ingredients of milk, sugar, flour and flavoring. Small pieces of ice were packed in the bucket around the canister. I was given the job of turning the handle which churned up the chilled mixture inside the canister turning it into rich vanilla ice cream.

During the dinner meal the family usually discussed issues of the day and any on-going news. Lately, of course, the talk was mostly about the war effort and what was going on in Germany and Japan, but that night Aunt Cora wanted to talk about how immigrants coming into America seemed to do better, and get ahead faster, than some native-born black Americans. She was making a point that in her opinion the immigrants worked with the idea of, "Do it on your own," and it was helping them succeed. "But all I hear from young blacks today is 'You deserve a break today.'"

Everybody laughed and Uncle Harry said, "I know where you're comin' from, sis."

Grandpa took up her cause. "You have to admit, Cora, that the liberal attitude does appear kindly. The hidden danger in it is that it undercuts a person's will toward independence."

"That's exactly what I mean. What happens to a man's self-esteem when you give him free meals and clothes? All you're doing is encouraging his passivity, keeping him quiet, keeping him *down!* " She looked around the dinner table, but everyone was busy with their plates

"It seems to me," Uncle William said, joining in, "a lot of my black friends — and whites, too — used to brag about their parents' personal advancement. Know what I mean? Like how they finished years of schooling, held a steady job, bought a home, raised a child and sent it on to college. I don't see much of that striving to achieve things today. Mostly I see young blacks with their hands out, expecting everything to be given to them... like they deserve it because they've been deprived."

"Well, immigrants are deprived too," Aunt Edna said emphatically. "They're deprived of correct English, knowledge of our customs... but they still make a go of it by hard work and will power. Know what I mean by will power? I mean I WILL learn to speak good English. I WILL improve myself. I WILL learn to read and write. That's "will power" as far as I'm concerned. No job is too menial, no work too hard, and it's making them tough. Slavery should have made *us* tough; able to take anything to get ahead and be somebody. *Nothing* was harder than slavery, but I don't see that happening. My God, wouldn't they rather *earn* five dollars than have some lily-face hand them a ten for nothing?"

"Well, I'll take the ten, thank you," Uncle John said with a wide grin.

"Yeah? And what will you do when there is no ten being handed out? If you work, you got the first five, and the next five. You can *depend* on it, John, because you can depend on *yourself.* You're gettin' it for yourself, not waiting on somebody else."

Just when the discussion was really getting interesting, I heard my dad's truck spit gravel outside in the drive. He was back from West Virginia where he'd been strip-mining coal. He came on into the dining room where I was sitting at the table and I saw his face was drawn with a sad expression.

"Charles," he said, putting his hand on the back of my chair. "I'm sorry, son, but you've got to go back to Minden tomorrow."

I think I just echoed his words without knowing what he meant. "Tomorrow?"

"Yes." He bent down and saw the bewilderment in my face. "Your mama's dying and she wants to see you one last time. I'm sorry. Grandma will help you pack up your things."

"Mama's dying?" I repeated like a fool, unable to grasp it, unable to move from my chair, unable to realize that my world was crashing down around me.

The next morning Grandma helped me pack up my things and after a tearful goodbye to the family, I had climbed into the family car beside my dad.

CHAPTER 35
Mama Recovers

All the way home to Minden I had been sitting quietly in the front seat, thinking about Mama's past and the misery of her beginnings. I had been lost in thought for hours. Now, as the familiar terrain of the coal camp met my eyes I began thinking about the life I was going home to, wondering if it was true that Mama was actually dying. I felt scared and worried, and full of an aching sadness at the same time.

It was a cold, late autumn day in October when we arrived back in Minden. Driving along the old highway, the cool evening air kept shifting in an uneasy manner as I did on the front seat of the car as we approached my old neighborhood. It looked the same to me, maybe even a little shabbier than I remembered. The steep mountainsides, with bare trees and scrawny, browned-out underbrush, looked bleak and still. Gray-black smoke from coal-burning fireplaces rose from the chimney of each shanty we passed.

The first sound I heard as we approached the camp community was the eerie whine of the tipple ringing out its abrasive noise as it churned the giant black chunks being fed into its belly from the long conveyor belts. The 'drift mouth' was clear, but I knew it would not be long before the coal-loaders lined up near the mine's entryway to haul the men down to the bottom of that ghostly pit. There was our shack. There was no smoke coming from our chimney. It looked like an abandoned old shed, with the weeds getting high on both sides of the porch steps and the torn window shades low on the sills; cold, gray, ghostlike and still. We got out of the car in silence. I kept glancing at the house, my heart pounding with fear, worried about what we might find. What if Mama was already dead? My dad didn't say anything as he took my string-tied cardboard box and walked me to the front door. We didn't knock; Dad just called out "Hello?"

"Mama? You here?"

We found Mama on a floor pallet, covered with a pile of dirty quilts, looking deathly sick and barely breathing. Sears Roebuck must have repossessed the furniture, including the bed. I could hear my sisters, Marguerite and Inez, and my baby brother, TC, crying in the back room… all too young to understand what was going on and too scared to come out and see who had just walked into their house. Mama's pretty hair was tangled and knotted, laying crazy-like all over her pillow; her eyes, sunken deep into her head, were closed. Hardly breathing, she just lay in her smelly mess of blankets, moaning, and moving restlessly.

The inside of the house was no different than it always was when Mama was drinking: cluttered with clothes and dirty plates and glasses strewn everywhere. This time, though, there was a pile of dirty diapers shoved into a corner giving off a powerful stench. Standing over Mama I spoke to her, but she only moaned and turned her head away. The filthy house horrified my dad. I saw him look around and noticed how his lips curled in disgust and his eyes went hard like they do when he's angry. I could see he didn't want to leave me in such a mess, but how could he take me away with Mama dying like she seemed to be.

First thing I did was go into the kitchen, checking to see if there was any food or powdered milk. Nothing. My heart sank. I had been yanked back into the same old problems… all the mess and trouble I thought I had finally left behind had caught up with me, only this time Mama wasn't just drunk and ornery; she was deathly ill, moaning there in her smelly quilts, lost in a fever. Looking around that squalid room I could not hold back the tears. In my mind I could still see the Ayers' farm, the loaded dinner table, the calm of neatness and order. I shook my head. It must have been a dream, a dream I had now harshly awakened from. Suddenly, it was like I had never been away.

Seeing my dad's car out front, the neighbor lady, Mrs. Myrtle, came in from the shanty next door. She and my dad talked for a while about Mama's condition. I went into the front room and sat near them on the floor. Mrs. Myrtle said she'd looked in on Mama and the kids every now and then. She said Mama had been vomiting for several days; couldn't keep anything, not even broth, on her stomach. Diarrhea and fever had turned her into a limp, listless, lump of misery. Mrs. Myrtle said that when Mama was awake, she cried incessantly, expressing herself in a nonstop series of whimpering, pig-like sounds that affected everybody around her. Nobody knew what to do for her. Dad asked if the coal-company doctor had been around to see Mama.

"Yeah, he come. Didn't stay long. Give her some pills or a shot or somethin'. I don't know. I was in here trying to fix some food for the children, and he tol' me there wasn't much he could do for her."

"Did you ask him about getting her into a hospital?"

Mrs. Myrtle laughed. "You kiddin'? If she was a white lady sick like this, then maybe they do somethin' for her, but in this coal-minin' camp ain't no hospital gonna do squat for no black woman. Hell, they'd let her die in the lobby before they let her near one a-them snow-white hospital beds. Besides, she ain't got any money and no husband to help her out."

"Yeah, I know. That man she married… Ledbelly… he still in jail?"

"Yeah, he is."

Just about then, Mama stirred, and in her dying voice she called out, "Where is my son? I want to see my son…"

I went to her and sat down on the floor by her side. She looked at my face, but I wasn't sure she really knew it was me, and she started crying. I hated to see her crying and sick like she was, but there was still something inside me that just couldn't accept that I had to stay there in that filthy house.

"Don't leave me, baby," she moaned. "I'm dyin'… I know I'm dyin'… Stay here with your mama, son. I missed you so much." Then she turned her head and her eyes focused on my dad. "Charles… please…" was all she said, but her voice was so small and faint and so full of pleading I knew he wasn't going to let me leave her. She closed her eyes again and I think she passed out. I don't know.

Dad came over to me and bent down. "You're going to have to stay with her, son. You understand?"

"Yes, sir." Tears were flooding down my face. I wasn't exactly crying, but I just couldn't stop the tears.

"Now listen. I've got some friends who live near here, over on the southern tip of this town. There's got to be somebody to take care of you… and the other children. I'm going to see if Alfreda and Shorty will help me out. You know I can't stay here with you. I've got to go on back to the farm and…"

"I know." I could hardly speak for the lump in my throat. "Will I be seeing you again?" The words came out of my mouth before I could think to hold them back.

"I'd… I'd like to promise you that… but…" He hesitated, not wanting to lie to me, but not able to promise either. "If your mother, uh, you know… if she dies, then…"

"Then I can come and live with you again?"

"Yes, son. That much I can say. But right now, we are all hoping that won't happen, aren't we?"

I hung my head and whispered, "I don't want my mama to die."

"I know that. Well, I'm going to go on now, like I told you, and see if those folks can come stay here a while. I'm counting on you to sort of, you know, take care of your mama and see if you can help with the other children. Can you do that, boy?"

"I'll try," were the only two words I could manage. I stood in the doorway and watched my dad walk back to his Packard, wave his hand at me and drive away.

Mrs. Myrtle left to tend her own family. She said Mama was sleeping and I should leave her alone and keep the house quiet if I could. Marguerite and Inez, hearing my voice, came out and were really glad to see me, but their noses were running from crying and they were hungry, and looking at me to do something about it. I wiped their noses and assured them everything would be all right and sent them back into the bedroom till I could figure out what to do. Dad had forgotten to leave some money with me so I could get some groceries at the company store, or maybe he just didn't have any to spare. Didn't matter. I knew I'd have to get used to being hungry again anyway. That's how it was living with Mama, and that's how it was going to be. All Mama's money went for whiskey.

I sighed and pulled an old paper bag from the pile Mama saved in a cupboard. I'd have to go begging from the neighbors or all four of us would go to bed hungry. God, I hated to beg for food like a bum or one of the hobos hanging out in the woods, but I'd go. My stomach was already growling.

I stopped to stare down at Mama. She didn't move, and she *did* look like she was dying, but something told me she'd pull out of this trouble. Mama was strong, more muscle in her than you'd think. I wanted to brush back her hair and talk to her for a minute, but Marguerite and the other children began to cry. I knew they were hungry. With my head down and my face flushed with shame, I went on out and began knocking on doors.

The lady who came to help us and take care of Mama was Alfreda Benedict, called Mrs. Freda. Her husband who came along with her was "Shorty." The way I understood things, when Mama died — if she actually did die — I would return to my dad's farm in Buckingham and Mama's sister, Samantha, would care for Marguerite, Inez and TC... at least until their daddy, Led, got out of jail.

It was not long after Mrs. Freda's arrival that Mama's bowels burst like a volcano erupting. Unable to help herself, she expelled a liquid stool of a deep green color more impressive than any I had ever witnessed. Yellow colored fluid oozed from her nose while she continued coughing-up dark mucus. Mrs. Freda said Mama's symptoms and misery came from alcoholic poisoning. I didn't understand about the poison part, but I knew — way before I went to Dad's farm — that Mama was drinking enough alcohol every day to float a barge.

I was very relieved that my dad had been successful in persuading Mrs. Freda to come take care of Mama and us children. I'd only been home alone with them one night and I hadn't been able to get much cleaned up. I'd gotten powdered milk for TC's bottle and cornbread from one neighbor and a jar of peach preserve and a jar of chicken soup. We ate it cold since I was afraid to start up a fire in the coal stove and there wasn't much coal anyway. I tried to feed Mama some soup, but she turned her head away and it spilled all over the quilt. TC's diapers were still piled up in the corner. I didn't know what to do about them. I picked up the dirty dishes and carried all the mess to the kitchen, but there was only cold water and no soap so I just left them in the dish tub.

Mrs. Freda was a very kind lady. A fat, pleasant, dark-skinned woman, about forty-five years old, she had an odd-looking wide mouth that pushed dimples into her round cheeks when she smiled. We kids were thrilled to discover she was an excellent cook and could make a tasty meal out of little or nothing. Her bread pudding was not only tasty but filling.

She cleaned up TC's dirty diapers by soaking them in a tub of hot water mixed with some kind of strong soap, and she'd found Oxydol somewhere and washed up all the dishes. The house was starting to look like Mama kept it when she was sober. Mama was still on her floor pallet, but Mrs. Freda gave her a hand-bath with a wash rag and put her in a clean cotton undershirt and spent all of one whole day washing her blankets, with me helping where I could, and hanging them outside on the porch rail to dry. She got TC cleaned up, put corn starch on his poor bottom where he was all puckered and red from diaper rash, and he finally stopped crying.

Because of the war going on, many foods were rationed, and commodities like butter, sugar and meat were hard to come by. Rationing didn't affect our lifestyle much, since we didn't get to eat that food anyway. But Mrs. Freda's husband, a short little runt of a man, was very good about bringing us wild game meat. Almost every day he would bring in rabbit, deer meat or a opossum, but mostly fish from the nearby river. Mrs. Freda would prepare the opossum deliciously with wild sweet potatoes which she knew how to find and polk salad — a wild green that was plentiful in the West Virginia mountains. Our drink was a flavorful tea-like drink Mrs. Freda made out of roots... sassafras, I think it was called. She would boil the roots in a gallon bucket until the water turned reddish. Then she placed the bucket outside on a bench in the cool air for an hour before serving it to us children.

Sacks of flour, farm eggs, powdered milk, oatmeal and canned spam meat was cheap, and that's about all the commercial food stuff we ever saw. Mrs. Freda was an expert at baking large biscuits, so when there was a dollar or so to spare, our breakfast consisted of eggs and biscuits, oatmeal and powdered milk.

Despite the delicious meals Mrs. Freda prepared, Mama ate very little, but it looked to me like she was feeling better. Shortly after I came home the diarrhea and vomiting disappeared. The mining company doctor visited her several times. He diagnosed her with a disease called "Delirium Tremens." Mrs. Freda called it the "DT's" and said it was from Mama's heavy drinking. She said that's what made Mama shake and tremble all over and made her see things that weren't there, like visions and ghosts. No wonder she screamed out in the night time, shaking and yelling about people being around her, and rats — she always feared and hated rats — and she'd scream that they were running all around her. I was standing right by her when that happened, but there weren't any rats. She was just seeing them in her own head Mrs. Freda said. Made me shiver just thinking about what that must be like for Mama.

The doctor also said she had pneumonia and bronchiolitis. "She's gravely ill," he said, shaking his head. He convinced Mrs. Freda that Mama was truly dying and needed to be watched carefully. I listened to all that, but I still didn't believe it. That doctor didn't know what my mama was made of. I saw her lift her head to take broth yesterday, and no matter about all that shaking and seeing stuff and her pneumonia and all, she was not going to die. She could lay there fevered and fainting and weak as a baby, but Mama had barbed wire in her backbone and a mean-streak that was too bulldog stubborn to let her spirit go before she was ready.

As dusk shaded into night, we retired to our pallet bed under the flickering light from the fireplace. Soon, everyone but me was asleep. I lay wide awake listening to Mama snoring and the crackling of the fire. I missed the farm something fierce. I thought back on the good life I had in Buckingham with Dad's family. I didn't feel hungry there and have to sleep on a floor pallet. I had a fluffy, feathery bed and a soft, hand-made quilt to keep me warm.

There's nothing left of all that now, I thought, feeling the miseries begin as they had for all the five nights I'd spent in that shanty. I looked through the torn window shade into the cold, dark and frosted night. The mountain ranges I could see appeared blurred and the landscape had no recognizable shape under the gray moon, like disconnected images rising from my own dark stream of memory. The chill of the room and the flickering of firelight made an eerie setting as the shadows danced on the walls and hovered like ghosts out of hell.

Suddenly Mama awoke screaming, "Lord help me! I want to die. Let me die!"

Mrs. Freda came and quieted her. "You don't want to die, honey. You just feelin' miserable now, that's all. Lay back down now." She stroked Mama's forehead.

"I can't take any more of this," Mama cried, raising her head. Her face had such a tortured look my heart ached for her. "What's left for me? I can't live like this any longer."

"Now, honey, don't carry on like that. You don't want to get your children all cryin'. Lay down now."

"I feel like I've lost my mind. I... I can't remember anything. If I could just die... and get past all this pain..." She started shaking all over and Mrs. Freda pulled up the quilt she had kicked off.. "My head feels like someone is standing on it," Mama groaned, finally laying back.

"That's right, honey girl. Close your eyes. We all right here with you." Mrs. Freda kept on soothing Mama till she stopped trembling and was breathing better.

I turned over on my side, pulled the covers back over my sister Marguerite, and went to sleep.

Three more days passed and Mama was suddenly feeling much better. Before anyone could stop her she was up and walking around, putting coffee on the stove, touching stuff and hugging us kids. She put her arms around me and held me close. "You grown taller, boy," she said, rearing back to stare at me. "An' you got some meat on your little bones." She hugged me again and I put my arms around her neck. For just a second it seemed everything was going to be all right. "I'm glad you are home," she spoke softly. "I need you to stay with me, Charles. You're my little man."

I kissed her cheek and fought the tears welling up in my eyes. She let me go and went on to heat up some of Mrs. Freda's biscuits. I walked out to the front porch and stood by myself for a few minutes, not hardly daring to breath the frosty air of that cold October morning. *I need you to stay with me,* was what she'd said. Inside my heart something snapped, just as plain as you'd snap a piece of kindling wood. My dream was over. My dream of going back to my dad's farm, to the fishing stream, to that clean school... over. *I need you to stay with me.* This... this... I stared around me at the mountains and the ugly shanties and the mist rising off the swamp ground and stood there listening to my mama singing in the kitchen. I stood there, so choked up with misery I couldn't even cry.

Everyone seemed surprised at Mama's recovery. Mrs. Freda and Shorty went on back home now that Mama was stronger. She'd lost several pounds, but she was able to be up and around. However, realizing how sick she'd been and what had brought it on, her self-esteem was very low. She kept saying how sorry she was and how bad she felt about causing such a lot of worry, and then Mama promised never to drink alcohol again.

"Never again, I swear it," was what she said. "I'll kill me one day," she prophesied, but she was smiling when she said it. "I'll kill me for sure."

I wasn't all that impressed by Mama's promise. I'd heard it before. She hadn't kept her word then, and I knew — come the first opportunity — she wouldn't keep it now. All there had to be was some reason to have a party. She'd always been that way and I knew she wasn't about to change her ways now.

CHAPTER 36
Evicted... And Nowhere To Go.

Word finally came to Mama that Led had been released from the county jail, but only with the promise that he leave the mining community of Minden. Looking back, I believe that was the kind of option the coal mine owners persuaded law enforcement agencies to oblige. But Led had not been in touch with Mama yet. While we waited to hear from him, we got an eviction order from the superintendent of the camp giving us thirty days to vacate.

That eviction notice stressed Mama severely. She cried and walked the floor, trying to think of what to do. "Where are we gonna go?" she kept moaning, over and over as she paced the bare room. We had no money, no food, no place to go, and no idea where Led might be.

It must have been sometime around midnight when suddenly a huge rock came crashing through our front window. Mama's screams awoke me from a deep sleep. Shattered glass was everywhere and we were all barefoot. The brutality of that act horrified Mama. In the darkness she yelled out, "Charles! Did it hit anybody? Are you hurt?"

"We all okay, Mama," I said, almost whispering from fear.

"Ohhh, them fools could have killed my babies!" she screamed. "Oh, God, what's happening here?"

Hearing the noise, Mr. Brooks, a neighbor from across the way, came running across the dirt road holding a long flashlight. From our pallet where I was holding on to my sisters and my little brother, I saw the rays of light crisscross our house as Mr. Brooks searched to see the damage and then came into our yard and up the steps.

Mama was open-mouth with shock, bewildered and terrorized.

"Mrs. Leadbetter, what happened?"

"Someone tried to kill us!" was all Mama could say. Her knees gave out and she sat down hard. "Someone tried to kill us," she said again like she couldn't quite believe it.

Mr. Brooks flashed his light around the room and across the floor, and there it was. The rock had landed just inches from Marguerite's head where she'd been sleeping. Shards of glass covered the floor under where the window had been and on out into the room.

Mr. Brooks returned to the front porch with his flashlight and walked all around our house. Returning to our front yard he called out to Mama, "I didn't see anything out here, Mrs. Leadbetter, but I'll keep watch from my window till it's light. In the morning I'll fetch the superintendent and the sheriff."

"Thanks, Ed," Mama replied.

"I think you and the children ought to move into the back room until tomorrow. By that time the company's carpenters may be able to replace that window pane."

"Thank you again," Mama called. Scrambling up, Mama bolted the front door and hurried the little ones to the back room. Then she and I pulled the pallet in there.

The night had been shattered, as well as the window glass, by the horror of the attack on us. Why had they done that? Did they want to kill us? Were they angry 'cause Led had been released from jail? Did they think he was here? Why did they want to hurt us like that? My head whirled with painful questions. It was almost impossible to sleep after that. I was tired, but I kept waking up, wondering what might happen next.

The night passed from the little back room where we lay. Half asleep, I could hear the ordinary sounds of the crackling fire and see the ghostly shadows flicker on the window shade. Soon I dozed off again and dreamed that I was running, pursued by a red-eyed devil monster. Terrified I awoke, screaming, in a cold sweat.

My screams woke Mama. "Charles, what's wrong?"

"I had a bad dream. I thought I saw someone in the window."

"It's just the shadows of the fire. Go back to sleep, honey."

Morning came abruptly after a long, restless night. The air was cold. The red and yellow flames that radiated heat from the fireplace were dead and now the room was freezing.

Mama got up and opened the door to the front room where the broken window glass lay in shards on the floor. Long, leathery leaves from a nearby crab apple tree were scattered about the floor too. We all stood in silence, thinking about what had happened. Only little TC was still asleep. Frighten and concerned, Mama seemed weary and shaken. My belly groaned with hunger. I had gotten used to eating regular meals at the Ayers' place. Marguerite and Inez begin to cry. Mama was still weak and not fully recovered from her long illness, but her natural colors had begun to appear in her light brown-skinned face. Her motherly instincts forced her into action. She was determined to pack our belongings and leave that dreadful house.

Before the late Autumn sun was overhead, Mama had wrapped our few belongings in a bed spread, dressed us children in almost all the clothes we owned to keep us warm, and we set out on foot to find Mrs. Freda Benedict's house, the lady who had cared for us while Mama was sick.

That was a hard time. Stumbling along, it seemed we walked all morning to reach our destination. Mrs. Freda's house, owned by the coal company like everything else in Minden, sat on a hillside right in front of a giant gray boulder that was as big as a locomotive. It was a drab-colored, one-bedroom house with a long, wooden porch standing on stilts at least twenty-five feet from the ground. The hillside was very steep and the ground was covered with dark, slate, ominous-looking, that covered the soil. Mama and we children labored hard to reach the front steps, having to stop several times to rest. It was pitiful to see Mama, holding my baby brother in one arm and our belongings bundled in that bedspread in the other, struggling to get up that hill.

We climbed the wooden steps up to the porch. From the porch the slate appeared even darker and more ominous than ever… it was like a dark valley below us, scattered with blackish-gray rock, shadowed by the glumness of dark clouds rolling overhead on this cold and icy morning.

Finally Mama set down the bedspread bundle and knocked on the green wooden door. She hammered on it loudly and waited. No sound came from inside.

She knocked several times. It was beginning to appear as if no one was home. Standing beside her I felt bewildered and totally dejected. Marguerite and Inez and TC were all crying. We were all hungry. There had been nothing in the house to eat before we left on this journey. All our stomachs were aching. Frustrated, Mama leaned forward with one arm braced on the door, leaned her head onto her forearm and cried.

I will never forget the sad look on her face. It was like she was giving up.

Like she just couldn't fight any longer. I couldn't help but feel sorry for her... and for myself. Suddenly I lifted my small fist and began to bang on the door while salty tears rolled down my cheeks.

They had to be home. They had to let us in. We were all shivering with the cold. White steam spewed out as we breathed into the cold air. If they did not let us in we would all die out here in the bitter cold. My mind swirled into a little boy's dream that an angel would appear and lift all of us out of this misery, for I could see no way out. We were lost and forgotten in a world of the unwanted. Standing there pounding on that green door I saw myself on the edge of a cliff looking down the path of darkness.

There was still no sound from inside the closed and forbidding house.

I pounded on the door again, knowing this was the only hope we had, as a million thoughts crossed my mind. I looked up at my mama. Tears were falling from her eyes, and I could see she was exhausted. Although I was only eight, an instinctive urgency signaled me to take charge. I had to be the one to be strong. Yanking on Mama's ragged coat, I said, "Please, Mama, don't cry. It will be all right." Desperately, I pounded on that closed door.

After a few more loud bangs, the door opened and there stood Freda's husband Shorty, wearing striped pajamas and making a face because he'd been so comfortable in his warm bed. Appearing immensely annoyed by our early intrusion he reluctantly said, "Hi, Nora. What's wrong?"

"Shorty," she said, "I need help. I have no other place to go. The children and I are hungry and cold. Will you help us?"

"Well..." Shorty hesitated, but he didn't have the heart to turn us away. "Come on in."

We enter the front room and stood there in our little group, huddled together, not knowing what to do next. The first thing that caught my eye was a family portrait that showed Mrs. Freda as a somber eight-year-old surrounded by her stepfather, her mother, grandmother, one sister and brother. I remember it clearly for it seemed somehow to remind me of things my Grandma Ayers had said about the whole hopeless history of black Americans.

I looked up at Mama. Her swollen, tear-stained face peered down at me.

"Are my babies hungry?" she asked, hoping to inspire an invitation from Shorty.

"Yes, Mama," I replied. "I am really hungry."

Inez began to cry. Her crying woke TC and he began crying. Before long, everyone was crying. Our commotion aroused Mrs. Freda who appeared from the bedroom wearing a long housecoat.

"Shorty," she called out, "put some more coal on the fire so Nora and the kids can get warm." She brought chairs from the kitchen and placed them near the fire for us. "Tell me what happened, Nora."

Mama told about the rock through the window. "They almost killed my baby."

"My God," Shorty said. "When did this happen? What time?"

"Stay out of this, Shorty." Mrs. Freda motioned him away. "You let me attend Nora and the kids. You go fire up the cook stove and get breakfast started."

While Mama and Mrs. Freda talked, the fire warmed the room rapidly. I felt like I was a thawing iceberg. When we were warm enough, we pulled off the heavy wraps Mama had put us in and tried not to notice the aromas from the kitchen that swirled through the house. Not having had a decent meal in days, my mouth watered as I smelled the bacon frying. Finally Shorty shouted, "Breakfast is ready. Come and get it."

At the table, the only sound was knives, forks and spoons clanging against the plates from the group of hungry eaters. There was eggs and bacon, biscuits and grits splattered with butter. After we'd eaten for a while Mr. Shorty said, "Nora, you look tired."

"I am a little bit, Shorty," she admitted.

"Are you sick?" Shorty always went to the essence.

"No, Shorty. I just feel like crying." And she did, right then and there, in front of us all. She just wept like her heart was breaking. Again, I felt sorry for Mama, and there were tears in my eyes too, but I was too hungry to stop buttering another biscuit and spooning up my grits.

Mama apologized profusely for being so emotional, but Mrs. Freda patted her hand and said, "It's all right, honey. You got good reason." She was a very warmhearted woman and Mama's problems touched her. "But I think it's time we found Led. He's got a responsibility here with his kids. When was the last time you saw him, Nora?"

"Well, he left, around May I think, to go into the Army, you know, but that's when they put him in jail. 'Course I went to visit a few times... then things got real bad with Led gone and Charles went to his daddy's place in June... and then I got sick and all. I guess it about five months... five months at least."

"An' you sure he's out now?"

"Oh, he's out. He just can't come on back to Minden, you know. I guess that's why we got evicted." Mama looked like she was about to cry again.

Shorty scraped out the last of his boiled egg and scrunched the shell down into the egg cup. "Knowin' Led," he said, "he probably hitch hisse'f a ride up to Kincaid. They's a mining company opened a new drift-mouth up there. Deep coal mining near Powellton. I'm gonna find out from the hirin' office if they hired Led."

"Aw, Led could be anywhere in West Virginia. Why would you go up to Kincaid?" Mrs. Freda asked, but Shorty had already left the table. When he got an idea into his head there was no stopping him. He went straight to his bedroom and prepared himself for a trip to Kincaid.

We watched from Mrs. Freda's front windows. Shorty galloped down the hill from the house, stumbling to hold his balance, but he didn't fall. Soon he was out of sight. We knew he was headed for the staging area just beyond Minden's tipple where coal was being loaded into the rail cars. Twice a day the freight cars were loaded with coal and pulled by two enormous coal-burning steam engines moving northeast to Kinkaid and then on toward Charleston and the big cities in the northeast. He'd have to wait patiently for several hours until late afternoon when the freight train would pull away and then he'd hop aboard the moving coal car. Shorty was taking a free ride like a common hobo, braving the chilling winds on that winter afternoon, on his mission to find Led.

Now that Shorty was gone, Mrs. Freda, Mama and we children were alone. It was a strange feeling for me to be in someone else's home. There were no toys around for us to play with, and we didn't know how to keep ourselves busy. We couldn't romp around and play like we'd do at home. Mrs. Freda gave us an old Sears catalog and we passed the time looking through those colorful pages.

That first day, with Shorty off looking for Led, Mrs. Freda appeared not to know what to what to do with herself and her unexpected company. She had spent her whole life working and mostly her only free time had come at the end of the day when she could knit a while or read a book. This kind of leisure, sitting around with no job to go to and with Shorty gone, was unusual for her.

Mrs. Freda and Mama began to talk, and reminisced the past. Even though I was turning pages of the catalog I was listening to them talking. Like many children, Mrs. Freda forgot about having any dreams when she was a child. All she did was wait from one day to the next, praying that the food would last through the week. Her family were sharecroppers from Alabama. They picked cotton for a living. She could not recall ever hearing her parents' talk about having any dreams either, but she sensed that they wanted their children to have a better life than they'd had. Finally she summed up her life as being "really simple." She didn't mean simple as "ordinary," she meant simple as no frills, no extras, only bare necessities. Her mother left her father because he was a hobo, going in and out of jail. For several years, she and her siblings were practically orphans. Consequently, her grandmother had to raise the family. She recalled how they had fished and raised chickens to supplement their meals, saying it was only by the grace of God they all got through that time.

Mrs. Freda made us a good lunch, cold biscuits with peanut butter and jelly, and served a fine dinner that night for Mama and us kids. She made two platters full of fried, batter-dipped fish Shorty'd caught the day before, with baked sweet potatoes, collard greens, sliced tomatoes, Kool-Ade and there was some of her delicious bread pudding for desert. It was a banquet to us.

That night Mama and all us kids slept on a pallet on the floor in the living room near the fire. Mrs. Freda didn't have a whole lot of extra quilts but we all cuddled together and got through the night. At least we didn't have to worry about a rock slamming through the front window.

The next day the air was still cold and breezy. Mrs. Freda made us breakfast, as good as the first one we'd so enjoyed. We did say thanks to her, but it didn't hardly seem enough. I knew we all would be starving and out in the freezing cold if she hadn't been kind-hearted enough to take us in. Mrs. Freda was a wonderful lady giving us all the comforts she could afford. She was feeding us delicious meals and she'd push those dimples in her cheek when she'd smile that wide smile of hers and say, "Go on, honey. Take a little more. I goin' to fatten you all up a bit." But Mrs. Freda herself, being a bit on the chubby side, ate sparingly I noticed.

After breakfast Mama and Mrs. Freda decided that we needed more groceries. After all, there were more mouths to feed. Moreover, they needed to arrive at the store early to get their portion of rationed meat, coffee, milk and sugar. I was left to baby-sit my two sisters and TC who was one-and-a-half. He still took a bottle and ate soft foods. Marguerite was six and Inez, barely a year older than TC, only two-and-a-half. Since there were no toys, Mama gave us some pencils and another catalog to finger through and draw on. Looking through those toy-saturated pages kept us dreaming for hours.

CHAPTER 37
Led's Back... We Move To Powellton

It was late in the evening when Shorty arrived. He had found Led, and they had been drinking together. The smell of whiskey filled the room when they walked into the house, and I still remember the intense feeling of gratitude that surged up in me when I saw him, half drunk as he was, coming through the door. It was so deep, so powerful it was almost painful.

Everyone seemed elated that Shorty had found Led, although the greeting between him and Mama was not a happy one. Right away Led said that Shorty had filled him in on the rock throwing incident and the eviction and all.

"Those goddam bastards couldn't wait one damn day, could they?" Led said, pulling up his chair by the fire. "They gonna make damn sure I know me and my family ain't welcome in Minden no more. Those stupid fuck-heads could'a killed my kid with that fuckin' rock." His eyes glittered wickedly in the firelight and I could see the revenge he was thinking of dancing like twin red devils in his eyes.

Mama didn't have much to say once Led showed up. She seemed detached and too calm, like a landscape after the rain when the thunder isn't done yet. They were acting very cold to each other and there was no show of affection, except in his greeting to Margaret. I could sense that trouble lay ahead, but I didn't want to think about that. In my young mind, my step-father Led always meant fried chicken with biscuits and gravy, his favorite down-home meal, and being with him meant eating again, and some kind of survival. In spite of his moodiness and his flashes of mean temper there was always a sense of security for me when he was with us and working regular. Without Led all we had was hardship and heartaches and near starvation.

I knew that as a family, our lives were very different from other families I saw around me. We were continuously moving from one camp to another and constantly without food to eat. Other children my age were not going through this kind of misery. That evening, in Mrs. Freda's house, I realized for the first time just how different our family was. I didn't know the word "dysfunctional" then, but that's what we were, and there was no one I could turn to for help.

The adults stayed up late that night, talking and drinking. From our floor pallet I watched Mama, holding TC in her arms, pour herself a drink from Led's bottle. I wasn't surprised. I just lay back and closed my eyes and knew what was coming. I had never believed Mama's promise to stop drinking. She'd had a bottle of white lightning in her hand three days after she'd gotten up from her sickbed. I hated these impromptu parties because I knew if Mama was drinking, and she'd already started, she would become very argumentative and it would end up in a nasty verbal fight with Led like it always did.

Led had settled back now and was explaining his being away for so long. After they let him out of jail, he reminded us, he could not come back to Minden — that was a condition of his release — so he'd gone off hoboing throughout the South, looking for his dad, Huddie Leadbelly. He said he went to Mooringsport, Louisiana, only to learn that Huddie was in prison for killing a man. Led laughed when he told that. "Like father, like son," he said, referring to the rumors about himself, since he had been accused of having killed men too. Anyway, Led claimed he went on looking for his dad. Huddie, a well-known blues singer, song writer and musician, also had a reputation for being a two-time murderer who traveled from town to town to sing and drink between murders. Of course, this kind of exaggerated talk made Leadbelly more interesting to his white audiences... much like the wildest animal in the zoo draws the largest crowd to his cage. Huddie seemed to enjoy being known as an uncivilized brute who had no respect for human life. At times, Led said, white audiences were actually afraid of Leadbelly. It was clear that Led himself took pride in his father's legend.

Anyway, Led's travels had brought him back to West Virginia and he finally found a job in Powellton, a small mining camp settlement ten miles southwest of Montgomery. The superintendent of that camp made arrangements for Led to sleep and eat at a boarding house that had been established for black miners. Two weeks passed before the company rented a separate house to Led down in the deepest part of Powellton Hollow.

I slipped off to sleep, happy that Led had been found, and wondering

what life was going to be like when we got to Powellton Hollow... for already
I knew that's where we were heading.

The late Fall mornings in Minden were always cold and uncomfortably-
damp in the low hollows where Mrs. Freda's house lay. Generally, it was the
afternoon warmth that heated the air as the sun rose higher in the sky. At that
time of year the weather changed only when a winter storm passed over,
leaving the ground frosted and the foliage with icicles. The rest of the day
would be lost in a freezing mist. You could usually count of those storms to
come at least once a week from October to February. Of course, the miners
were always glad to have cooler weather because that meant that deep in the
mines the working conditions were pleasant.

Just after breakfast there had been no knock on the door, but Shorty wasn't
surprised when he looked up and saw a square-jawed man standing there.
Pegleg Bates was a large-chested man, tall and wide as a barrel keg, who
walked with a noticeable limp. He dwarfed Shorty in appearance. The little
yellow book Pegleg pulled from his pocket was the tell-tale sign of a numbers
runner. Pegleg was a shady character who enjoyed pimping women, but he
knew his place around decent folks and mostly stayed in it. Well dressed, in
a flashy kind of way, he had a broad smile which could distract you from his
extremely cold eyes.

Mama blurted out, "525 is the number for tomorrow."

Mrs. Freda called from the kitchen, "367 is mine!"

"How much you puttin' on these numbers?" Pegleg's gravel voice came
from the doorway.

"Twenty-fi' cents." Mrs. Freda came with the money. "Here's a quarter
for me and a quarter for Nora."

Pegleg collected the money, including another quarter for Shorty's 377
lucky number. "Okay. See y'all tomorrow," Pegleg growled, leaving quickly.
Playing the numbers was big business in mining camps, especially among
black folks. The number's racket gave a glimmer of hope to those with a few
quarters to throw down and a dream of hitting a big score. Men like Pegleg,
who ran the game and collected the money, got wealthy off the players. All
the players got out of it was a lift, and then a let down, but they still enjoyed
the game.

Meanwhile, the grownups sitting around the fire began talking about
Pegleg's routes. One said he was a quick-tempered gambling man, who bluffed
his opponents in most poker games. Somebody else claimed Pegleg was

nothing but a fancy pimp who kept a bevy of young girls in the houses he rented, or owned — whorehouses as they were called — in several different mining camps to service the miners. He drove around from camp to camp in his brand-new Packard, taking care of business and collecting the girls' money. Each mining camp had its pimps; but a man like Pegleg would pimp two or three or more camps.

Finally they all ironed out their differences of opinion on what Pegleg Bates' exact role was, and decided that since he traveled from camp to camp like he did, it would be a good idea to ask him to carry Led and Mama and us to the mining camp of Powellton. He'd be going there in his new car anyway.

The day wasted away in some drinking and mostly idle conversation. Darkness soon cascaded upon that tiny one-bedroom house. Finally, everyone was asleep except TC and me. The sound of him sucking on his bottle echoed through the night. I laid awake thinking about our move to Powellton. I could hardly wait for the coming day.

Soon daybreak peeped over the mountain as the sun began rising. The grownups began stirring about. I lay on the makeshift pallet, half-asleep, listening to the sounds of the morning. Led cleaned the dead coal-cinders from the fireplace and stirred the firebox with a long iron poker. He finally awakened some glowing embers and in a little while flames began to warm the room. Shorty was in the kitchen starting a fire in the cooking stove, and the smell of ham soon filled the little house. He was making a breakfast of eggs, grits, biscuits, ham and cheese and coffee. Even the aroma of the perking coffee made me hungry, although I was too young to enjoy it like the adults did.

Soon everyone was up and breakfast was ready. I felt jubilant in a way because I had a feeling Pegleg would agree to helping us move to Powellton. He wouldn't do it for nothing, but I was pretty sure he'd do it. Inside me was this wild, restless urge to get away from Minden, away from whoever it was had thrown that rock, get a new start somewhere with Led back home again.

Although I was thankful that Mrs. Freda, and Shorty took us in when we had on other place to go, I still had a terrible unhappiness in my heart, and a dark feeling in my soul…which was driving me to think ugly things about grownups, especially since I'd overheard the discussion about Pegleg and him pimping with those young girls.

It was midmorning when someone knocked at the door. Expecting Pegleg, Shorty rushed over. He was always expecting good news about his number, hoping it was his lucky 377 that hit.

"Who's there?"

"The one-two-three man," answered Pegleg, signaling that indeed it was the numbers runner. Shorty opened up and there was Pegleg, a giant of a man, tall and broad as the door.

"How much I win?" Shorty enthused, assuming he was a winner.

"Not your lucky day, Shorty. Rubin hit the number. Won $500 bucks."

"Damn! I can never win a goddam thing!" blurted Shorty. "I been playin' for…"

"Oh, Mr. Bates," Mrs. Freda interrupted Shorty. "We all been wondering if you would help us out and move Led and Elnora and the children to Powellton Hollow. They have a new place to live."

"Powellton Hollow?" Pegleg repeated, like he was weighing whether or not he liked the idea of Led being in one of "his" towns.

"Yes, Powellton Hollow," Led said forcefully, like he was really asking "You givin' me a hard time?"

"How much you willin' to pay?"

"How much you charge?" Mama spoke up.

"I guess five dollars is a fair price." Nobody objected. "When you want to leave?"

"How about this evening?" Led asked, in a less aggressive tone.

"Okay. I'll be back here around 4:30. You all be ready to go," Pegleg barked.

Mama nodded. "We'll be waiting for you."

With that settled, Pegleg opened the front door to depart when Shorty called out, "Hold on. You didn't take my number."

"Oh, I'm sorry, Shorty. How much you putting on your favorite 377 today?"

"I'm puttin' down a quarter. I feel lucky."

"You always feel lucky." Pegleg hurriedly wrote the numbers in his book and ripped out a yellow copy for Shorty. "Anybody else?"

Mrs. Freda said she was broke, and, of course, Led and Mama were going to Powellton anyway.

After Pegleg left, the grownups began to drink the last of the moonshine that had suddenly appeared. I believe the joy exhibited by Shorty and Mrs. Freda was a kind of a secret celebration because we were soon leaving their tiny little house. They had been very good to us, but I'm sure our family caused them considerable hardship.

Mama did not have very much to pack up. Again she threw the few items we had in a bed spread, then she folded up the ends and tied them together. That was it. We were ready to go.

As the day went on, Mama and Led were still not talking to each other very much. They did not even have the usual eye-to-eye contact between them. It reminded me of the on-going anger that used to erupt like a volcano in our Minden shanty, and even though they'd been apart for several months, it was still there, smoldering between them and ready to catch fire any minute. I knew something was wrong and I dreaded what I feared was going to happen between them. I'd never had this strange sensation before, and being only a child, there was no way I could explain or discuss it with anyone else in that house. No one would understand the strong feelings that were prodding me with anxiety. I didn't know how to express the danger I sensed hanging over my parents, and it made me feel like a trapped animal.

The late afternoon passed slowly as I sat waiting for Pegleg to come and take us away. Uneasiness hung over all of us and the grownups had already started drinking to calm their restless nerves. Fortunately, Mrs. Freda had thoughtfully prepared a food box for us. She fixed several peanut butter and jelly sandwiches and red beans with rice. She poured the seasoned beans and rice into a quart fruit jar and then placed it all in a box. Watching her in the kitchen reminded me of some of the stolen lunch buckets Novello had stolen from the miners a few months earlier when I'd played lookout.

At a quarter after four, knocks hit the door like a jazzy drum beat. Half drunk now, Led wobbled to the door and opened it without first asking who was there. Even I knew better than to do that. Opening the door to anyone without saying "Who is it?" is not a good habit in any West Virginia coal mining community. State Police and mining officials periodically raid houses looking for racketeers, bootleggers and number runners. Fortunately, it was Pegleg. He was right on time, a common trait of numbers runners who had many places to go and many quarters to remove from the seedy pockets of "lucky" prospective winners.

"You ready?" he asked with no greeting or other salutation.

"They ready!" Mrs. Freda said, unable to disguise the joy in her voice.

Everybody went through the usual ritual of thank yous, goodbye's, take care and hope to see you soon, and all that, but it was the same old phony words used by people who are really glad to be getting rid of you.

In minutes, Led and Mama and us kids were all sitting in Pegleg's brand new tank of a car, a spiffy 1942 Packard. Us kids and Mama were packed in the back seat like a cargo of slaves. Led was up front with Pegleg. As we pulled away, Shorty and Mrs. Freda stood on their porch, high on the hill, waving in the chilly air. Everyone bade each other a last good-by with effusive formality. The car moved onto the two-lane highway, and I leaned back to watch the mountain ridge and the clouds vanish as darkness fell.

The trip was not a quiet one. Led and Mama were in a continuous argument about past problems, some of which I had never heard before. They seemed to forget all about us kids listening to them and started accusing each other in harsh words of being unfaithful.

"You think I believe you sittin' home all by yourself while I in that jail cell?" Led snarled.

Mama came right back at him with, "And the minute they let you out, I guess you got in touch with me right away. Huh? Right. You think I believe you were all this time lookin' for some job? Just holdin' on, waiting to see me?" She forced an ugly-sounding laugh. "You took off running for the nearest piece you could find wearin' a skirt."

"Don't start up with me on that, Nora. You the *last* one to talk to me about shit like that."

"I was home," Mama said, but the lie was in her voice. "Charles here knows I was home. He can tell you…"

"Don't bring that young boy into this mess. He don't know squat about what we're.."

"Sure he does. Charles, tell Led I was home."

I didn't answer, just kept staring out the window.

"Tell him!"

"Nora, you leave that boy alone. It's me you're talking to. Charles, you mind your own damn business and stay out of…"

"Don't talk to my boy that way…"

And the bickering just went on and on, about stuff that happened years ago, especially before Inez was born, and all kinds of mean talk. I kept my head turned away and said nothing. Even Pegleg tried a couple of times to stop the argument, but they ignored him. His voice betrayed his anger and impatience, but he knew Led's vicious reputation so he just drove on in silence. Soon I drifted off to sleep, not knowing what to expect. It seems to me that there was no end to the darkness of the path we were traveling.

It was still dark, around four a.m., when we reached Powellton. As we entered the Hollow, Led coached Pegleg about where the house was located. Just before we crossed a one-lane bridge to the Hollow, we passed the Mining

Community township. It was a lonesome little place with four street lights, and a narrow paved road flanked by company houses that were surrounded by white-washed fences. The mining company store stood bleak against the tall, dark mountain range. An old railroad coach-car, which had been converted into a snack bar where miners and their families hung out, sat on the hillside just above the company store. It was open to serve the miners who kept the mines going twenty-four hours a day.

Once we had crossed the bridge, I automatically knew we were in the Hollow because the conditions appeared so lifeless, so dark and deserted, so worn down and lived out. Typical of all coal mining communities of that time the Hollow was where the black folks lived. On our side of the bridge there were no street lights and no paved roads, no stores, no conveniences of any kind. Just shacks and tumbled down houses and beat-up old cars and chimneys blowing out black coal-smoke.

Finally we reach the place they'd rented to Led. It was a two-story building that had four, separate family apartments. From the outside it looked like one of the cleanest places we had ever rented so far. Pegleg stopped the car and we all got out. Led grabbed up Mama's bedspread carryall. Almost immediately Pegleg pulled away. He never said "goodbye," and he never looked back. His car disappeared into the mist.

Standing in the dirt road I looked up at the house. The windows were dark and without curtains. I mounted the wooden steps leading up to the second floor behind Led. Our apartment was upstairs on the right. He tried the front door, found a key and unlocked it and we all entered the apartment. The dwelling was owned by the Mining Company, and as usual, the interior was far from well kept. Roaches crawled about and we could hear what sounded like huge rats squeaking and scampering in the walls. Our footsteps, and TC's whining, resounded in the dark rooms. Led shouted, "Hello?" as if he expected someone to be there, but the only answer was a broken echo. The rooms were almost bare. The previous tenants had removed almost everything of use that was removable. They'd only left an old, heavy oak table and four dilapidated chairs, an old fashioned iron bedstead in one room, a stained mattress sprawled on the floor in another.

An antiquated stove made of solid iron stood in the small kitchen where a half-size couch bed had been shoved against one wall. I was still glad to be in our own place. Being with Mrs. Freda had been what Mama called a "Godsend," but it was better still to have your own.

We slowly explored the apartment. Led tramped on through the rooms saying, "Hello?" and "Is anybody here?" Mama looked for some light switches, but she couldn't find one. Led manage to find one switch, but all I could hear was a "click," "click." The electricity was not on. The walls of the small kitchen were covered with peeling wallpaper that hung loose from the ceiling. Then I found the bathroom. There was a sink with running water and an inside toilet. I had never seen a water commode already installed. The instant water taps, the magic of bright, odorless electric lights were exciting novelties and a welcome sight to me, especially since I'd lived most of my young life using candles and inhaling the smell of kerosene lamps.

The kitchen windows faced the dirt road. In the kitchen pantry we found some cornmeal, some cans of sardines, garlic, a half-full jar of jelly, potatoes that had started to sprout, and a bottle of bootleg whiskey. There was a fireplace in each bed room, but the house was supposed to be centrally heated. It was cold in the rooms because they had not turned on the heat for our particular apartment. We picked the largest bedroom to settle in and pulled down the window shade since it wasn't yet dawn. Led started a fire in the fireplace and we began to eat the peanut butter and jelly sandwiches Mrs. Freda had made for us. However, there were no spoons to use for eating the rice and red beans, so Mama used a butter knife to dip into the jar and shovel the rice and beans into our mouths.

The atmosphere of that bedroom was ghostlike and enchanted from the firelight. Inez and Marguerite were a little afraid of the tall, dark shadows playing over the walls like spirits from some tormented world... and even I found them evil-looking and scary, but that was probably just my own, worried and fearful imagination. Finally, the sun came up enough to take the chill out of the roof and the room warmed. Mama urged us to sleep.

CHAPTER 38
School Again

The next day when Mama woke us, I took a good look around the place. In our apartment the floors were hardwood and we had a long porch to play on. Tall mountains stood to the east of the building. On the west was a dirt road, and just to the west of that was a one-room school surrounded by a whitewashed fence. Behind the school was a wide creek which could have looked pretty if it weren't for the man-made slate dump towering gray and ugly beside it.

Remembering her experience with the truant officer in Minden, Mama wasted no time enrolling Marguerite and me in grade school. Like most kids, I had some fear and anxiety about starting another new school. For Marguerite, who had turned six last April, it would be her first experience. The teacher's name was Mrs. Grace and she made us feel welcome.

One significant thing I remember about Mrs. Grace is that she required each student to bring a spoon to school. Every morning during school days the children would line-up and march past Mrs. Grace's desk where she would pour out a spoonful of vitamin syrup for each child. It was always very embarrassing for me and Marguerite because we were the only kids in class who did not bring a teaspoon to school. We could not afford one. But that was not the only thing we could not afford. Sometimes, especially when Led was not working at the mines regularly, we didn't have money for lunch. Mrs. Grace proved to be a very kind-hearted lady, because on the days we did not have a lunch, she would give Marguerite and me her lunch to share. I remember eating those lunches, her lunches, and I remember feeling bad about taking it from her. My conscience told me she was being deprived for me and my sister's sake, and it made me feel guilty, but my hungry belly would not allow me the pride of refusing those thick, delicious sandwiches.

Knowing how good her sandwiches were, I admit there were times I was tempted to lie about not having my own lunch because those sandwiches she brought flashed memorably in my mind. I didn't, but I wanted to.

Meanwhile, the atmosphere at home was getting worse. It seemed like every day Marguerite and I came home from school to hear loud voices and our house in frightening disarray. There were endless arguments going on between Led and Mama and both of them were drinking heavily.

One weekend, around midday, Mama and Led had a terrible confrontation. All I know is that they were arguing and Mama screamed out to Led, "I can't help it if she is not yours!" That prompted my curiosity as to what, or who, Mama was talking about.

"You're a no-good woman," Led shot back, and his black face grew pale. He was in one of his ugly moods and I knew to stay far away from him. I kept Marguerite and Inez and even TC with me in another room. But I still could hear Mama and Led shouting at each other.

Then, for about an hour or so Led just sat in the chair, staring off into space, drinking steadily. Then he spoke up. "Nora, tell me..." He began grinding his teeth like he always did when he was about to explode.

"Led, please. The children..."

My heart sank. It was coming. Any second now. That volcanic explosion. I pleaded a little prayer that they would stop fighting and tiptoed to the door to hear more.

Led saw me and shouted, "Get the hell out of here, boy!"

I ran to the porch. Then I heard Mama scream, "Don't you talk to my child that way!"

Their voices were loud and heated. Suddenly I heard furniture falling over and a piercing scream. Rushing back into the room, I found Mama lying on the floor in the living room, blood trickling from the corners of her mouth, her eyes puffed, her face bruised. She thrashed wildly back and forth, screaming uncontrollably, catching her breath, then sobbing and screaming again.

Led had one, long, bleeding gash on his face. Mama had torn his shirt and he was slumped on one of the wooden chairs in the kitchen, his eyes glassy, and the bottles of liquor were sitting on the floor next to his chair. He moaned to himself, "Goddam lyin' arrogant bitch!"

My emotions raged high and I could barely restrain myself from leaping on him like a mad demon to choke and hurt him in any way I could. I wanted to gouge out his eyes and cut off his breath. I knew better than to actually attack him, but that's when the fires of hate began burning in my eyes every time I looked at his mean, surly face. If I'd had any weapon in my hand I'm not sure if I would have been able to stop myself from trying to kill him. My heart was pounding with the cry of vengeance. All I wanted at that moment was the exquisite pleasure of blowing his damn brains out for beating my mama. I spent the remainder of the day running between the living room, where my mama lay weeping and moaning on the floor, the kitchen where Led sat staring blindly at the wall and drinking, and the rear bedroom where my two sisters and little brother were sitting on the old stained mattress, frightened and crying and hungry. I gave them some crackers I found in the cupboard, but my hands were trembling so hard I kept crumbling them before I could get them out of the box. I went and got a wet rag to clean up the crumbs because I didn't want the rats to come sniffing around us in the dark. It took a long time for me to get calmed down that afternoon. I don't think Led had any idea how much I wanted to kill him.

In our fragmented home there was little love or affection shown by anyone. Led was only working three nights a week at the mine, and that wasn't enough to buy food and pay our rent. He began drinking more and more. Mama couldn't take his bad mouth and his meanness, and she began leaving the house and staying away for hours. By the time she'd come home she was already drunk, but she'd start drinking again.

I opened cans and fixed whatever I could for us kids to eat, because neither one of the adults knew what day it was or what was going on around them. Mama would get flushed and angry at the sight of us, so I kept Marguerite and Inez out of her way. In her drunken stupor she'd sit on the wooden kitchen chair, sprawled and sloppy looking, her hair undone and uncombed, and ramble on until all hours, talking to herself. She was incapable of staying on a single subject for more than one minute, veering off into her past, ranting on about men — some names I'd never heard before — who had wronged her, lied to her, cheated and mistreated her. She cursed them all, mainly Led. And then she began crying about Inez. "Poor little thing," she said, her eyes pouring tears. I didn't know what she was talking about... until later when I began putting things together about her past.

Then on a Monday afternoon, Mama dressed Inez in her warm clothes and took her to stay with some lady who lived in the lower Hollow. That's when I learned that Led was not the biological father of Inez. He was the biological father of Marguerite and TC, but not Inez Interested, because it seemed a curious thing to me, I began putting facts together. Mama and Led had been together since 1935 when they'd taken off to get married and left me with Mert and Kemp. I knew that because I was born early in 1934 and Mert and Mama always talked about how Mama met Led when I was only one year old. Marguerite was born in April of 1936, and they'd been together for all that time. Then Led went off on the road looking for work. That's when we were all starving, and he came on home with BigFeet and we had that fish fry party where those people got killed and the sheriff came, and Led and that man, Crooks, had that knife fight. And Led went to jail for cutting Uncle Henry. Inez was born in July of 1940. Then Led got out of jail again and TC was born in May of 1941. And yet Led was not the father of Inez? I was too innocent to see the significance of Mama being gone all those hungry times and Led off in another part of the country looking for work to connect it with nine months before Inez's birth. I don't know how Led learned that Inez was not his own child, but during one of Mama's wild rages she could have unintentionally told him the truth. I was glad I was the only one among us kids who had even a shallow idea about what had gone on with our parents. Because I kept them out of the way most of the time, the younger ones seemed to be oblivious of the alcoholic horrors going on around them in our household.

CHAPTER 39
Lloyd Robinson... A Savior And A Sad Memory

The situation became so bad at home that I began to feel somehow I had become the head of the household. Day after day we were at home alone and had to fend for ourselves. Led and Mama seemed to have forgotten us. There wasn't any food in the house to eat, not even soap for bathing. Marguerite and I were absent from school days on end. We got up a few times and dressed for school but our clothes were so dirty, we took them off and stayed home. Since there was no one else, I had to go out looking for food for Marguerite and me and milk for TC. We missed little Inez, but it was easier having only three of us to feed. From one apartment to another and house to house I went begging for food. It was unbelievable to me that I was frequently turned away with a slur or an angry curse.

One chill winter evening, I sat on a bench along the outside fence waiting for one of our parents to come home as we children hadn't eaten in two days. For a time I simply sat with knees drawn up under my chin, not thinking about anything specifically. I sat there for a least three hours waiting in vain, going back into the house every once in a while to check on TC and Marguerite. When TC cried, Marguerite would struggle to hold him, or she'd give him a bottle with sugar water in it. Seeing that they were all right I rushed outside again. Finally, the lowering sun glowed like a distant, unreachable orange, and again I felt betrayed by my parents.

There was a young black man who lived deeper in the Hollow than we did who passed our place twice a day, going and coming back from work. His name was Lloyd Robinson. The kids called him Mr. Lloyd. Mr. Lloyd worked with electricity for the mining company. He was tall, intelligent and articulate. He had a very pretty wife and two young children. A polite person, he always spoke very gently to us children whenever he saw us as he walked past our house.

Just as I was about to give up and suffer a sleepless night from the torment of hunger, Mr. Lloyd passed our place. He said, "Hi, son," in his pleasant, low-keyed voice.

"Mr. Lloyd, would you give me something to eat, please?" I begged.

He looked astonished. His mouth opened wide as if he could not believe what he had just heard. But I must have convinced him for there was agony and true anguish in my voice.

"Why, sure, son." He stopped and looked carefully at me. "Where are your parents?"

"I don't know."

"Where do you live?"

"Upstairs," I said, pointing in the direction of our apartment.

"Take me there." He seemed to be angry and yet bewildered.

"All right." I got up from my bench dispiritedly and led the way. So hungry I couldn't think straight, I figured I'd probably made a mistake. Maybe he would tell my parents that I was out begging for food. Confused and starving, I just wanted to break down and cry.

We reached our place and I opened the door. Mr. Lloyd walked in and seemed shocked at the mess and the empty bottles piled in the room and the rank smell in the place from TC not being attended to properly.

"Stay here, young man. I will be right back."

For some reason I felt he was going to let us down. Hungry and too weak to run after him, I dropped down on the floor and just let the tears roll from my eyes. If he didn't help us then there was no one else to turn to. The taste of salt coated my lips as the tears flooded down, but I didn't want Marguerite to see me crying so I hid my face in my arms. I believed we had come to the end. Though my stomach growled with hunger, I dared not let out a sound.

Suddenly I heard a soft knock on the door. Immediately, I was relieved because some inner telepathy told me something good was coming. I hurried to the door and unlocked the latch. There stood Mr. Lloyd and his wife with boxes of food and powered milk. My eyes lit up and opened wide. My mouth began to water. There is no way to say how happy I was to see these people at our door. They'd brought us something to eat and it smelled like heaven. There was fried chicken, biscuits, home made jelly and peach preserves, powdered milk and chocolate cake. How could I ever forget that meal!

Mr. Lloyd's wife's name was Charlotte. She took TC into her arms and cuddled him and kissed Marguerite on the cheeks. She washed out the nursing bottle and prepared powered milk for TC. After they had both been fed, she gave Marguerite and TC a bath.

Before that evening ended we had all eaten a big meal, had a hot bath and been readied for bed. Mr. Lloyd and Mrs. Charlotte left us then with a promise to come back and check on us.

It's hard for me to say this, but even though I loved my mama in spite of everything, that night I wished with all my heart that the Robinson's were my parents.

The weeks passed and the situation between Led and Mama grew more bitter and more explosive. They were barley speaking to each other, but suddenly I noticed a change. He and Mama started being more careful about us kids... remembering to feed us most nights and thinking about us having clean clothes; trying to be more of a parent. I believe their drunken and neglectful behavior toward us children — especially since I had gone out begging for food so many times — had finally gotten neighbors and townfolks so outraged that the community leaders strongly chastised them and shamed them for leaving us like they had. Still, in spite of their being more careful with us, there was angry talk and streams of profanity and cursing in our house as they barely spoke a civil word to each other. Through all that, Led was noticeably warm and tender to TC and Marguerite, but his attitude toward me was growing more contemptuous. I'm sure, thinking back on it now, he saw the blazing hatred in my eyes that had been there ever since he'd beat up my mama. I know it showed every time I looked at him, but I couldn't hide it.

Both Led and Mama kept on drinking whiskey every day. It seemed like Mama had totally forgotten how the whiskey had almost killed her only a few months ago, or if she remembered she just didn't care that much about living. Either way, she made sure she got intoxicated almost daily. Led didn't drink when the mining company scheduled him to work, but Mama had no such restriction. As parents, they were still embarrassing and irresponsible. They were like little kids who were unaware of the seriousness of life, doing things that even I knew were self-destructive and hurtful, and I was only eight. During that time I saw Mr. Lloyd as often as possible. His son was two years younger than me, therefore we had something in common. We two boys built go-carts and rode them down the hills, we made sling-shots, even some bows and arrows, and managed to harass the birds. The creek that ran through the community always harbored ducks, and we often saw muskrats along the creek bank.

It was Mr. Lloyd who took me and Marguerite, along with his kids, to our first motion picture show. It was a war movie and William Bendix was one of the stars. The movie fascinated me, and not understanding the technology, I remember thinking that the actors were actually behind the movie screen performing. Another time Mr. Lloyd took us to see a Western where, for the first time, I saw famous cowboys such as Tom Mix and Hoot Gibson.

In late November, fog poured in from over the mountains. The day was gloomy and dark and the wind whipped icily off the wide creek. Rains drizzled heavily and milky smoke from the nearby damp slate dumps, wrapped the community in an eerie white winding-sheet. Finally, the drizzling rain swirled into sleet, and then icicles hung motionlessly from naked trees. As the wind rose, it became an intense storm that ripped through Powellton like a howling freight train. Trees fell across power lines knocking out electricity, leaving the Hollow in darkness. Realizing the chaos that the lack of electricity in Powellton was causing, Mr. Lloyd, being the good Samaritan he was, donned his jacket and gathered his tools and went outside to see if he could restore the electric power. As he approached the downed power lines, believing them to be dead, something terrible happened. The downed lines were still alive and Mr. Lloyd was electrocuted on the spot.

The whole community was stunned and could hardly believe what had happened to such a good man; a man who had worked so hard to help his community. When I heard the news, I was plunged into deep shock. Life is habitually lived, especially by the very young, with the feeling that it will go on indefinitely, without end. A person's death, especially someone extraordinarily humble and kind as Mr. Lloyd, destroyed my feelings of immortality very quickly and made me see how vulnerable we humans are. Never in this world had I ever imagined that anything bad could happen to that good, loving man. I was overcome with sadness, and could hardly fight the deep depression that gripped me on hearing the news.

There was wake for Mr. Lloyd. Most everybody in the community came to view his body and pay their last respects. I didn't get to go to his funeral, and I'm not sure I would have wanted to if I had been asked. I was still having trouble thinking of him as dead. I kept looking to see him come walking up the road at his usual time after work... knowing full well what being dead meant, but not able to accept it. At our church the Reverend Green spoke eloquently.

"Here was a man who gave of himself without a fee, gave willingly to try to help others without asking "What's in it for me?" When the need arises, there are those who step forward and give their best. Brother Lloyd was one of those. We could depend on Brother Lloyd, depend on his love, his ability to share with others, until the very end." I knew exactly what the Reverend meant when he closed with the words, "A giant oak has fallen at this hour." Mr. Lloyd was that protective oak to me, sheltering, comforting, nurturing, and strong. He was even more than that, he was a savior who had stepped in when I was at the end of my ability to cope. I vowed, as I sat in that church with hot tears streaming down my face, that I would never forget his generous and loving deeds and his kindness to me.

Mrs. Charlotte and her children went home after the funeral, pulled down the shades in their house and had a good long cry together, and a few days later they moved away from Powellton Hollow. Long after he was buried over in Montgomery, I found myself sitting out front of our building on that little bench where I first met him, looking down that road, and then I'd remember Mr. Lloyd wouldn't be coming by after work any more. It still hurt, remembering he was dead.

CHAPTER 40
An Ovation… And A Broken Jaw

Thanksgiving came and went without celebration, since the cold attitude and the sharp hatefulness between Mama and Led had not changed. To hurt Mama and me as much as he could without physically attacking us, Led had become a sadistic and cruel, devil-of-a-man. To show Mama and me his contempt, on Thanksgiving Day he purposely brought home just enough food to feed Marguerite and TC, leaving Mama and me to go hungry.

From that moment on, my hopes and dreams were centered only on getting from day to day without being hungry. At home the atmosphere was tense and crackling with anger in the air. The two grownups were psychologically attacking each other every way they could and anyone could see there was no love between them.

During these sad times school was a terrible struggle for me. Without anyone at home to help with my homework, plus the fact that I missed so many school days, I was always lost as far as what was going on in my class group. Naturally, the class room became like a prison to me and a place of constant shame and humiliation for I could not read well, I could not answer Mrs. Grace's questions on the work book, and I was having trouble with my handwriting. The only two things I grasped was music and arithmetic. Those two positive and dependable things I could understand.

As I watched the boys playing games in the school yard and I was deeply hurt when they did not include me. Despite my urging for acceptance, they ignored my sister and me. When the little girls played, they would not include Marguerite. I remember seeing her stand a distance away from the group, watching them. That poor little child was forever sucking her thumb, probably to help ward off her constant hunger pangs, and weaving her hand between her legs as if she had the urge to urinate.

One afternoon, Mrs. Grace uncovered an upright piano that stood half-hidden in a corner of the classroom. My eyes grew large and my heart pounded heavily when I saw it. I knew if I had a chance to play that piano the other children would begin to like me. I was confident that there was no other kid in our classroom who had the talent, or the passion for music, that I did.

"All right, children," Mrs. Grace announced. "This afternoon we are going to have a talent show. Everyone who wants to participate should come to the front of the class and do so."

"Can I go first?" a girl named Shirley asked.

"Of course you can, Shirley. What are you going to do for us today?"

"I will sing 'Twinkle Twinkle Little Star.' "

"All right, young lady. I will accompany you on the piano."

When Shirley finished her song, the teacher asked, "Who wants to be next, children? Please raise your hand."

I quickly raised by hand. "I will, Mrs. Grace."

"Why, Charles," she said with a surprised look. "What can you do?"

"I play the piano," I said with no further explanation.

"Oh?" she said suspiciously. And then she did something I thought was strangely prejudice. She turned to the student body and asked, "Has anyone ever heard Charles play the piano?"

Most of the students looked surprised at hearing my claim. They turned their heads back and forth, indicating "No."

"All right then, Charles. Come on up here and play the piano for us." Then she abruptly asked, "What are you going to play?"

"'Pine Top Boogie Woogie.'" I nervously rose from my desk and made my way to the piano. My hands were shaking, but I managed to get started. In a little while I could hear feet tapping to my beat. It appeared that everyone was enjoying my rendition of that old standard.

When I finished playing, everyone gave a thunderous ovation. The children clapped their hands for five full minutes. I never felt so pleased and happy in my entire young life. That was a supreme moment of satisfaction for me.

Mrs. Grace called for more volunteers... but there were none, so Mrs. Grace spent about a half-hour discussing the life of a great military musician who was currently a prisoner of the Japanese in the islands of the Philippines... a black American named Walter Loving.

After telling of his rise through the ranks during his three separate enlistments, she described what happened one night at the St. Louis Exposition in May of 1904.

"It was a warm spring evening that year, but the men of the Philippine Constabulary Band — of which Walter Loving was the revered conductor — walked on stage dressed in full khaki and red uniforms. They strutted proudly in true military style to their places, very much aware that they were entering competition with the world's best bands. On a cue, the men sat and immediately assumed the concert posture, poised in readiness and awaiting the conductor's signal. On stage walked a handsome black American man, six feet one inch tall and resplendent in his white conductor's uniform. After acknowledging the audience, he turned to his musicians and raised his baton in preparation for the first piece. As he gave the downbeat for the opening strains of Rossini's "William Tell Overture," the electric power snapped, plunging the exposition grounds into total darkness.

Suspicion flashed through the audience, sitting in the dark, that someone purposely cut the electric power to sabotage the performance of Walter Loving and his Philippine group. However, Walter paused only to knot a white handkerchief to the tip of his baton. Then he went on to lead his band through piece after piece, until the entire program that they had planned was finished. It lasted an hour, and the musicians did not miss a note. When the lights came on again, the Philippine Constabulary Band had established world celebrity status for itself. The highlight of the entire concert was that unforgettable performance. In total darkness, the band was soundly applauded for their musicianship, their extraordinary ability to play from memory, and for their success in capturing the subtleties of each composer. Walter Loving became known as one of the world's great band conductors.

"Sadly," Mrs. Grace continued, "at this very moment Walter Loving and his wife, Edith, are both trapped in the Philippines. Reportedly, they are prisoners of Japanese soldiers. We all pray that Mr. Loving and his wife will return safely to America."

With a wave of her hand she dismissed the class. "That is it for today, children. Donald, pass the wraps."

I went home that day, holding my sister hand, feeling inspired by my own sweet success and by the proud achievement told about in the Walter Loving story. I felt so good about it that I wanted to tell my parents. But, of course, as soon as I was within earshot of our apartment I realized they would not be interested in hearing about my piano performance, or about Walter Loving. They were wrapped up in their own torments... the torment of beating on each other.

We reached home and up the steps we went. When we got to the door, we could hear Mama and Led fighting. I opened the door and stood terrified. Led was on top of Mama, holding her straddled between his legs. He was pounding her with his balled fist. Without thinking I flew into a rage and attacked Led, kicking at his back and flailing my fists at his head, screaming for him to stop beating my mama. Led jumped up, grabbed my arms and slammed me against the wall so hard I saw stars and could not breathe. A jolt of panic hit my chest as I saw his wild-looking face. He was out of control. Mama screamed.

"Don't hit my child like that!"

Led's eyes were fiery red and he was grinding his teeth. I had seen him that way before when he slashed Uncle Henry and cut the other man's throat. I was almost nine years old then and up to that moment I thought I'd seen so much brutality I was numbed by it, but Led's unchecked anger was so terrifying I started shaking and crying, knowing the hate I had for him was dangerously intense, but I was helpless against him. Perhaps, we all were lucky that day. Led was so insanely angry I believe he could have killed us all without thinking about it. But suddenly he grabbed his cap and slammed out the door leaving us all crying.

Mama was bloodied and her eyes and face were swollen enormously. Me and Marguerite quieted down after Led was gone and Mama somehow found the strength to open a can of Spam and prepared some sandwiches for Marguerite and me before she went off to see a doctor.

Mama returned late that same evening with bandages wrapped around her head and face. She had been badly hurt. Nothing left to do but watch her suffer and complain of the pain from her broken jaw. It was sad to see those bandages on her and the blood oozing from her mouth.

Those injuries laid up Mama for several days and she lost a lot of weight as she could only eat by drawing her food through straws. She was sober during this time, and it was strange because I remember thinking that no one could have a sweeter mother that she was when she wasn't drinking. We had a few good days together, then the lady who was boarding Inez came by to see Mama and left Inez home with us.

CHAPTER 41
It's A Blue, Blue Christmas

A whole week went by and Mama was up and about again. Led showed up several times, but he only stayed around for a short while. Once he brought groceries for us that included fruit, nuts and candy. Nothing had really been resolved. It was an off-again-on-again situation, but sometimes he stayed over night with us.

One Saturday afternoon, in a gesture meant to impress Mama, I guess, he borrowed a wagon from a neighbor, loaded all four of us children on board and away we went to the company store. The popular railroad car restaurant, the one I had seen in the white folks section of town when we first arrived in Powellton, was our first stop. The railroad car diner was situated on a hillside about a hundred feet from the main company store. Led pulled the wagon up the blacktop path where we unloaded and went into the old diner and took a seat in the small area reserve for colored folks. Then Led went to the counter ordered hotdogs and fountain sodas for Inez, Marguerite and me and a vanilla milk shake for TC.

Christmas was only a week away, and from my seat by the window in the diner I could see that most of the white folks walking by were already in the mood for the cheerful holiday. People were buzzing around carrying brightly wrapped Christmas packages and there were Christmas decorations and ornaments in the diner and on the streets and in all the windows. Everybody had the Christmas spirit and we'd seen colored lights lining the tree branches along the entire length of the shopping area. As it began to snow lightly, I wondered if a white Christmas was in the making.

Daylight had almost disappeared when Led decided to take us back home. Walking through the dark we reached home safely, but unfortunately Mama was not home when we arrived. Led got irritated about that, returned the wagon to our neighbor, and was back in a flash. Abruptly we children were sent to bed and he left the house, storming out and talking to himself as if he knew where Mama was.

Morning came, and we woke up to an empty house. It was Sunday and I guessed that Mama and Led had been partying all night. We were all hungry, so I had no choice but to try my hand at cooking us some breakfast. Just as I was about to start, a knock hit the door. I opened the door cautiously and there they were, Mama and Led, swaying on the porch.

They were arguing again, throwing nasty accusations at each other. One look at Led's face and I knew he was getting ready to pound on Mama again. Once they were in the house the screams began. They grabbed at each other, tussling, shoving, pushing, swearing loudly and cursing, hurting each other as much as they could. Led's fists landed twice, but Mama wouldn't fall down. She had a hold of his coat and she was kicking at him with her feet. All of a sudden something exploded in me.

"Stop it!" I screamed hysterically. "Stop it! I can't take it!" I grabbed the frying pan I had put on the stove and with all my might I threw it between them, trying to separate them. The pan crashed against the wall. Marguerite and the babies began to cry loudly at the racket. Mama and Led were both startled. Mama swung around to face me, stepped close and suddenly she slapped me hard, knocking me to the floor.

"You mangy little bastard! Don't you *ever* lift your hand to throw anything at me again! Do you understand me?" Then Mama began to cry. I believe she suddenly realized that my action had saved her from a beating... possibly saved her life. I stayed where I was on the floor, curling myself into a ball under the kitchen table. Led showed no remorse. He pulled out a pint bottle of moonshine from his back pocket and took a quick drink and then another. Led could drink a gallon of alcohol and not appear intoxicated, although he would be totally bombed out of his skull. He was grinding his teeth like he always did when he drank heavily. Mama was still crying, so Led grabbed his jacket and walked out, slamming the door behind him.

On Christmas Eve Day, Mama left the house early in the morning. I told myself that she was going off to do Christmas shopping — because that's what I wanted desperately to believe — but in my heart I knew, just from the way she left the house like she did, she was going out to find something to drink. She was a helpless alcoholic. But hope for something good to happen seemed to grow in my heart anyway, in spite of what my own eyes were telling me. All the other kids I knew were talking about what they expected Santa Claus to bring them, and I couldn't help but wish for something too. Maybe a heavenly angel would see our situation and bring us something... maybe God would... maybe Santa... maybe Mama.. I knew better, but my childish hope burned feverishly just the same.

We kids were again left alone that day, and as always I was the babysitter. Only Marguerite and I were old enough to understand the significance of Christmas and all we knew about it came from exaggerated stories told by other kids and by advertising pictures in magazines we had seen. We thought Christmas was a very special day in the year when children got plenty to eat, lots of fruit and nuts and candy and new toys to play with. And we knew that children had to be especially good, because Santa Claus was coming to every house. It seemed strange, since we were lacking in any Christmas spirit at our house — no Christmas decorations of any kind had been strung up — but we never thought that we'd be left out of the celebration. All around us we saw people going about with Christmas trees and packages wrapped in bright paper. Snow was falling and all seemed joyful outside.

I did not have much confidence in my parents, but I did have confidence in Santa Claus. Previously — when times were better — our parents had taught us to believe in Santa Claus and therefore, me and Marguerite were depending on Santa Claus to make our Christmas a happy one.

By late evening on Christmas Eve, we had still not seen our parents. In fact, we did not have supper that night because there was nothing in the house to eat. As the last bit of daylight disappeared, we kids crowded the frosty window looking for Mama or Led. But there was only bleakness and two feet of fluffy whiteness outside. Nevertheless, we believed the snow was a blessing as it would make it easy for the reindeer to glide their sled to our residence.

Marguerite and I prepared for the arrival of Santa Claus. We took the only four chairs we had in the house, washed them clean, and arranged them in a row, one chair for each of us children. Then we went to bed, happily thinking that when we awoke on Christmas morning we would find whatever Santa Claus had seen fit to leave us.

We woke up on Christmas morning expecting to find Santa Claus had left toys, gifts and lots of Christmas goodies for us. Instead, we found Led stretched across the chairs. He was snoring and sleeping off his intoxication. We children were stung bitterly to the heart. Santa Claus had let us down like our parents had. As the eldest of the four children, I searched my mind for an answer. In my own mind, I tried to rationalize an excuse, but it was no use. I was too hurt and puzzled. I quickly lost confidence in Santa Claus, for he had been my last hope to make something good happen for us. The thought "Santa Claus dislikes us too" arose in my mind and wouldn't go away, although I could not guess what we had done to deserve such rejection. I don't believe anyone ever experienced such a blue Christmas as we did that year. Marguerite and I were grief-stricken and profoundly hurt, mainly because we kept thinking we'd done something wrong. We could not conceive that Santa Claus would be so cruel to us. The day passed and we had neither food nor toys on Christmas Day.

CHAPTER 42
Led Is Killed In the Mine... Accident or Murder?

Two months passed, and living continued to be a struggle. Led and Mama were always yelling at us children and snapping at each other. The only time I saw Mama happy was when she was drunk. But even in her intoxication she was unkind and cruel, and she seemed to pick on me particularly.

The only time I saw Led happy was when he had his knife in hand, whittling away pieces of wood. The presence of the knife frightened me, though he'd never threatened me with it. But it was there... in his hand... and his temper was so quick, and his hands so strong... I was afraid to get near him.

Confused and unhappy, there was no one to turn to for help. I knew something was wrong, but I was not sure whether the problem was me, or my parents. Was I so wicked with all my dark thoughts that just being around me made Mama and Led mean? Did they hate me so much they stayed away from the house just to avoid me? Were they starving me because I was being punished? These seem like such unreasonable questions now... but they plagued me in my confusion and insecurity and I couldn't help but wonder what I had done to cause all of this unhappiness. The only measurement I had was to watch other kids, but they seemed so carefree and happy-go-lucky. They didn't seem hungry and sad like I was most of the time.

It was the last Monday of February in 1943. I would be nine in another month. The day began with strong winds, sleety rain and snow flakes. If the quarreling between Led and Mama was not enough, the rain and blizzard-like winds were just one more thing for us children to try to deal with. The night before Mama had slipped away after another fight and being beaten by Led.

Despite the weather, a mining supervisor came around the community ordering men to work. Reportedly, an unusual amount of water was seeping into the mines. The pumps were not efficient in pumping out the excess water to keep it from flooding the mine. There was a rich coal bed, with a seam ranging 25-feet thick and several miles long, which would be covered by a river of water, making it more expensive and difficult to harvest. Men were needed to shore-up pillars with timbers and blast the coal seam into smaller chunks so it could be loaded onto special-made coal cars and hauled to the surface via the vertical shaft.

Led was always willing to respond to an emergency. Perhaps it was his way of gaining some small amount of recognition and respect. Anyway, he put on his mining gear and set out for the mines. As Led departed for work, we children crowded the foggy window and watched as he disappeared in the swirling wind and rain. We had no way of knowing it was the last time we would see Led alive.

Regardless of the weather, the coal companies — driven by the greed of the owners — coerced the workers to enter the elevator that would sink them hundreds of feet below the surface via a vertical shaft. To the superintendent, excavating the coal in this dangerous environment was more important than the danger to the miners' lives. Since all the miners needed work to support their families, and most of them were already deep in debt to the company stores, they were compelled to ignore the water-soaked ground and potentially dangerous flooding conditions occurring in mine. If they refused to venture into that deep dark pit, they would be fired immediately.

The men reached the bottom of the quarry via the main shaft that was twenty-three stories below the surface. At the bottom, there were several underground tunnels, called drifts, that strayed like tree roots from the main intake road or haulage road. The drifts were dug as the workers followed the seams of coal. Ventilation came from a current of fresh air in the "downcast shafts" or airducts. In the Number Two mine, the coalbeds were too deep underground for sinking multiple air ducts, and it was too expensive, so air was pumped into the mine at that level by one common airduct. Number Two mine was 10 years old and the drifts' vertical spaces were barely adequate for the men to crawl about on their knees. Sometimes they had to slither around on their stomachs. In these small spaces the coal was shoveled by hand onto conveyor belts which moved it to the coal cars on the haulage road. A locomotive then hauled it to the main shaft where an elevator took it to the surface.

Deep underground, there was no evidence of the rain and windstorm that raged on the surface. However, there was a strange quietness among the flickering yellow glow of the carbide lamps mounted on the miners' helmets. Number Two mine was one of the richest and largest coal deposits in that area, and the men were committed to excavating it.

In that part of Appalachia mines, the "room and pillar" methods were used to excavate coal. Timber was brought in to shore-up the pillars and the shafts. Dynamite and fuses were set and then the wire was laid and connected to the blasting machines. Finally, all was ready.

The warning sign was given and the men rushed to safety.

They gathered in rooms near the vertical shaft where they would be hoisted up by the elevator if anything went wrong.

Men working outside the mine were lashed by swirling winds, rain and sleet, as they prepared for the final moment.

The order was given, the plungers of the blasting machines were shoved downward. There were low rumblings from the depths of the mine. The miners listened intensely, then grinned at each other. It was over. Hundreds of feet down, there was now a pile of rubble, ready to be loaded and hauled to the surface. Picking up their tools, the coal-miners loaders onto coal cars and scuttled back into the tunnel.

At first no one noticed the water as it seeped through the shattered coal face at the site of the blast. Unknown to the men, water began to rush in. When the first miner felt the dampness through his boots, he was more annoyed than worried. But then the water began rising, and soon the miners realized what had happened. Somewhere in the depths of the earth, there was a pocket of water, and the blast had disturbed it.

The miners began hunting for the source of the leak.

Someone went to the surface and brought back the shift supervisor. More lumber was brought down, and the walls and pillars of Number Two mine were quickly shored up. But even as they worked, the water rose higher and soon the miners were wading.

"At the back," someone cried. "It's coming in from the back where the seam thins!" The men surged forward to see what was happening. Suddenly, they saw it.

What had started as a tickle was now a raging torrent, spewing from a gap in the wall of the shaft. The men watched as great chunks of coal broke away to be replaced by ice-cold crystal-clear water that was quickly stained inky black by the pulverized coal over which it flowed.

Suddenly, the walls of the haulage road caved in and water rushed over the men, flattening them on the floor of the shaft and pinning workers to the walls. Other men were swept along in the water's powerful current and savagely crushed instantly as the walls collapsed.

Perhaps, the fortunate victims drowned in the first few moments of the flood. For the rest, it was an even more horrible death.

For them, the flood played tricks, picking them up and sweeping them along, then, pressed them up near the roof of the mine, where pockets of air were trapped. The survivors kept their heads above the tide while the icy water numbed their bodies, allowing them to hope for a way out where there was none.

The pressure of the rushing water began compressing the pockets of air, and for the men trapped against the roof, a new agony began. Their ears began to hurt and they swallowed over and over again, trying to clear the pain from their heads. But as tons of water drained into the unnatural shaft that the men had created by blasting, the pressure grew; the pains increased.

A few of the miners plunged into the depths of the water, then fought back up, their fingers clawing instinctively at the roof of the tunnel, trying to find a way out, even while their lungs filled with water. Soon their struggles ceased.

For the few who grimly clung to life, even when they knew it was over, the mine had saved one last torture.

Finally, the current stopped flowing, and suddenly stillness loomed in the blackness. Each surviving miner, unaware that he was not alone in his survival, began to listen in the bleak silence. None of them knew what he was listening for. The voices of friends, calling out for help. Or perhaps, the voices of rescuers. The sound, when it came, was low, A distant murmur at first that grew and swelled to a chorus of voices. Like the voices of children, crying in the darkness. Crying for their mothers. Crying a lonely requiem of abandonment. One by one the miners began to die. Outside the mine, dusk fell. The wind ceased as if some weird evil-had passed over.

But it was not over. The water began to subside, and faint moans could be heard. On the surface and around the mine's shaft at least sixty men were readied to be lower to the accident scene and rescue the living and the dead bodies.

All day and all night people of the community gathered in front of the mine's shaft to mourn as lifeless bodies were raised from the depths. The wind blew down from the mountains, and with it came the sound of sadness.

At the shaft's bottom, rescuers searched the darkness with beams of light, looking for survivors. It was not long before the powerful light beam spotted an incline or dip where three men had found refuge. Unfortunately, the incline had caved in, trapping the men under heavy dirt and slate rock. One of those men was Led. The fallen slate had crushed him. He was barely alive.

The day the accident occurred in the mine, they did not tell us children about it until late the next day. As it was many a time, we were left home alone. On that late winter evening, we huddle at the window, hoping to a catch some glimpse of one of our parents coming home, but neither of them showed up. I went to the kitchen to search the cupboard for something to eat, thinking maybe I'd find some canned food or something that I could fix for us kids. I sensed that we had to survive on our own somehow. But there was nothing in the cupboard. Nothing at all.

The day after the accident Mama returned home intoxicated and crying profusely. At first I thought she was into one of her dipsomania spells. She soon explained, in her alcoholic stupor, that Led had been seriously hurt in an accident in the mine. But Mama, in her drunken daze, wouldn't accept that it was an accident. She kept insisting it was murder.

"It was a conspiracy to kill Led," she said, weeping, and her voice harsh. "He's a union member and they want him dead." Over and over she said those words... "They want him dead..." Later, the union authorities did speculate that Led and other union members had been forced to work in that dangerous situation which would kill them. "If water was already seeping into the mine, any amateur would know that an explosion would aggravate the seepage more," the union authority said.

Mama took a cold bath, slipped into her best dress, and off she went to the Montgomery Hospital. We learned later that she arrived to find Led unconscious and near death.

Later, Mama received an official report regarding the accident from the mining superintendent: "Explosions are common in mining operations. Dynamite is used to bring down coal from the slate. Usually, when an explosion occurs, it does not open cracks in the wall of the mine's tunnel. Unfortunately, this time, when the explosion occurred the vibration jarred an already fragile wall and caused a river of water to rush into the shelf where the men were working."

However, and to the contrary, the union representatives believed that many accidents were occurring because they purposely made working conditions unsafe for certain miners. His suspicion was that similar instances had caused the death of many union sympathizers and especially the black union members, who seemed to have a chip on their shoulders. This scenario fit Led, and Mama was always certain they had deliberately tried to kill Led.

For several days Mama traveled back and forth to Montgomery Hospital to visit Led. Yet, somehow she also managed to find whiskey. Consequently, she was consistently intoxicated. Little by little we learned that Led's body had been crushed beyond repair. The slate rock had crushed many of his bones, his liver had been severed and his skull cracked. He laid unconscious for several days before death took him.

The day he died, Mama came home after dark, sober and sad, but too depressed to tell us anything about Led's condition. Later, several neighbors visited our dwellings. People were standing around on the porch and in the yard. I had never before witnesses so many people visiting us at one time. I looked around to see if I knew anyone... still wondering why so many were at our house since no one had told us that Led had died. Suddenly, Uncle Henry and Aunt Samantha appeared. It was then that my heart sank to my stomach. That was the instant I knew he was gone.

It was a sad time for Mama and us children. Mama was consistently crying and for the rest of her life she believed Led was murdered. I noticed that my Aunt Samantha and Uncle Henry did not cry, nor did they express much sorrow about his death. Uncle Henry never forgot that Led almost killed him. Subsequently, he felt no remorse.

On the other hand, Aunt Samantha seemed angry and disgusted and acted cold toward Mama. I believe she was upset about the plight of us children and our living conditions. The first thing she did when she arrived at our house was to give us all a good bath and prepare a good meal and then, while Mama sat crying and moaning in her grief, Aunt Samantha began to clean our house. Uncle Henry stayed busy chauffeuring Mama around in his Ford, arranging various business issues with the coal company, and making preparation for Led"s funeral.

On the third day, Led's daughter from his common law wife arrived. Her name was Castmay. She was twenty years old with large luminous black eyes, pearly white teeth and built small and petite. She came with her boy friend. Both cried a lot as they grieved her father's death. Led's funeral was held on the 9th of March in 1943... my ninth birthday.

The preacher spoke eloquently about Led and several of his friends eulogized him regaling his artistic nature, the abundant talent he possessed, and asked for understanding of his quixotic, impulsive personality.

After the funeral we all went home. Mama lowered the shades in all the rooms and had a good long cry. She was carrying a bouquet of yellow and white chrysanthemums somebody had given her at the grave side. She smelled their fragrance and she must have forgotten all about how she and Led had been fighting and trying to hurt each other… "Lord what will I do now?" she sobbed as she wiped her tears on the flowers. "There is nothing in the whole wide world worse than losing the man you've counted on to support you." Discouraged and heartbroken, she moaned inconsolably, "It is a damn shame, that's what it is," Mama muttered to herself.

Personally, I felt no great loss with Led gone. I could not forget his evil ways. Especially the times he beat Mama unmercifully and the time he slammed me against the wall. I didn't want to show it, but in my heart I felt that some of our heartaches and our sorrows were over. Still, I worried over what the future would hold. If I had been older I would have known that the darkest doubts and worries never change the color of the sky nor turned the tide. While Mama and the other children sobbed, I stared remorselessly at the slit in the window shade where rays of late afternoon sunlight fell upon a tall, bluish vase on the center table that contained a spray of flowers someone had given us. It was the last item brought into our house in memory of James "Led" Leadbetter.

The evening after a funeral is always difficult. Led was dead, buried and gone forever.

Visitors and well wishers were all gone. I stood, somber, looking out the window at the wide creek as it rushed past. Swans slumbered on the banks of the stream, shrouded by giant oak trees where brown leaves were still present and where birds cuddled close to each other. Squirrels slept in their hollows as their furry tails floated with the intermitting gusts. The natural stillness was broken only by the ghostly clatter of a window shutter assailed by an aggressive March wind.

All I could think of was it was over. All the fighting , the bitter yelling and the screaming and the hitting on each other… the horrible arguments that went on and on. It was over. Led was in the ground. It might have been mean-hearted of me, but as I stood staring out that window… I sighed deeply and almost smiled.

CHAPTER 43
Startin' Over In Harlem Heights

Now that Led was gone, Uncle Henry and Aunt Samantha persuaded Mama to leave Powellton and move near them in a newly developed community for black Americans called "Harlem Heights." This black community was three miles north of a little town named Oak Hill and two miles south of Fayetteville in West Virginia. In 1940 they had divided this particular stretch of farm land into parcels and sold the lots off to blacks who were seeking a rural and quiet environment. When we came in 1943 there were only ten or eleven black families living there.

My uncle and aunt lived off a gravel road in Harlem Heights which is now called High Street. They owned a white house with red shutters. It had one bedroom, a front room, a small kitchen, a pantry for storing canned foods, and a small clothes closet where Uncle Henry kept his hunting guns.

In the front room there was a large Turkish rug covering the varnished wood floor, a blue satin living room suite and two tall floor lamps with ivory-colored shades. They covered the bedroom floor with linoleum and furnished it with a maple bedroom set. In the kitchen was a maple wood breakfast set, an iron coal stove, a sink, and a white cabinet that held silverware and beautiful dishes. Aunt Samantha owned a white washing machine with a "wringer" — rollers you turned manually with a handle. It sat in one corner of the kitchen covered with a red-checkered table cloth to keep the dust off. When Aunt Samantha was ready to wash, she rolled the machine to the back porch.

The dwelling was perched on a down-sloping hillside, consequently the front porch and entryway were at ground level, but the rear of the building was about ten feet off the ground. They enclosed the bottom portion of the home with red-painted planks which therefore formed a large basement area with two doors. There was a garage about 20 feet east of the house. I remember they had four rain barrels sitting on planks at the rear of the house to catch rainwater as it came off the roof.

Aunt Samantha's idea was to settle Mama and us children nearby so she could keep an eye on us. She and Uncle Henry picked out a nice hillside lot — off a road now called Lewis Street — which was just across the canyon from their own house. They made a down payment on the land and then Uncle Henry commissioned and an old friend of his, Mr. Eddie, to build a house.

Mr. Eddie was a jackleg carpenter (unlicensed) who did very good carpentry work. He was a strange Christian man who had purchased his own coffin and kept it stored it in his basement. Anyway Mr. Eddie began to build our house in April of 1943. I remember being very excited about all the activity. Trucks loaded with lumber arrived from a local sawmill and more lumber came from another yard in Oak Hill. Mr. Eddie brought a helper along who dug deep holes in the ground for the pillars of our house. After few days, the foundation took shape and then the frame went up. Several men who lived in the community found time to help Mr. Eddie. I even got to hammer a few nails to attach the long oakwood planks to the frame. Then they covered the frame with thick tarpaper shaped like red bricks.

Three weeks passed and the house was finished. It consisted of two rooms, a small kitchen and a small back porch and a wider front porch. It was a cute little house and the only thing it didn't have was a toilet — not even an outdoor toilet — and we had no running water in the house either. We did have a deep well they had dug 100 yards west of our house. To answer nature's call we had to run out into the bushes, whatever the weather.

The interior of the cottage had not been finished when we moved in. Uncle Henry and a man name Bill Bruce worked on it daily, sealing it with sheet rock. When all the sheet rock was up, Aunt Samantha and some of the other neighbors gave us what furniture they could spare. A lady who lived across the canyon, named Fannie Tensely, arranged to give several pieces of living room furniture to Mama. It was not long before we had enough furniture to satisfy Mama and us children. We all enjoyed having the little cottage, and didn't even mind going out in the bushes to relieve ourselves.

Ours was the very first house built on the half-mile red graveled road called Lewis Street. The west end of Lewis Street intersected Old Fayette Road. Across from our front porch was a long field of hayweed; tall, brownish grass-like weeds that swayed in the wind. Before April was over, the sun burst though with unusual warmth. In our cottage side yard the new grass sprang green and tender, and I found crocuses belled purple and yellow amid jade spears. Just after moving into our new house I stood alone beneath the branches of a copper beech tree, looking around at the cottage, the neat yard and the fresh green of nature, and something within me wept soundlessly for the years I had spent in dispair. However, the spring tide matched the surging in my veins and with the natural joy of a nine-year-old I inhaled the fragrance of the golden hayweed wafting from the nearby pasture.

When we first moved to Lewis Street there were only about twenty white families living along the Old Fayette Road. Of course they'd never say they lived in Harlem Heights no matter where their home was situated along Old Fayette Road. There were the Crouses and the Haywoods — the Haywoods had a large, white goat that nibbled the grass in their front yard — and across from the Haywoods was a beer garden, what you'd call a tavern now, with a sign on the door, "No Colored Allowed." Further on were the Richardsons who owned a huge farm. Along with their pigs, cattle, and chickens they raised corn, potatoes, many other vegetables and a variety of fruit trees and grapes. They sold their produce to the smaller black community.

Mr. Richardson had a hump back and was a mean, unfriendly and hateful man. Most of their children were grown but they had one redneck, alcoholic son named Clint who would walk down Old Fayette Road through the black community on his way to the beer garden and when he met any black person along the way he'd stick his flat nose in the air like he smelled something rotten. Behind his back he was called "nigger hater."

Once we'd moved in to our little cottage Mama quickly heard talk about the Richardsons. "Find the old white lady who lives in that big green farm house on the north end of Old Fayette Road," people said. "She's got plenty of farm stuff for sale."

Everybody called her "Old Lady Richardson." Mama bought buttermilk, eggs, and butter from Mrs. Richardson who charged ten cents each for a gallon of buttermilk or a pound of churned butter or a dozen eggs... and 25 cents for a slab of hickory-cured bacon. Mrs. Richardson was a very generous lady and the food she often gave us kept us from hunger.

Once again Mama enrolled me, and Marguerite, too, in the Minden school, since it was the nearest school to the Harlem Heights Community; and once again, lunch time was a problem for us. We had nothing but a peanut butter and jelly sandwich every day. Mama tried to buy one loaf of bread a week along with the peanut butter and jelly, but now that there were two of us she could not always afford the loaf of bread. Instead she bought ten pounds of flour, rather than the five pounds she usually bought, and each night she would make biscuits. She fixed two biscuits with peanut butter and blackberry jelly for each of us. When I pulled my peanut butter biscuits out at school during lunch time, my classmate would laugh at me. I was the only boy among all those black children whose family was too poor to buy a loaf of bread.

Times were really hard at home. Mama tried to buy clothes for the two of us, feed all four of us and herself, and keep us in school, but it just could not be done on $20 a month she got from "compensation" because of Led having been killed in the mine. Day by day the food got scarcer and scarcer and we got hungrier.

When Mama could scrape-up ten pennies, she sent me to buy a gallon of butter milk from Old Lady Richardson. Then we would eat cornbread crumbled in buttermilk for several days at a time, or until Mama could scrape-up enough money to buy some other food. On some days, when Mama could only afford to buy one piece of meat, she spent 25 cents for a slab of bacon from Mrs. Richardson. Then she would fry a few slices and use that to supplement our cornbread and milk.

I recall many days when we had no money at all and nothing in the house to eat. Unwilling to sit home with an empty belly, I took off and climbed the mountains and the ridges around the community looking for dew berries which helped ease my hunger pangs. As I walked along the ridges, my thoughts wandered far away to memories of having feasted at the Ayers' farm… to the fried chicken dinners Mama used to make when Led was working full time in the mines… to the candy kisses an old white lady used to toss at us kids back in Leslie just to see us scramble in the dirt. I combed the hills for walnuts and hickory nuts left over from the previous season. When I found one, I searched for two stones to crack it, praying all the while there'd be a nutmeat hidden inside. I remember resting in the blooming blackberry patches, wishing for a miracle of rapid ripening. In that moment of quiet, the full impact of my need was upon me, more profound than ever before, and I wept for I could not escape the burning hunger.

When Mama had money, she sent me on the half-mile journey to the Richardsons' farm to buy buttermilk. If we could afford them I also bought eggs and an occasional chicken. I enjoyed doing that because soon Mrs. Richardson — who couldn't help knowing of our poverty — started giving me dinner leftovers to take home for my family. Sometimes, too hungry to stop myself, I started eating them before I reached home, swallowing everything I could in great guilty gulps, ending up with only a few scraps. Mama would look in the paper bag when I got home, glance at me and give the scraps to Marguerite and the babies. She never yelled at me for eating some of the food before I got home, although I'm sure she knew, or at least suspected, that hunger had won out over responsibility.

One Friday I went to get milk and butter for Mama and Mrs. Richardson offered me breakfast. When I sat down she served eggs, pancakes, bacon, cheese and a basket of hot biscuits. I was surprised at this white lady allowing a black boy to sit at her breakfast table. After I finished eating, Mrs. Richardson asked me to clean up their yard where old grapevines and dead tree leaves had accumulated. Then she asked me to pull the weeds from the walkways around the house. After I finished, she gave me a fifty-cent piece. She did not take any of the money Mama gave me to pay for the items I was to purchase. When I returned home and told Mama about Mrs. Richardson's kindness and my working, she laughed until tears rolled down her cheeks. I laughed, too, for I was so proud that at nine-years-old I had been hired to do my first job. In the weeks that followed, I often did little jobs for Mrs. Richardson.

CHAPTER 44
A Billy Goat And Eighteen Relatives

In May of 1944, the West Virginia schools of Fayette County took a summer break which lasted through July. As the days got warmer, the entire community was plagued by millions of swarming flies from the adjacent cow pastures. Mama could not afford to buy a screen door for our cottage so we had to spray fly-killer twice a day. The smell of that spray was on everything in the kitchen and strong on the window sills where they congregated and then dropped motionless on the sills.

I was ten years old in 1944 and I didn't care too much about the damn flies. All I could think about was the white goat I'd seen in the Hayward's yard. It was for sale. I don't know why I wanted that goat, but I did. I'd never owned a pet of any kind and I just wanted him. I liked the way he looked, stubborn and tough, and the way he walled his eyes around at me without turning his head when I walked by. I liked his white hairy coat, silky-looking in the sunlight, and I liked his little hooves. He had two large curved horns on the top of his head and they intrigued me... making me think he was part devil.

The Haywoods were asking five dollars for him. After hearing me going on and on about that goat, Uncle Henry took pity on me I think and he somehow managed to purchase the animal for three dollars. He led him down the road to our house and gave him to me. I was delighted and I promptly named him "Billy." To me, Billy was the smartest and the most beautiful creature I'd ever seen.

Billy gave me a rough time at first for he was always trying to butt me, however it did not take me long to learn how to handle him. I would grab him by one of his horns and he and I would wrestle it out. Billy was strong, and once I got hold of his horn I knew I had better not let go, so I held on for dear life. Mostly he was a mild-natured, intelligent animal. Occasionally, after chewing his tether-rope in half, he'd run away to his previous home, but the Haywoods were always kind enough to bring Billy back to me.

I learned a lot from Billy. He drank hardly any water; he was a natural lawn-mower; in fact, he ate almost anything, so we did not have to spend money to feed him. Billy became a fine pet and a playmate.

Seeing how much time I spent with Billy, Uncle Henry built me a two-wheel cart and then made a little harness for Billy. Soon I had him pulling me wherever I wanted to go around the community. Sometimes I let TC, who had just turned three, have a ride with me because he was small and skinny, but not often. Folks got a big kick out of seeing me riding in my little cart behind my goat. But the more Billy pulled me around, the sorrier I felt for him. It didn't seem right, putting that harness on him, making him go by switching, even lightly, on his legs, making him do what I wanted like he was a slave. He was only a poor little goat and he shouldn't have to pull me in my cart. Weeping with angry guilt one afternoon, I destroyed the harness, parked the cart behind the house, and never again used Billy like that.

We'd been living on Lewis Street for about a year when Mama found a job working in the nearby town of Oak Hill as a cook. They did not pay her much money, but they generally gave her left-overs to bring home, which to my mind was almost a better deal. I was still afraid that she'd start buying her white lightnin' again, although lately she'd been easing up on her drinking and taking care of us kids and our new house. Sometimes those left-overs Mama brought home from the restaurant were all we had to eat, and we looked forward to them.

Mama had been working at the restaurant in Oak Hill for only two weeks when she got word that her sisters, Aunt Ruth and Aunt Sally, were coming from Alabama to visit at Aunt Samantha's house across the canyon. Aunt Ruth was Mama's favorite sister and they had not seen each other in over twenty years. Aunt Sally, Mama's oldest sister, had visited Aunt Samantha and Mama three years earlier.

It was a trying time for Aunt Samantha, for suddenly she had eighteen people in her tiny one-bedroom house. Aunt Ruth came, and then Aunt Sally arrived with her four children. In addition, Selma — Uncle Henry's daughter from his first marriage — and her eleven children came on too. They all arrived simultaneously. Thinking back to that time, it seems impossible that so many people could survive in a one-bedroom house, but they did. At my young age I did not realize how much work and effort was involved in feeding and bedding down three extra adults and fifteen extra children. To me, having so many relatives in one place was fun, but it must have been a nightmare for Uncle Henry and Aunt Samantha. At night people were sleeping on the porch, in the front room, in the basement, and in the garage. Every day we children had to scramble for food, and every night there was good-natured competition for sleeping spaces. Until this day I do not know how Aunt Samantha managed enough food to feed eighteen relatives, plus her and Uncle Henry, and sometimes Mama and us four kids too, but she did, and I don't remember hearing a cross word among them except one time when the ladies got into a heated discussion over the best way to cook catfish... batter dipped or in plain cornmeal. I didn't care how they cooked my catfish, as long as I got to eat some.

My cousin Simon was thirteen years old and he was the most flamboyant of all my male cousins. He loved females and made it a point to flirt with every good-looking woman, young or old, he saw. He flirted passionately with pretty Mrs. Elizabeth (Aunt Samantha's next door neighbor). Finally Aunt Samantha and Aunt Sally scolded Simon about it, telling him he was headed in a bad direction with all that flirty stuff and that it would get him a cheap reputation. He grinned and let it go in one ear and out the other.

When Aunt Sally arrived with her four children, the first thing Simon did was to tease my Billy goat. He grabbed Billy by his horn and tussled the animal to the ground. I didn't like Simon teasing my goat, but unless I was ready to fight him, which I wasn't, I couldn't stop him.

One day Billy got tired of Simon's teasing, butted him as hard as he could in the rear, gave his tether a good tug and broke lose, ran away and went back to his previous owner. Simon, yelling and hollering at Billy, chased after him, with me hard on his heels, following the goat to the Haywoods' house way down the road.

While he was there, he met one of the Haywoods' young daughters, a pretty blond girl with blue eyes, about fifteen years old named Lucy. I do not know how it started between them, but after that day she and Simon began to meet secretly in one of the nearby corn fields. Simon was an adventurer, and sometimes he would disappear for several hours. One day Theron, another of my cousins, followed Simon and witnessed his rendezvous with Lucy.

They met in the thickets of the corn field situated across from Lucy's house where they could not be seen through the green corn meadow. Young Simon's confident eyes wandered slowly over the inviting shape of Lucy's sleek body before he ripped off his ragged checkered shirt and pulled the white girl toward him. She gasped and tried to draw away from him, but there was no strength in her feeble gestures. It was as if she were afraid the feeling of his bare chest against her would unleash her deepest longings. Pretending to struggle in his arms, she let him pull her close and it was clear that touching his gleaming black body and being touched by him was what she really wanted. The sight of Simon's bronzed shoulders, his muscular neck and his dark eyes so close to her face started her blood racing like a gushing river, flushing her white cheeks to the brightest cherry red.

Hiding only a few feet from the couple, Theron felt his own heart raging and wondered at how slowly Simon was moving as he touched the white girl's face and body... touched her like he owned her, like he wasn't doing something wrong at all, like he wasn't scared or nervous about doing what he was doing, and like he had all the time in the world. Theron was so close he could hear the sharp intake of the girl's breath, see her body begin to jerk under Simon's hands as her pulse jumped in her slim white throat.

Slowly, she slipped down the shoulder straps of her sundress and let the garment drop to her ankles. Then, stepping on it with her bare feet, she sank low to Simon's muscular thighs and pressed her wet mouth to him. Indolently, Simon's eyelids drooped to half-closed as he felt the heat of her tongue and gazed down into her shining blue eyes. Soon blackness covered whiteness on the bare and fragrant earth. They lay between the corn rows, pressed together, hidden below the dirt heaps, as they became one, slipping into the frenzy of their passion.

Theron rushed home and told Aunt Sally, Simon's mother, what he had seen. Aunt Sally told Aunt Samantha and they were both terribly frightened for him and outraged. The two adults understood that a young black boy carrying on, especially in that way, with a white girl could get himself lynched in that part of the country.

I don't know what happened, but they must have told Simon something that scared him half to death for he stopped seeing the Haywoods' daughter... at least as far as we knew. But Simon was a daring adventurer even then, and with him there was no telling what he might truly be up to.

CHAPTER 45
Mr. Coy Comes Callin'... My Sisters Go To Aunt Ruth's

One warm Saturday evening Mama and Aunt Ruth went out to party. They just wanted to go dancing and have a good time and there were several beer gardens around the county which catered to black Americans. The most popular, and the most roughneck one, was called Red's Tavern. It was two miles south of the mining community called Glen Jean and two-miles north of the small town of Mount Hope. Of course, Mama and Aunt Ruth headed straight for Red's, leaving my cousin Samantha, named for my aunt, to babysit me and Marguerite, Inez and TC.

We were put to bed early that night, Marguerite and I sharing the day-bed in the front room which had been pushed over in a far corner and Inez and TC sharing a crib in Mama's back bedroom, but for some reason I couldn't get to sleep. Cousin Samantha went outside on the porch to talk to some friends in the warm night air, and I tossed and turned till Marguerite started fussing at me. Then I lay like a stone, staring up at the ceiling. I was worried about Mama. She hadn't gone off like this since Led's funeral, and I was worried that she'd start drinking again. The hours dragged by but she didn't come home. Finally I fell asleep.

She wasn't in her bedroom the next morning when we woke up. In fact, it wasn't till way after Cousin Samantha gave us lunch that Mama came trailing home with Aunt Ruth, laughing and talking kind of shrill, and bringing home a man.

Coy Douglass was a tall, handsome black man with deep cowlicks and a wide smile. My Grandma Ayers had shown me pictures of a man named Frederick Douglass several times in the photo albums she kept on the farm. Grandma was proud because Frederick Douglass had been a great orator and a credit to his race in the fight against slavery. This tall young man Mama had just walked in with looked very much like Frederick. Same wide grin and the same cowlicks curling his hair on the left side. Coy Douglass was a strongly-built, big-chested and broad-shouldered man standing six-feet-three-inches tall — I know because I made him laugh when I asked him how tall he was. Mama must have admired him a lot for he was the first one she ever bothered to introduce to us children. We were to call him "Mr. Coy."

She pestered him a little, in a light-hearted, flirty kind of way, to meet the rest of the family across the canyon at Aunt Samantha's house, but Mr. Coy appeared shy and politely rejected the idea. He'd meet the rest of the family some other time he said with his brilliant smile.

Big as he was and fit looking, Mr. Coy had recently been discharged from the Army because of some health problems. He was well dressed and had a very mannerly demeanor. What struck me most about him, outside of his height, was his very large feet. He wore what looked like giant shoes to me, and when he let me put my own small foot beside his you could see it would take about six of mine to make the length of one of his. He told me he wore a size fourteen-and-a-half shoe.

As I remember Mr. Coy had on a beautiful, long-sleeve silk shirt of a golden color that afternoon, and it almost glowed against his bronzy-looking skin.

I admired Mr. Coy. I guess it was because he exhibited enormous strength and power to a frail little ten-year-old like me. He was vibrant and extremely pleasant to us children. Then, as he relaxed and draped his long frame into one of the front room chairs, I discovered he was a drinker and a smoker. That greatly disappointed me because I knew from experience that one drinker always encouraged another drinker... and I'd had about all I could stand of Mama's drinking.

Anyhow, Mama served him a drink, and somehow she spilled bourbon on the sleeve of his gold shirt. She apologized and promised that if he would take off his shirt, she would wash it for him. Well, it was very warm, and I am sure Mr. Coy did not mind taking off his shirt, since it would give him a chance to flaunt his extraordinary physique.

Mama washed the shirt in clear water containing a teaspoonful of vinegar and soft soap. The shirt turned out beautifully. She hung it in the sun on a makeshift clothesline situated at the bottom of the front porch to dry. After a while, she went out to the porch to see if the shirt were dry. However, to her surprise, Billy the goat was just about finished eating the shirt. He had the last bite of it in his mouth.

Mama couldn't apologize enough and I was embarrassed about my goat chewing it up. Now Mr. Coy had no shirt to wear. He had been planning to take a Greyhound bus over to Hill Top — another mining community about 15 miles south of Harlem Heights — but it wasn't hard to imagine what would have happened to Mr. Coy in a rural community where white folks were scared of black men if he'd gone running around half naked. Mama sent me across the canyon to borrow one of Uncle Henry's shirts. It barely buttoned across the chest, but it covered him and he was a good sport about wearing it.

Mr. Coy was ready to leave, but he kept hesitating, holding onto Mama's hand and saying he simply could not leave without her. This made Mama laugh, but I noticed she didn't encourage his leaving, either. Looking across the canyon Mr. Coy happened to see Rubin Puryear, a man he'd known for several years. He knew Rubin would be traveling toward Hill Top, so he called out across the ravine and asked Rubin to give him a ride. Mr. Rubin obliged, saying he'd pick up Mr. Coy in a half an hour. Mama and Mr. Coy came on back inside and had another bourbon, and then true to his word, Mr. Rubin drove his car over to our house. Mama and Mr. Coy piled in the front seat and off they went, laughing like two kids on a picnic. Aunt Ruth, who'd come home with Mama and was suffering from a slight hangover from their long night of partying, had gladly waved them on their way and agreed to stay and watch us children.

During all the excitement Mr. Coy dropped a $20-dollar bill.

I spotted it in the dirt, picked it up and instantly decided to keep it. He would never miss the money, I was certain, because it was only one bill off the big roll of twenties he had in his pocket. But then I had a problem. I did not know what to do it, since I'd never had so much money in my hands before in my life. I couldn't resist telling my cousins Theron and Simon, and of course, Simon said he knew exactly what to do. Give him the money, he said, and it would then be safe with him. Being a young and trusting soul, I believed him and handed it over, not seeing the smile of satisfaction curling his lips.

The next day the three of us made our way over to Oak Hill and went to a movie house called The Kings Theater. Simon took out my twenty and paid for our tickets, three bags of popcorn and some candy. He put the change in his own pants pocket and we all went in to see the movie. While we were watching the movie star Lash LaRue, Simon sneaked out and was gone about a half an hour. He came on back carrying a small package.

When we left the theater Simon refused to say what was in the package, but Theron and I guessed that Simon had spent my money. A loud argument followed, during which Simon acted like he always did, overbearing and arrogant, refusing to tell what was in the package and refusing to show me "my" money he was supposed to have in his pocket. We started walking back to Harlem Heights. Simon wouldn't walk with us, saying he didn't want to argue about the money any more. Theron and I lagged back, talking quietly about an alternate plan. We knew that one-on-one with Simon we didn't stand a chance. The only way we might get the money away from him was for us to double-up and both of us jump him at the same time.

Apparently Simon caught on to what we were up to because when he noticed we were trying to catch up to him he took off running like a scared rabbit. Until this day, Theron and I argue about what happened to that money. The speculation is that Simon spent it all to buy a gift for that white girl, Lucy Haywood, but we'll never know.

It was two whole days before Mama returned from her outing with Mr. Coy. When she did come home, she and her sister Ruth sat down together in the front room and Aunt Ruth was doing a lot of talking... most of it having to do with Marguerite and Inez. It seems that while Mama was gone Aunt Ruth had become deeply attached to four-year-old Inez and sweet-natured Marguerite and didn't want to part with them. Furthermore, Aunt Ruth didn't like how we were living, in such a hand-to-mouth way — trying to get by on $20 a month — and she didn't like Mama doing so much drinking, which she had noticed since she'd arrived from Alabama. The point was that Aunt Ruth wanted to take the two girls home with her to Alabama. It would be a burden off Mama, she said, and Mama would know they'd be eating right and going to school regular and being raised properly.

Mama refused to listen to Aunt Ruth at first, saying she couldn't stand to lose her precious girls, but Aunt Ruth kept at her. "What kind of a life you giving them here, Nora? Trying to feed four kids on $20 a month? I know it's a strain, honey, and it's gettin' you drinkin' too much already. Don't make a face at me; you know it's true. My husband and I got a nice little house and I love these darlin' children, Nora. Jim's gonna love them just as much as I do. You know they be better off with us. Tell me the truth, Nora... you don't want them livin' like this, do you?" Aunt Ruth glanced up and noticed me standing by the door, listening to them. "Charles, you go outside and play with Marguerite now. Your mama and I want to talk."

Reluctantly I did as I was told, taking Marguerite with me, but I sat very quietly on the front porch for I felt that something was about to happen and I wanted to know what it was. Aunt Ruth went on talking about Mama and Mr. Coy. I couldn't hear all they were saying, but it was something about Mama starting to think about her future... about needing a man to support the family. Mama and Aunt Ruth got into a kind of a shouting match then and Mama was crying, but then she finally agreed to let her sister take Marguerite and Inez home with her to Alabama.

Sitting on the porch I was listening so intently I didn't realize I was tilting sideways until I fell over in front of the open front door with a crash. Mama got up saying something about "little pitchers have big ears," and she closed the front door with a reprimanding bang. I didn't care. I had found out what I wanted to know. It wasn't me who was going to get away from Mama's dark pathways... it was my two little sisters.

After three weeks of visiting, all the relatives left Aunt Samantha's house. Selma took off with her brood and Aunt Sally gathered up her four. Aunt Ruth came to our house and packed up Marguerite's clothes, what few she had anyway, and Inez's little baby doll she played with all the time, hugged Mama and marched them out the door. Marguerite didn't seem too unhappy to leave... she glanced back at Mama and me only once, looking a little fearful and bewildered. Mama didn't make any big show about them leaving, no crying or carrying on, because she knew it would only get them all upset, but there were tears shining in her eyes. I smiled and waved like they were just going off on a picnic. All Inez knew was she was going for a bus ride. In a way I was glad to see them go, for even I knew they would be better off with Aunt Ruth and Uncle Jim. At least they'd get fed and they'd be far away from Mama's mean temper when she started drinking again. And I knew that was just a matter of time.

CHAPTER 46
Billy's Gone

Once the company left it was right back to the old times again, Mama and her white lightnin' and me and my three-year-old little brother trying to get through the day without being hungry. School was on again in Fayette County, but now the one loaf of bread Mama bought for my peanut butter sandwiches lasted through the week. I missed Marguerite a little, we had played a lot together, and now there was only TC and my Billy goat for company.

Somehow we got through that difficult fall and winter season and before I realized it my eleventh birthday came on March 9th of 1945. As I recall, there was a lot of talk at that time about Germany being on the verge of surrender, but in early March the war was still raging. My concerns at that time, however, were far more personal than the distant war overseas. I was concentrating on my daily problem of getting enough food to eat.

I remember thinking how glad I was that we didn't have to share what we did have with Marguerite and Inez. And then I'd wonder about what they were eating, remembering Aunt Ruth's ample body, and that she had a husband working, and I'd get a little envious of their good fortune.

TC was going to be five in May, and the two of us still didn't get along very well. I don't know all the reasons why, but I think he sensed that I just plain out didn't like him. It wasn't his fault — how could I blame a five-year-old? — but the truth was I still carried such a tight-chested, hateful memory of his father, Led — TC resembled Led in looks as well as his sullen nature and his single-minded stubborn ways — that I just didn't feel like going out of my way to be friends with him. Young as he was, TC liked to slip away from our house and go on the footpath through the high brush leading across the canyon to play with the Puryear kids. TC had a way of wanting to do

252

things only his way, and if you wouldn't let him, then he wasn't interested. Even at five when he was frustrated he'd lash out and kick me if he could, or smack me with his fist, knowing I was forbidden to smack him back. I was just as glad he didn't care much for my company either. The Puryear kids were far more accommodating to him than I was.

But there was one bright spot in my life. I still had my Billy. I had owned my goat since just after my 10th birthday and all during that year I had grown more and more attached to my little pal. That sweet-natured animal had become my precious pet and he followed me everywhere I went. I combed his long white hair sometimes with Mama's hairbrush — of course I never told her I did that — but it curled up so nice and silky and he seemed to like when I groomed him. When I called for him, I would say "Billy, Billy, Billy," and he would always come running. Some days when I came home from school, I would begin calling Billy while I was still several blocks away and he'd always come running to meet me. I would give him a big hug with both of my arms flung around his shaggy neck and then we'd slowly make our way home with him stopping every foot or so to nibble on the wild grass and flowers.

One day on my way home, just down the road from our house, I called for Billy, but he did not come running. I called again. He didn't appear. I remember stopping on the road, wondering why I felt such a overwhelming sense of foreboding, and knowing something bad — something terrible — had happened. I sensed it as I went flying home and did not see Billy on his tether out in the yard. I slammed into the house and one look at Mama's face told the story. Mama had slaughtered my goat because we needed food to eat. My worse nightmare had come true. My Billy was dead.

The truth hit me like a lightning bolt. I think I opened my mouth and screamed some awful scream; it just poured from my guts, from my primordial self, from my torn soul. I couldn't believe it, and yet there was his carcass, red and bloody, hacked into chops and slabs of his ribs, leg and rump roasts, on the kitchen table. My Billy.

"I had to do it, Charles," was all Mama said, and her eyes swam with tears but I only saw the cold set of her mouth. Then she added, "You knew this was gonna happen, didn't you?"

I shook my head. Numb. Unfeeling. Dead. My Billy.

"I told you, when Uncle Henry gave him to you... I told you we'd keep him for a while... a while, I said... remember?"

I looked at her in shock. Yes, she'd said that, but I hadn't realized what she meant.

"I thought you understood." She turned her guilty eyes away.

I ran outside, unable to bear the sight of my pet's dead body a moment longer. She knew damn well I had never thought anything of the kind. Nobody loves a pet like I loved Billy with the "understanding" that he'd be slaughtered after a few months. I ran and ran and ran, my feet taking me to wherever they might. Somewhere in the woods I fell, exhausted, weeping, raging and screaming against the unfairness of life and mourning my terrible loss. She had slaughtered my Billy. I would never forgive her for that. And I swore I would rather die than swallow one bite of his poor dead flesh. I would rather die.

Oh God, how I hated my world at that moment. How I hated everything about my life and everything and everybody in it. Shaking my small fist at heaven I was ready, in my anguish, to challenge God Himself for letting that happen to my pet. Never in my life had I experienced such a sense of loss. Curled under one of the sheltering oaks I wept bitterly for my lost playmate.

To my shame, my vow of abstinence did not last long once hunger gripped my stomach with its unrelenting iron fist. The smell of roasting ribs and the emptiness in my belly conspired against my resolve, wearing it down like a river of tears over stone, and I steeled my emotions as my hands reached for my dinner fork. He was already dead. If I didn't eat, I would sicken and die too. I could not bring Billy back. So I ate him. I chewed him up in my watering mouth, I forced myself to swallow his flesh, making him part of my flesh, and even as tears rolled down my cheeks, I plunged my fork into him and I ate him.

CHAPTER 47
Hunger Gets Me A Beating... And Mama Marries Mr. Coy

Again Mama's drinking got worse.

She craved her bottle so much she even sold some of Billy's meat to get money to buy her whiskey. I hated that. I hated her doing that to Billy. I could almost grasp the necessity of her having him slaughtered for us to eat, but then we were obligated to eat him, eat all of him in order to justify his sacrifice to the Gods of our hunger. But to kill him and sell his flesh for whiskey was hateful, wicked, wrong.

There were things happening now between Mama and me, things she was doing that were making a hard and bitter impression on my soul. Like selling Billy's flesh for whiskey money. Maybe I saw things differently because I was getting older, and I could understand more. But I didn't like a lot of what she was doing and I was beginning to withdraw from her. I didn't count on her anymore for anything. If she said she'd be home, I didn't wait for her anymore. I just stopped expecting her to show up. I began to think about my life, my needs, and I was able to see past all her stories and her moaning about her sad life while she was sitting there with her whiskey. I didn't give a damn anymore. I had a hard life too. If I was going to feel sorry for anybody, I was going to feel sorry for myself. And I hated feeling sorry for myself, so little by little I began to open my eyes and change my life, by myself... and for myself.

Mama's boyfriend, Mr. Coy Douglass, had stopped coming around. I hadn't seen him at all lately, and the more Mama was left alone, the more she drank. I thought maybe they'd had a lover's quarrel, or some kind of a disagreement, but very soon things got so bad that she was leaving TC and me to fend for ourselves like she'd done when we lived over in Minden. Day after day I'd come home from school and find her drunk and too angry to talk to. The moment I walked in she'd take off, leaving TC crying because he was hungry and no food in the house and no money. I didn't accept that now like I used to. I trailed her to the door, grabbing at her purse. "Come on, I've got to buy some food, Mama! You just goin' after booze. Give me some money." I shouted the words for she was already dazed looking and almost past hearing me. I wanted to stop her, shake her hard to make her hear me, but I wasn't strong enough yet.

"Get outta my way, boy." Her face crumpled into a mean-tempered mask. "You *know* better'n to raise your voice to... ME!" And she'd slash at me with her purse, but I ducked the blow and kept at her.

"Damn, Mama, we're hungry. We need food! Come on..." But she was already out the door and I didn't follow her out of the house because I didn't want to shame her in front of the neighbors for leaving us like she did.

But time and time again I had to go begging for food. In my need, I remembered Old Lady Richardson's generosity, so I sent TC across the canyon to play with the Puryear kids (maybe he'd get something to eat over there) and made my way to Mrs. Richardson's house to ask for work. She had nothing for me to do. Embarrassed, with my stomach groaning loudly, I asked her if she would give me buttermilk on credit. She was very kind. Not only did she give me the buttermilk, she gave me the family left overs too.

For once I managed to get home without eating any of it and I yelled across the canyon for TC, saying I had something good to eat. He came running and we gobbled-up every scrap. Then we tried to drink as much buttermilk as we could because we had no way of storing the milk to keep it from spoiling. Our stomachs were full and I was able to sleep that night. Mama didn't come home, and I didn't even care. I was through worrying about all that mess.

The next day the hunger came on me again.

That's the terrible thing about hunger. You get rid of it today, it's right back on you tomorrow. It's a battle every waking day . It just won't let you rest. It won't let you forget it. You find yourself doing all kinds of things just from the fierce drive to fill your belly. There is no drive as strong as the drive to preserve life, to fight hunger and save yourself. The problem was, I knew where there was food. But I couldn't have it. I couldn't even ask for it. Everything in me wanted to go to across the canyon to Aunt Samantha's house, for I knew she'd feed me and TC too. But I didn't dare. If I did, and Mama heard about it, she would beat me within an inch of my life. And then, after she started drinking — like she did every night — she'd remember what I'd done and beat me again with anything she could find to hit me with, screaming, "You don't go to my sister's house for food," giving me a blow on the head or my body with every word.

I knew why.

She was ashamed. She was ashamed that she spent our food money for whiskey; she was ashamed she was letting us kids go hungry while she drank up the money… and her pride was more important than our empty stomachs. No, I didn't dare ask Aunt Samantha for food.

One early evening Mama came home, and she was drinking heavily. There was no food in our house, and there hadn't been any for two days. I looked at her, staggering around in the kitchen, looking for her glass; I studied her face. It used to be such a pretty face, but now it seemed drawn down into sullen, angry lines, her forehead wrinkled with frown lines, her eyes — so sparkling brown when she was happy — dull-looking and almost glazed over like she was half blind. She was slamming cupboards and banging drawers. She couldn't see the glass that was sitting right there on the table where she'd left it and she didn't like swigging out of the bottle.

TC and I hadn't eaten since yesterday afternoon when a neighbor took pity on us and gave us some cornbread, beans and buttermilk. TC was hiding under Mama's bed — that's where he went whenever he was scared or upset about something — and I thought maybe I could get Mama to see what was happening to us. I eased over to where she was standing unsteadily by the table, and I pushed her glass back out of the way, like I was taking it away from her, I suppose, and I said, "Mama, please don't drink anymore tonight. Please. TC and I are starving hungry. We need something to eat. Can't you see that?" I did not expect the rage that my request generated in her. She wheeled around in a fury and slapped me several times in the face and on the head and arms when I tried to cover up. Then, madder still because she couldn't smack my mouth, she grabbed up the water dipper — a heavy, long-handled, metal, cup-like utensil — and slammed it across my neck with full force. The sharp edge brought a stream of bright blood gushing down my shoulder and back. Again and again she brought that dipper down on me, striking any place on my body she could reach. Her eyes were dead-looking and suddenly I knew she didn't even know what she was doing… it was like she was hitting a snake that had already been broken apart, like she was sullenly — and not even with anger — trying to beat me to death. I shoved her away from me with all my strength and ran screaming out of the house to the gravel road and down the Old Fayette Highway to Mrs. Simm's, the first house with a light on. I was bleeding badly and my body was covered with marks and bruises from the dipper's sharp edges. Mrs. Simm's held a towel on my neck wound and half-carried me to my Aunt Samantha's. My aunt managed to stop the bleeding and put a thick bandage on my neck held on with adhesive tape. She also gave me one of Uncle Henry's old under-shirts to wear because my own shirt was soggy with blood. I was trembling all over and I felt like I was going to throw up. She made me lie down on the floor, afraid of staining her blue satin couch, and covered me with an old quilt.

Uncle Henry was pacing up and down in their front room, furious at Mama for beating me so badly. "She could have killed that child!" he ranted. "That woman should not be trusted to raise kids. She's gone too far this time." He turned to Samantha. "This is child abuse, no other words for it. I'm not going to let Nora get away with this kind of behavior. She's got to learn there are consequences for such vicious acts. I'm going to report this and let her learn a lesson." Aunt Samantha wouldn't let me stay at her house that night, even though I begged to, for she was worried about TC being alone with Mama and her being drunk like she was and in such a violent mood. "Just stay away from her," she said. She sent me on home after feeding me some cold chicken with biscuits and buttermilk and giving me a bag of food for TC. "Just keep out of her sight. We'll take care of it."

I went on back and crept into the house — Mama was in the kitchen, talking to herself like she did a lot of the time, not making any sense that I could understand — so I got TC and pulled him out on the porch and let him eat his chicken and biscuit in the dark with his fingers, and then we just went inside and lay down on the daybed in the front room and tried to go to sleep. The gash in my neck burned under the bandage, Aunt Samantha had put some iodine on it I think, and my mind was spinning with all kinds of questions, and frustration, and anger of my own... but I finally slept.

The next morning the state police came to our house and arrested Mama.. She was hung over and sleeping when they arrived. They pounded on the door and when I opened it they took a look at my bandage and at the blood, dried now and caked, on the kitchen floor.

"Your Mama did that, son?" one asked.

I looked down, ashamed to answer.

"With this?" The policeman picked up the still-bloody dipper.

I nodded. What were they going to do? "You going to take Mama away?"

"I think a little rest in the county jail might do her some good, son. You okay here with your little brother?"

"Yes, sir."

The two officer went back to Mama's bedroom where she was sprawled in her clothes across the bed. They woke her and made her get up. When she saw who they were, she started screaming and crying and she begged them to leave her alone, that she'd just been drunk and didn't know what she'd done, and all like that, but they took her out the door anyway. Aunt Samantha was standing out in the yard, her arms crossed over her chest and an angry look in her eyes, when they put Mama into the police car. Aunt Samantha took TC and me to her house where she gave both of us breakfast and a hot bath.

They made Mama stay in jail that whole day, bringing her back only after supper time.

Mama was very apologetic to me. She cried and told me how she loved me, and tried to hug me and cried when I hollered because she'd squeezed my neck where my cut was. "Oh, I'm sorry, I'm sorry," she kept saying, but for the first time I wasn't moved. I didn't care if she was sorry. She had been sorry the last time she got drunk and beat up on me, too... so what did "I'm sorry" mean to her? Nothing. They were just words as far as I was concerned. "Oh, you know I love you, Charles." She loved me? Sure she did. She acted like it, didn't she. She had nearly killed me in a drunken rage. My heart was growing colder and my intense need for self-protection was growing stronger.

Oh, I knew my mama loved me. Deep down inside her I knew she cared. But there was something wrong with her. Something wrong that reared up and came to life inside whenever she drank whiskey. It was like the devil possessed her. She was terrifying in her blind rages, and uncontrollable in her screaming fits of destruction. She had been seeing rats again, like when she was supposedly dying that time — and having what Mrs. Freda had called "hallucinations" of ghosts and evil eyes on her. I knew it was a sickness... a terrible sickness, but I had reached a point where I had no more sympathy in my heart. I knew it wasn't a matter of her just trying to stop drinking. I knew she couldn't stop drinking. It had her solid, locked up and no exit. Mama was a prisoner. But damn, I wasn't going to be her victim any more.

After that day in jail, for a little while — maybe a week — Mama tried to act like a mother to TC and me. And then Mr. Coy started coming around again, visiting on a regular basis. Once they started seeing each other again, things got a little better. Mama seemed happier and had tried to straighten up our house — which she'd let go something terrible — not wanting Mr. Coy to see how she'd been living. I'm pretty sure Mama never told Mr. Coy about her being put in jail that day. I never mentioned it and TC never cared if I lived or died anyway so he just crawled under Mama's bed and kept to himself. I don't think Mr. Coy ever found out. When he asked about the bandage on my neck, I just shrugged and said, "It's okay. I just ran into something." He didn't ask again.

As I remember, Mama was still trying to feed us on that $20 she got, and what food she brought home from her part-time job at the restaurant. Now that things had improved between her and Mr. Coy, she started making more of an effort with us kids. To supplement our meals, she went out into the forest and picked armfuls of wild greens she called "poke salad." She found the same red roots Mrs. Freda used to use — sassafras, I believe — and boiled them to make a refreshing drink for us. She would clean the poke salad greens and boil them with salted pork, a little wild onion and a small bit of vinegar. When this mix was partly done, she added corn cut off the cobb. Then she fried hickory-cured bacon to a brown, hard crisp and added the crumbled bacon to her cornbread batter. I remember sitting down to that meal. I remember how the table looked, how the plates were arranged, the heavy pot Mama used for the greens with saltpork, the pan of hot cornbread … the smell of it with the bacon pieces crumbled in… I remember it like I was sitting there today. When my mama was sober she was without doubt one of the finest cooks in the world. I remember that meal as one of the best, and one of the last, she ever made for me.

Mr. Coy Douglass kept on coming around to be with Mama. I was always glad to see Mr. Coy, because when he was around Mama made an effort to keep our house nice and to remember to fix our meals. I knew they were getting very close — he always had his hands on Mama, patting her or kissing her face, holding her hand, just touching her a lot — but it was only after they came back from the ceremony on Saturday afternoon that I learned Mr. Coy had asked Mama to marry him. Later I found out he'd asked her that morning and they had gone out that very afternoon to tie the knot. Officially now, Mama was Mrs. Elnora Douglass, and I had a new stepdad.

The whole black community was happy for Mama. After she showed off her ring and announced their wedding that afternoon, she began receiving gifts from friends and neighbors. Over the next few days she got some beautiful cooking items, linens and housewares.

TC and I were happy about their marriage, for both of us admired Mr. Coy. But the main benefit was that we now had a stepfather who was working. That meant money would be coming in. That meant food on the table. We would not have to go hungry again.

Mr. Coy moved into our house, putting some of his things in our front room — a lamp he liked, a chair he'd bought that fit his gangly frame, a few photographs of him and his family — and he hung his nice-looking clothes in Mama's closet and set his big shoes under her bed. He was kind-hearted toward us kids, going out of his way to smile and joke around with us boys, but I tried to keep my distance with him. I wasn't trusting anybody anymore.

I was glad for the change, glad to be eating regular meals, but my heart was still cold toward any great plans for a happy future. Sure things were better now. But I wasn't fooled anymore. I was way past thinking all our problems were solved because Mama had married Coy. I just watched Mama and Coy and in my secret heart I made my own judgements, thought my own thoughts and wondered how long it would last.

CHAPTER 48
Lewis Hilliard, My Neighbor, My Inspiration

Mr. Lewis Hilliard was a long-time neighbor of ours in Harlem Heights. His first wife had died several years ago and he lived with his second wife in their big house. He was a light-skinned, crinkly-eyed, one-armed man of many convictions and he loved to talk. Mr. Hilliard knew my father, Charles Ayers, very well for they had grown up together as kids and were still great friends. I didn't know him all that well when I was nine, but now that I was almost a man … going on twelve… I was aware that he was taking a great interest in my welfare as he had long been aware of my dysfunctional family.

When I first saw him, I thought he was a devil man, for every other word out of his mouth was a curse word… goddam this… goddam that… and he'd swing that one arm of his for emphasis and you could just imagine how he'd look if he more than just a stump for a left arm. Coming home from church on Sunday, which in spite of Mama's own personal feelings she made me attend, I passed Mr. Hilliard's house, and every Sunday he'd be out on his porch with his paper and his silver-rimmed glasses just dying for me to stop by so he could talk about all that was on his mind.

First of all he didn't like the preachers in our black community who carried on non-religious activity in the name of Jesus Christ. "Life is too short to deal with all that goddam nonsense," he said. "Goddam waste of goddam time."

Second, Mr. Hilliard was critical of those preachers who claimed to be prophets who spoke from the scripture. Yet, those very preachers could not read the English language or any other language. Mr. Hilliard believed that if a preacher could not read, then, "How in the hell can they speak about what's written in the goddam bible? You think they memorize what some other jackleg preacher told them? They don't know what they talkin' about. It's shameful how them illiterates get folks to listen to their goddam hogwash."

I remember my first understanding of what "pimping" meant came from Mr. Hilliard's vivid conversations. He was always talking about someone doing something like a "jackleg preacher pimpin' off Jesus." I finally figured out that he was referring to the self-proclaimed preachers who took money and gifts from the black community in the name of Jesus Christ. He was most incensed about the preachers who took pleasure and leisurely advantage of the religiously inspired young women of the church. And it was common knowledge that one married woman in the community had borne a child belonging to one popular preacher. Mr. Hilliard's negative ideas of preachers also included those who took advantage of public hospitality.

He spoke spectacularly about one preacher who was the pastor of a church, enjoyed an excellent reputation, but was living off one church family and then another, taking their money and gifts, eating at their tables, dallying (some said) with their young daughters. Sometimes Mr. Hilliard would repeat his beliefs and his harsh comments to other adults in an effort to give them what he said was a "wake up call"... but it never did anything to flush the culprits out of their cover holes.

As I look back, I consistently heard rumors about the carrying-on of the local clergy, and I myself witnessed some ugly happenings engineered by a few jackleg preachers trying to lead folks into a guilty feeling where they'd be obliged to pay their way out, with contributions they could not afford, for the benefit of the preacher. Mr. Hilliard called it, "pickin' black folk's pockets in the name of Jesus," and he thought it was a "goddam shame."

It was true that in the community, and surrounding areas, churches were able to ordain so-called preachers. Unfortunately, the congregation gave them the title of Reverend, just because the wanna-be-reverend announced to the congregation "I got the call... I got the call and it came to me as I was half-asleep... dreaming. It came to me in a vision." Mr. Hilliard thought that was pathetic, and unfortunately it was common, in the black community especially, and it had been going on for as long as I could remember.

Mr. Hilliard had nothing but contempt for those preachers he called religious pimps and parasites, saying "They are some blind niggers leadin' the blind down a path of failure. They are out there in the community leading by goddam guessing games and using the opportunity to pilfer from those they lead. They say they tryin' to change the world. Bullshit! They actin' just *like* the world."

One of the things he hated most was when the churches in the community got involved with "Prayer-Bowl Duels" and preach-offs that brought out all the "pimpin' preachers" from the nearby mining camps. They would all come together, whoopin' and hollerin', and not teach the gospel or deliver any message helpful to black Americans. Mr. Hilliard said it was nothing more than a "preachin' contest... a goddam feel-good session." And I thought he was right, because having attended several I discovered there wasn't much counseling, teaching, praying, pastoring or leading done. Like Mr. Hilliard, I believed — as I'd heard my father say — that black folks required more than preaching to solve their problems.

I was impressed with outspoken Mr. Hilliard because he admitted he himself was a sinner, but he was doing the best he could "from a Christian heart" to speak up, basing his opinions and beliefs on his own experience, knowledge and insight. He told me he had gained all his knowledge through the inner experiences of his own conscience, from the tragedies of life, and from "the school of hard knocks." Another reason I began to seriously listen to Mr. Hilliard was because he had a lot to say about the plight of black men as concerned with black women. When he said that most often black women were single parents who abused their children, especially their sons, my ears perked up because now he was talking about me. I understood exactly what he meant for I believed my mama was abusing me, beating me at every opportunity when she was drunk.

Mr. Hilliard listened to my stories, sometimes with tears in his eyes, and he understood the consequence of physically and mentally abusing a child. He tried to explain Mama's behavior... saying she had been taken by the devil of alcohol and didn't have the strength to escape that demon's grip.

I remember telling him how Mama seldom went to church, or attended school meetings, and if she did, she was intoxicated, creating another humiliating scene for us children. He knew what I was talking about, and it did my heart good just to have one grownup, one calm and sensible adult, listening to my side, who I could unburden myself to without being called names or being made to feel bad for talking about my mama. He was the first person who ever really listened to me, except for Mr. Lloyd Robinson back in Powellton, and poor Mr. Robinson had died before I was old enough to get it all together like I was doing.

Mr. Hilliard would say, "Look around, Charles. Look at the young black women today. They are rude, they're over-sensitive, and they like to play mind games. Do you see them takin' responsibility for trainin' their sons?

Do you see them teachin' them to be respectful by showin' a little respect? Goddam if they do! Women want respect from men, but how do you get any boy to respect women when his own mother calls him all sorts of names, beats him just because she's feelin' mean or had too much to drink and takes no interest in his education?" He shook his head. "How do you think that boy starts to behave toward women?"

"I think they start to hate them," I said, reaching deep inside myself for the truth, knowing that was exactly what was happening to me.

"Right. Goddam right, Charles. And they start feelin' resentful, too. Even toward the ones who might be sincere. Now it ain't right, a boy feelin' that way to his mother, but it ain't right for her to keep at him and keep at him till he got no other way to feel."

"I don't want to hate my mama. But when she gets crazy like she does, I... I don't know. I feel this... this rush of anger in me now... and it's getting stronger."

"That's pride, boy. That's your black pride rushin' up on you and sayin' nobody gonna make you lick dirt when you done nothin' to deserve it. But you got to keep it under control. You can't never forget she your mama. No matter what she does. You may feel like it, but you never gonna hit back at her. Never."

"No, sir. I've never done that. But what do I do when..."

"Get away from her. That's all. You say yourself she don't know what she doin'. Just get away. She'll cool off. Keep out of her way."

"Yeah. That's all."

Our Sunday talks developed into more or less every-other-day conversations. I believe Mr. Hilliard saw my deep-seated need to relate to some adult and knew that I was reaching out for some kind of understanding of the hellish life my mama had put me through. Now that she had married Coy our lives had straightened up a little, but the two of them still got drunk together nearly every weekend, and there was very little attention paid to me and TC as Mama devoted herself to her new husband's wants. It was still a matter of Mama beating on me if I crossed her on anything, or even asked her a question she didn't like. That part of her hadn't changed. I was the one who was changing, and my new attitude was happening fast.

One day Mr. Hilliard came over to talk to Mama ... I think he got really worried after she'd hit me with that metal dipper and cut my neck open. I was wearing a red handkerchief around my neck to cover the scar. I waited out on the front porch and he found Mama alone in the kitchen. Coy had left for work across town and Mama had already started on the jug of white lightning.

Their conversation started politely enough, and then after he sat down at the table for some coffee she'd offered, he just plunged in like he always did, coming right to... as he would say... "the goddam point."

"Nora, you got to stop smackin' that boy around. You gotta stop hittin' on him like he's your punchin' bag. All you're doing is driving him away from you. Hell, would you come near a coiled snake ready to bite you? Would you want to be around a crazy-acting woman who smashed you to the floor every time you took a wrong step? Don't you see what you're doing? You a respectable married woman now. You want to be takin' an interest in Charles' education and well-being. Don't you see what you're teachin' him to think about how society views black men? Do you think you're helping your son feel good about himself? An' what do you believe he thinks about black women?"

"He better respect black women, Lewis. He better respect me."

"Respect you? Nora... look at the way you were living. Do you think you are showing him love and dignity and respect? When that boy goes out in the world what's he gonna get? *'Whites only here! Get out, nigger! You sit in the back of the damn bus! Get your black face outta my drinking fountain!'* That's what he gonna get. Nobody gonna give him the time of day, so what are you doing, bringing him down any lower? You want him to grow up mean-minded and nasty? He's gonna have a hard time fightin' those chains he still wears, Nora, just because he was born black."

"It ain't like that anymore, Lewis. It's changed."

"Yeah, Nora, the world is changing, but it ain't changing that fast. You forgot that black men today are still struggling with the marks left on them by their own uneducated fathers — the fathers who are gone off somewhere else — and the transient boyfriends that come and go."

"I'm a decent married woman, Lewis, and you better watch your mouth. You're in my house and you can't..."

"You know what I'm talkin' about. It's your goddam drinkin', Nora... it's makin' you..."

"Aw, shut up, ol' man. You don't know half a what you sayin'. I love my boy. He knows I do. An this is my house. If I want to drink, I damn well gonna do it."

"Sure you will. Ain't nobody gonna tell you what to do, Nora. I'm just letting you know what you're doing to your son."

"I ain't doing nothing to my son."

"That's right. You're doing nothin'! NOTHIN'! you hear." He got up and was ready to leave. "Go on, turn your face away. I'll say it again. You doin NOTHIN' for your son. You ain't raising him, you ain't showing him any respect for his young manhood."

"He's still a baby... he don't..."

"He ain't no baby anymore. An' you ain't givin' him any goddam help at all. You doin' NOTHIN', and it's a damn shame." He walked out and I caught up with him on the road.

"What happened? You tell her about not hittin' on me?" I asked, although I'd heard every word.

"She ain't gonna change, son. She already carrying half a load this morning and it ain't even ten yet. I'm sorry." And then he stopped still in the middle of the road and turned around to me. He put his one hand on my shoulder and his eyes were flowing tears, which I didn't understand, and he said, "Listen to me. I don't care if you never heard another word I ever said, but you goddam well remember this. It's up to you from now on. Your mama can't help you. She can't do anything because of her demons... you know they've got her." His gnarled fingers got tight on my shoulder. "It's up to you. Don't look to anybody except yourself. You're nearly grown now. An' you're smart. Christ, you're Charles Ayers' son, ain't you? "

I nodded, my own eyes getting teary. I felt like he was giving me a benediction... like I was swallowing some secret information from the grownup world.

"Well, act like Charles Ayers' son, then. Be somebody."

We walked in silence then back to his house and I waved as he went on in. I knew then why he was crying as I watched him bang the screen door behind him. He was disappointed... and he'd been disappointed so many times. He'd been hoping he could change Mama, make her see... give me a helping hand, but he knew now he was just talkin' , like he said, "to the goddam wind."

All the speeches in the world weren't going to change Mama's way of thinking.

I walked on back to our house, my hands shoved deep into my pockets, thinking and making some decisions for myself. What Mr. Hilliard had said was true. Young black women did have their mothers and sisters as role models, but many young black boys, like me, had no father to emulate, or

267

one, like mine, who was physically and spiritually absent.

I could feel the deep resentment within myself as I tried to fight the memory of Led, my common-law stepfather whom I'd hated all those years, and the memory of all my mama's men friends who had come and gone during the long weeks when he was away... and all before. It didn't help all that much that now she had Coy and was trying harder. I was stuck with all those bitter feelings and memories. I tried to fight the hatred I felt, but I just couldn't get over it. I viewed them all as no good S.O.B.'s They had given me nothing of value and, in fact, they had all helped to bring my mama down, encouraged her drinking and her running around and leaving us kids alone. Their interest lay in the gutter common to all alcoholics.

The closer I came to my house the slower I walked. I was thinking more clearly than I had ever been able to before. Suddenly much was clear to me that I hadn't been able to grasp before. Now that I thought about it, I didn't believe that Mama was all that much in love with Coy. Oh she probably did love him — he was tall and good-looking and brought home money — but I began to see that to her, a man was only something she had to have to help serve her needs. I don't think she saw him as a man who deserved respect... as a person in his own right. I think inside herself somewhere she wanted a husband, but even deeper down she thought all men were no good bastards. All of them. Just pawns to nurse her addiction to whiskey.

What chance did a young black male have in her house?

What examples did I have to follow beside that one, brief glimpse of my father... and my Grandpa Ayers? But that was so long ago. I had grown up so much since then. I was still bitter about having to leave the farm, and I was aware that my dad had never come back for me. Something in me kept whispering that he could have if he'd wanted to, but he never did. That had hurt me too. Thinking he didn't want me either. Who did I have to show me how to be a man, much less a black man? All the men running through my mama's house lacked the will to fight for their value, to show with courageous efforts their own personal worth as men. All they had was the same old slave mentality of being beaten down and powerless. Suddenly I remembered what my Grandma Ayers had said three years ago. Me and Grandpa were sitting with her at the kitchen table and she was talking about black women and their needs. *"Maybe black women need to be shown good examples by honoring those among us who have struggled and won... those who have educated themselves... like you did, Daniel. There are plenty of decent black women who have escaped poverty and oppression, who have walked away from drunkenness and worldly living, who have made hard choices and lifted themselves out of... of the downward spiral of low self-esteem.... and the terrible, self-destruction of acceptance that sucks so many young black girls down to the depths of depression."*

I stood still, struck by the truth of her words and finally understanding. *"Those who have educated themselves, like you did, Daniel,"* she'd said to my grandfather. And Mr. Hilliard's words fit right in: *"It's up to you from now on,"* he'd said. *"Your mama can't help you. You're nearly grown now. An' you're smart. Christ, you're Charles Ayers' son, ain't you? Well, act like Charles Ayers' son, then, goddamit. Be somebody!"* That's when it happened. That "click" that went off in my heart, and in my mind. I wasn't going to let Mama pull me down along with her. I wasn't going to let life toss me away like a dirty rag. *"Be somebody!"* Mr. Hilliard said. That was exactly what I planned to do.

CHAPTER 49
FIRE Across The Canyon!! Alone With Heartbreak

I knew something was going to happen that day. Something bad. I could just feel it in my bones. My great-grandmother Elizabeth had been a "seer" and I always thought that same ability was running in my blood, like it ran in hers. All through the morning I tried to shake off the feeling, and just go on about my daily work, but it festered inside me and I kept waiting and watching...wondering what was going to happen.

My Aunt Samantha's house across the canyon sat between two neighbors; the Barretts were to the east, and the Puryears were to the west. The Puryear's dwelling was close to Aunt Samantha's, but there was a clearing in between. It had been the fifth home built in our area. They'd used some very old, dry lumber to construct the building. It only had two rooms: a front room where the bed and the fireplace were, a small kitchen and a back porch, high enough off the ground so they also had an enclosed basement like my aunt's place. There was a spectacular view of the canyon from their porch. In the kitchen stood a small wooden table and an iron stove used for heat and for cooking. Around the stove, a rocking chair and a couple of wooden, straight-back chairs formed a sitting area. Wallpaper hung loose from the walls and made big bulges in some places near the ceiling. The exterior had been covered, like our own house, with tarpaper made to look like dull, yellowish brick. Most Harlem Heights houses built in those days had no inside plumbing, but they did have outhouses about fifty feet away.

Rubin Puryear's wife was young and beautiful, and at only 21 years old, she attracted every man in the community. We called her Mrs. Elizabeth. She was brown-skinned, tall and slim, and had long, thick, black hair. She was very friendly and would offer a smile whenever she was spoken to, but to me she always seemed lonely. I assumed that was because her husband worked long hours and was always coming home late. Sometimes he would not come home at all. Rubin Puryear was an astute business man with interests in several businesses. He and his brother, Tom, were considered two of the wealthiest black men in Fayette County.

Rubin Puryear and Mrs. Elizabeth had two children, a five-year-old boy named Raymond and his four-year-old sister, Iris. Both children were around my brother TC's age. The Puryears' house, and several others on that side of the hill across the ravine, could be seen from our kitchen window, and even better from our small back porch. Many a time TC slipped away and rambled across the canyon to play with Iris and Raymond. Mama would go to our kitchen window, look across the canyon and see TC on the Puryear's porch playing there.

Usually, whenever Mrs. Elizabeth went off shopping or whatever, she asked someone in the neighborhood to babysit her children. She frequently hired me for that job and early on I had discovered that little Raymond enjoyed playing with matches. He had a passion for watching the bright flame after he'd strike the match. I lit into him about that, took them away from him several times and put them where I thought he couldn't reach them, but he'd get them somehow and I'd catch him at it again. I remember telling his mother about that habit of his, and I know she gave him a good whipping, but I don't think it stopped his fascination.

Most of the time when I did various shores for the Puryears they paid me off in pennies. Mr. Puryear kept a bucket full of pennies on a high shelf in a locked dinning cabinet. I was pleased that they paid me in pennies because it gave me a feeling of having a lot of money. Besides, I could buy a piece of candy for a penny. Sometimes I could buy two pieces of candy for one penny. Occasionally, Mrs. Elizabeth hired me to go shopping for small items. I was happy to do this and I'd go next door and ask Aunt Samantha if she wanted anything from the store, too. She usually wanted a box of Argo starch that cost 11 cents, and she'd let me keep some change for making the trip.

When I had everybody's list, I walked the two miles south to the store on Highway 19, called East End, and after getting their items, I'd buy my penny candy or an ice cream stick. My favorite candy came on a stick and was called Cow Lick. I always enjoyed doing some errands for other people... it made me feel important.

Anyway, that fateful morning when I was just standing on the porch, getting that hair-raising feeling of doom, I was surrounded by lilac-colored mountains huddled under the warm sun and off in the distance a low rainbow marked the end of an early morning shower. I could see Mrs. Elisabeth and her two children on their porch. It appeared that she was tiding up the place because she had a broom in her hands. Raymond was playing with his sister.

Mama came out from our kitchen and called across the canyon form our porch, asking Mrs. Elizabeth if she would lend us her washboard.

"Sure. Just come get it," Mrs. Elizabeth called out.

"I'll send Charles."

"Okay."

I saw that Mama was preparing to go shopping with Coy, who had promised to buy us some food from the mining company's store. Before leaving, Mama instructed me to get the washboard from Mrs. Elizabeth and to wash the pile of dirty clothes she left on the porch in the tin washtub. Mama and Coy finally left, headed for Lochgelly, another mining community three miles east of Harlem Heights where Coy worked. I knew they wouldn't be back for a long time so I didn't hurry getting to the laundry. I fooled around doing some other stuff until it was gettin on late in the afternoon. Remembering my job, I made my way across the canyon to the Puryears' house and knocked.

Raymond opened the wooden door, but the screen door was latched high on the door frame, too high for Raymond to reach it. I coached Raymond to pull one wooden chair from the table to the door, stand on the chair and unlatch the screen door. Raymond unlatched the screen with some difficulty, but he managed to open it. Inside, I found the two children had been playing on the floor with the bucket of pennies that Mr. Puryear usually kept on a high shelf. They had scattered other toys and things about the floor, but I do not recall seeing any matches or anything that could cause a fire. The coal stove was hot, but not unusually so.

I asked Raymond where his mother was and he said she'd gone next door to the Morrises' house. I found the washboard and left.

As I was on my way home, I heard loud music coming from the Morrises' house. That wasn't unusual, but it did suggest they were having a late afternoon party.

Back home, I put the washboard on the porch next to the pile of laundry and then went to the community well for a pail of water, poured it into the tin tub and went back for more. Then, dumping in some soap flakes, I was just ready to scrub the clothes when I glanced across the canyon to the Puryears' place. There was a person on their back porch, just leaving, going down the steps. I don't know if they'd been in the house or just spoke to Raymond and Iris through the screen door. The person had on a long, black coat with a colorful scarf over their head. From the distance I couldn't tell if it was a woman or a man, but I didn't think anything of it because lots of folks were always coming and going to the Puryears.

Anyway, I had the washboard and was beginning to wash some white clothes when I looked up and saw flames leaping from the roof of the Puryears' house. The old, dry lumber was burning fast. Some man came running up. He was hollering as he broke down the screen door and tried to rush into the house, but the flames shooting all around him forced him back. I heard Raymond screaming out for his mother. Horrified, I stood on my porch as the fire engulfed the entire house. Within half a minute, Mrs. Elisabeth showed up from next door. She broke a window on the east side of the house. She was about to crawl into the flames and smoke when a neighbor grabbed her and yanked her back. Just as he pulled her away, the roof fell in with a terrifying crash and a roar of flames. I could still hear Raymond's voice calling for his mother. I stood frozen, listening, watching, hardly breathing, as Raymond's voice faded in the smoke and the leaping flames and went silent.

The fire burning away at the tarpaper covering on the exterior of the house intensified. Suddenly the blaze exploded as if a devil-wind had swooped in, twisting and crackling like all hell had broke lose. Mrs. Elizabeth had collapsed on the ground, her eyes round with terror and pain.

In minutes, the fire swept in on Aunt Samantha's house, licking, but not quite able to reach, the walls of her kitchen. By now, people from all over the community had rushed to the scene. Unfortunately, in those days there were no fire hydrants in the black communities. People were trying to put out the little catch-fires by running back and forth with cans and pots from the rain barrels.

As I stood on our back porch watching that drama unfold before me, I felt my heart plunge down into my shoes as I suddenly thought of TC. Where was he? Had he gone over there to play? I left the porch and searched frantically for him, finally finding him asleep under Mama's bed, his favorite place. Now that he was safe, I went back to the porch to watch the tragedy across the canyon unfolding. The little house was now a full-blown inferno, red and orange flames roaring, black smoke billowing like the pit of hell.

I begin to cry. Hopping back and forth from one bare foot to another, unable to hold myself still with the pain that gripped my heart. Tears cascaded down my cheeks and my teeth chattered. My whole body shivered as if a cold frost had suddenly crushed in on me. I was a total wreck, helpless as I stood, weaving back and forth in my agonizing grief, my heart drumming in my ears as if a million horses were trampling over me. It was the darkest day of my life, listening to Mrs. Elizabeth screams for her poor burned children.

There was nothing anybody could do. The house was gone. Luckily the flames had only licked at Aunt Samantha's house and hadn't caught, or it would have been gone too. Raymond and his little sister Iris had been burned up in the fire. Mrs. Elizabeth was on her knees, still screaming and moaning and flinging herself at the smoking rubble, calling out for her babies. My heart broke for her.

Seeing that fire, so fast, so powerful, stunned me.

I forgot about the wash. I forgot about everything.

My knees gave out and I almost fell down on the porch… so I sat there, staring across the canyon at the tragic scene. Raymond was dead. I had just talked to him, no more than ten minutes ago and now he was dead. My head spun with unanswered questions.

Could a tragedy like that happen to me?

Could life be snuffed out like that, on one bright and sunny afternoon, in only a few moments, with no warning? And right then, right then my eyes opened, and the fragility of human life dawned on me. I was alive; feeling; thinking; seeing. Raymond was dead. He was only five. What a very short time he'd had. I was eleven. And like a bright vision I saw myself on my own path of darkness… it stretched before me, twisting, turning, hiding its pitfalls, as it had been for all those eleven years, stretching now into the black smoke and shadows. And there I was, walking on that treacherous path leading nowhere. I watched myself, like watching a movie of myself, and I was afraid for the flames were reaching out for me… and then suddenly in a sheet of flame and a puff of smoke I disappeared. I wasn't there on that dark path any longer. I had disappeared. Gone. The old, frightened, shy, self-doubting, self-hating Charles was gone.

I blinked and heard myself say, "That is not my path any longer."

I looked around and knew that I'd just experienced some sort of an inner dream-flash, a mind vision, for only about five seconds had passed. Across the canyon the smoking ruins of the Puryear's fire were still smoldering, and my heart was beating like an anvil, but there was a singing sound behind it all. I wasn't the same frightened little boy I'd been only five seconds ago. I held out my hands… Steady. No more trembling. I stood up. My legs were strong. My stance was sure. My heart had made up its mind. I was going to do something with my life before it was too late, before some fire, or some flood, or some other tragic accident made me miss my chance.

Pausing a moment, I thought about heaven then, wondering if what the preachers said was true. Wondering if there was a heaven, and if Raymond and Iris were… Well, I wasn't sure about that. I was only sure that I'd watched Raymond burn to death in only three minutes of real time. Time. There suddenly seemed to be hardly any time left.

I started walking across the canyon. I wanted to see close up… to remember… to feel the heat.. My bare feet slapped on the dirt path. Hurry. I started running.

Some hours later, a fire engine appeared. The fire had burned itself out by then, and they sprayed water on the site to cool it down so the investigators could look into the cause of the fire. Many curiosity seekers stood around, shocked and stunned by the disaster.

The investigators poked around with their rakes until they discovered the burned bodies of the two children. It appeared that Raymond had his sister by the hand. Judging from where the bodies lay, they were only three feet from the window where their mother had called out to them. They'd almost made it to safety. When they pulled the baked bodies from the rubbish, many people fainted. I didn't. I wanted to see. I wanted to remember.

It was late evening when I reached home.

Everything had left my mind except my experience about the fire. I do not remember walking home. I was simply dazed from the tragedy, and so keyed-up I did not sleep all night.

Over and over I keep seeing myself on that dark pathway, disappearing into a dark cloud of smoke and coming fresh, to myself, to my *new* self on the porch in the sunlight. Over and over I kept hearing Mrs. Elizabeth moaning for her children. "I was only gone a minute," she cried. "Only a minute… Oh, God, how cruel. How cruel to take my children…"

Only a minute. Anything could happen in a minute.

The next morning, the sun came from behind the mountains as it always had and I watched it make a new morning begin. I was not exactly crying. It was just that I could not stop the tears that kept forming in the corners of my eyes. I could not seem to hold them back. Every couple of minutes one would slip lose and start its quick run down my cheeks. I would catch it before it got too far by wiping my forearm across my face. The house was quiet. Mama and Coy were still away. They had been gone all night. For sure, they had gone out drinking again. TC was still asleep and I let him slumber on, knowing he was too young to grasp what had happened.

I believe the whole community mourned for the Puryear's loss. Mr. Puryear was never the same man again. I never saw Mrs. Elizabeth after that terrible day either. The last time I saw her was when Mama called across the canyon to borrow her washboard. Mama kept that very washboard for ten years and then it disappeared.

CHAPTER 50
A Visit To·Alabama… I Escape My Own Path Of Darkness

Mama and Coy never did come home the day of the fire, and I no longer gave a damn if she came home or not. They finally showed up two days later and were shocked to see the burned out place where the Puryears' house had stood… and how close the fire had come to taking Aunt Samantha's house too. Mama cried for Mrs. Elizabeth and for the poor dead children, and Coy comforted her. She asked me if I'd seen it happen. I said yes, I saw it. She was about to ask me something else, but she looked close at my face and whatever it was she saw in my eyes stopped her. She never asked about the fire again.

Mama was always talking about how she missed Marguerite and Inez. She wrote to them just about every two weeks or so, and to her sister Ruth, telling her about being married to Coy and all about her gifts from the community. Watching her, I could tell Mama got a kick out of signing her name, "Mrs. Elnora Douglass."

Maybe it was the Puryears' fire that put the idea into Mama's head.

Maybe the idea came after she found out how close that fire had come to taking Aunt Samantha's house too.

Maybe it was just something she'd had in the back of her mind for a long time. I don't know, but all of a sudden Mama was talking about going to Alabama with Aunt Samantha to visit her sister Ruth and see Marguerite and Inez and to visit her other sister Aunt Virgil whom she hadn't seen in years, and also her oldest living sister Sally.

I didn't care all that much about the visit, but I was interested in seeing where Aunt Ruth and Uncle Jim lived, and what, if anything, they might be able to do to help me with my new goals. I was determined to go on with school To go every single day, and to excel. I was going to let nothing stand in the way of my getting an education. Mr. Hilliard said that was the one thing in life I had to have. I didn't need a lot of money. I didn't need fine suits of clothes. I didn't need fancy tools or material things. I only needed an education and the determination to excel. After that, I could get all the rest. And he reminded me to never give up. "You gonna get stalled now and again," he said, "everybody does. But don't let nothin' stop you. I don't care how long it takes, son, but never... never give up."

During this period of change for me, I remember listening to the radio a lot over at Uncle Henry's house, especially Arthur Godfrey's show and the one where the millionaire gave away money with Marvin Miller. I loved listening to the radio. It helped me learn how to pronounce words better and gave me a better vocabulary, and I was interested in all that improvement. One time I heard a statement — I never was able to recall who said it — but it impressed me deeply. A man on the radio was talking about how people differ, one from another, and he said, *"Comes the many... comes the few. A few rise above their fellow men and become great."* I remember thinking at the time how much I wanted to be among those few. Of course, at eleven, and coming from where I was coming from, I wasn't thinking about rising to greatness — that was far beyond my dreams or expectations — I just wanted to *rise*... rise to whatever it was I could achieve.

As I was making all these new decisions in my head and planning out my future, I began to feel sorry for Mama. I knew there was nothing I could do to rid her of her alcoholism, but it made my heart ache just the same. I loved Mama, in spite of everything, but I was through with the old ways. I realized she was ill and helpless to escape her own paths of darkness. After all, I started my young life going on that same path beside her, dragged along by her alcoholic sickness, her men friends, her chaotic life style, her needs, her changing moods, and constantly subjected to her drunken beatings until I was only a shadow of a boy-child with low self-esteem, low confidence, guilt and confusion, unable to find my own way.

But all that was in the past. I was different now.

As I thought about what happened to me on the day of the Puryears' fire — that inner vision I'd had — I became curious and wanted to know if other people had had them too. I asked Mr. Hilliard about it, explaining in detail what I'd seen and how it made me feel, and he said yes, lots of other people spoke of a "life changing" experience like that, and he told me there was a name for it. He could not recall the word exactly at that moment, but he said it sounded like "e-pit-any," or near that, and he was pretty sure it started with "e-p-i-something." It took me most of the afternoon, but I finally found the word in Uncle Henry's dictionary which he let me borrow. I had to read all the listings beginning with "e-p-i," but the moment I saw "epiphany" and read the definition, I knew that was the word. The dictionary said:

"E-PIPH-a-ny. 3 a (1) : usually a sudden manifestation or perception of the essential nature or meaning of something (2) : an intuitive grasp of reality through something (as an event) usually simple and striking."

I had to look up "essential" too, and the word "intuitive," but when I studied on it, I was certain that's what I'd had. An epiphany. It got me off that dark pathway and changed my life. I was going on twelve, coming into my manhood at an early age and I could feel the change in my body and in my growing bones. I actually felt reborn, and I liked thinking for myself, educating myself, depending upon *myself*!

As Mr. Hilliard said, "*Act* like Charles Ayers' son. Be somebody!"

Over the next few weeks, while the talk was going on about Alabama and whether or not to take a bus or the train, I closed myself off from my mama's sicknesses, from her angry, drunken words that still managed to cut my heart, and from her incoherent mutterings that were only going to tear me down. I took over the far corner of the front room, folded a blanket there near the light from the window, and began teaching myself how to read better. Once more I borrowed Uncle Henry's dictionary. I started out with the same Third Grade Reader I had in Buckingham, the one which my Grandma Ayers hid in the box she packed for me when I left that day.

Taking Mr. Hilliard's advice, I started on my own personal agenda of change, beginning with the very basics of living that, as a child, I'd always taken for granted. The first thing I did was to wash my clothes and my body as if I were washing away all the old garbage. I was on a new road, a higher road, a brighter road where there was a future for me. Mama noticed the change in my behavior. She said, "What's wrong with you, boy? You gettin' pretty uppity around here, aren't you?"

"Yes, Mama," I said, and I smiled because that was exactly what I was feeling about myself. Uppity. And it was about time.

While Mama and Coy made plans — he was going to stay at the house in Harlem Heights and keep on working while Mama and us kids went visiting — I made my own arrangements. I was tall enough now to pass for twelve or thirteen and I walked all over town asking for work and I found small jobs. I wasn't feeling scared anymore; not scared of my future; not scared of going without food. I earned money now. And I wasn't scared of Mama and her smacks.

I learned to dance away from her hands and laugh at her, which made her crazy, but being drunk she couldn't touch me anymore. Then she'd cry in her frustration, and I forced myself not to care about that either. Her crying got to me at first — it used to just break my heart — but I learned to steel myself against it, for most of the time it wasn't even Mama talking... it was the whiskey.

Of course, she was different when Coy was around. She showed only her best side to him, and I guess that was smart, but she wasn't fooling me anymore. I was pushing hard on growing up. The war was over in Europe and as far as I was concerned, it was over at home too.

I couldn't know then as I was packing my clothes — along with the three new books I'd bought for myself — that within five short years I'd graduate high school at Dubois High in Mount Hope, West Virginia. I only had an inkling that during my high school years I would be a musician who enjoyed playing jazz and ragtime hits on the piano, and a vocalist for a popular band that entertained throughout Appalachia.

Remember the day I raced that freight train and nearly got killed for my trouble? Eventually that ability made me a World Class sprinter and co-holder of the World Record for the 100-meter dash.

When I climbed aboard the train with Aunt Samantha and Mama and TC headed for Alabama and Mama's beginnings, I never guessed that somewhere down the line I would become an esteemed member the international organization called Mensa — the schools I attended up to that point in my young life never tested kids for intelligence or I.Q. and therefore, the idea that I might actually be "smart" had never occurred to me — or that I'd achieve twenty-two years of military service, including a stint with the Army's elite military forces, combat in Vietnam, earn more than a few medals in active service, including the Purple Heart, the Bronze Star and a Presidential Citation, or that I would take an MA in Business Administration from Central Michigan University or a masters in Public Health from the University of Hawaii and finally my doctorate in Human Behavior/Industrial psychology.

Of course, there were a lot of stops along the way, zig-zags, pitfalls and detours, but in the end I survived.

The story of how I stayed true to my goals from age eleven to sixteen, of how I was able to remain on my higher road (with more than a few tumbles from grace) and negotiate the twists and turns of my dangerous, chaotic journey through life with my sometimes-loving, sometimes diabolical, alcohol-addicted mother would fill another book.

AFTERWORD

Dear Reader,

I know there's no longer any lift to the statement, "I did it, and you can too," because it's been said so many times. You've heard it before and nobody believes it any more. It sounds hokey. It sounds like a just another scam.

"Yeah, yeah," you say. "All I got to do is believe in myself. Man, that's shit! I've heard that so many times, I can't stand it. What good does believing in yourself do when you're hungry? What good does believing in yourself do when they evicting you and repossessing your damn car and when you get downsized out of your job? Huh? You think believing in myself is gonna make somebody want to hear my music? Is it gonna put food on the table for my kids? Or pay my rent?"

I hear you. And the answer is: No, of course not.

Faith in anything won't do a damn thing for you if things have gone that far. At that point believing in yourself is good for the soul, but getting off Your butt and develop a sense of courage, determination to be an honest, faithful productive and dependable citizen. You must find a way to earnest, keeping in mind that we all must crawl before we can walk. Most often we must start low to get to the high. This means it may be necessary to swept floors clean toilets or what ever to make our way to the top. Sitting at the table, waiting for God to bring you groceries won't feed you.

Faith has to be there, inside you, a whole lot earlier than that.

Faith when you are only 12 and feeling real tough about going into the high school. That's when belief is supposed to kick in and help you get your head together. That's when you need it. That's when it will do you some good. That's when your kid should read a book like this to see that a deprived black kid like me who lived in squalor, slums, filthy mining camps, often starved for food, with a mother who was so deep into her bottle she didn't know she had kids — made it. I survived. I walked away from that path of darkness. It can happen in your life too. I wasn't any better than you. Maybe I wasn't any smarter, either. I sure as hell didn't get any special breaks, or favors from anyone that gave me a leg up. I had nothing at the start. Nothing..

Maybe I did have a little luck though.

I'd say I got lucky when I met Mr. Hillard and started believing in myself. I'd say I was lucky that it wasn't my house that burned that afternoon when the Puryear kids died so horribly, and I realized the vulnerability of my life and saw myself on that long, path of darkness. But all I really had was my belief in myself. I believed I could learn. I believed I could achieve. I believed I could turn my life around. That is what I'm telling you.

Start early.

Start before you cut your own legs out from under you with drugs, alcohol and low self esteem.

Start believing in yourself and what your goals are. Just being black is not enough, man. You've got to be black and proud.

Who was I before I started believing in myself? A punk black kid with no idea at all of how to get through life, or what life would do to me. With no hope, no plan, no goal, no faith in a damn thing. A kid coming up from a history of slavery, probably like your own family.

I wrote this book about my life because I knew I had a story that needed to be told, and because maybe what changed me, what lifted me, what helped me get off my rotten, lousy road to hell, what gave me back my self respect, and my self esteem and my self pride, will help you too. Good God, man, if a punk like me could rise above my childhood, could find a way out of my own dark pathways and get an education by sheer will and determination, then you can too.

Take hold of your own life.

Stop waiting for somebody else to help you out… like I was hoping until I got my head on straight when I turned eleven.

Believe in yourself.

Start now.

I wish you well.

Charles Williams, Ph.D.

P.S. If you want to write, let me know how you're doing. I'd like to hear from you.